Handbook of Parapsychology

Compiled by

Maci Valerio

Scribbles

Year of Publication 2018

ISBN : 9789352979585

Book Published by

Scribbles

(An Imprint of Alpha Editions)

email - alphaedis@gmail.com

Produced by: PediaPress GmbH
Limburg an der Lahn
Germany
http://pediapress.com/

Contents

Appendix   **167**

Article Licenses   **199**

Index   **201**

Introduction

Parapsychology

Parapsychology is the study of paranormal and psychic phenomena, including telepathy, precognition, clairvoyance, psychokinesis, near-death experiences, reincarnation, apparitional experiences, and other paranormal claims. It is identified as pseudoscience by a vast majority of mainstream scientists.

Parapsychology research is largely conducted by private institutions in several countries and funded through private donations, and the subject rarely appears in mainstream science journals. Most papers about parapsychology are published in a small number of niche journals.[2] Parapsychology has been criticised for continuing investigation despite being unable to provide convincing evidence for the existence of any psychic phenomena after more than a century of research.

Figure 1: *Photographs which purportedly depicted ghosts or spirits were popular during the 19th century.*

<table>
<tr><td colspan="1">This article is part of a series on</td></tr>
</table>

This article is part of a series on

Fringe medicine and medical conspiracy theories

- $\frac{v}{t}$
- $\underline{e}^3$

Terminology

The term *parapsychology* was coined in or around 1889 by philosopher Max Dessoir. It was adopted by J. B. Rhine in the 1930s as a replacement for the term *psychical research* in order to indicate a significant shift toward experimental methodology and academic discipline. The term originates from the Greek: παρά *para* meaning "alongside", and psychology.

In parapsychology, **psi** is the unknown factor in extrasensory perception and psychokinesis experiences that is not explained by known physical or biological mechanisms.[4,5] The term is derived from the Greek ψ *psi*, 23rd letter of the Greek alphabet and the initial letter of the Greek ψυχή *psyche*, "mind, soul". The term was coined by biologist Berthold P. Wiesner, and first used by psychologist Robert Thouless in a 1942 article published in the *British Journal of Psychology*.

The Parapsychological Association divides psi into two main categories: psi-gamma for extrasensory perception and psi-kappa for psychokinesis. In popular culture, "psi" has become more and more synonymous with special psychic, mental, and "psionic" abilities and powers.

History

Early psychical research

In 1853, the chemist Robert Hare conducted experiments with mediums and reported positive results.[6] Other researchers such as Frank Podmore highlighted flaws in his experiments, such as lack of controls to prevent trickery.[7,8] Agenor de Gasparin conducted early experiments into table-tipping. Over a period of five months in 1853 he declared the experiments a success being the result of an "ectenic force". Critics noted that the conditions were insufficient to prevent trickery. For example, the knees of the sitters may have been employed to move the table and no experimenter was watching above and below the table simultaneously.[9]

The German astrophysicist Johann Karl Friedrich Zöllner tested the medium Henry Slade in 1877. According to Zöllner some of the experiments were a success.[10] However, flaws in the experiments were discovered and critics have suggested that Slade was a fraud who performed trickery in the experiments.[11,12]

The Society for Psychical Research (SPR) was founded in London in 1882. Its formation was the first systematic effort to organize scientists and scholars to investigate paranormal phenomena. Early membership included philosophers, scholars, scientists, educators and politicians, such as Henry Sidgwick, Arthur

Figure 2: *Henry Slade with Zöllner*

Balfour, William Crookes, Rufus Osgood Mason and Nobel Laureate Charles Richet. Presidents of the Society included, in addition to Richet, Eleanor Sidgwick and William James, and subsequently Nobel Laureates Henri Bergson and Lord Rayleigh, and philosopher C. D. Broad.

Areas of study included telepathy, hypnotism, Reichenbach's phenomena, apparitions, hauntings, and the physical aspects of Spiritualism such as table-tilting, materialization and apportation.[13,14] In the 1880s the Society investigated apparitional experiences and hallucinations in the sane. Among the first important works was the two-volume publication in 1886, *Phantasms of the Living* which was largely criticized by scholars.[15] In 1894, the *Census of Hallucinations* was published which sampled 17, 000 people. Out of these, 1, 684 persons admitted to having experienced a hallucination of an apparition.[16] The SPR became the model for similar societies in other European countries and the United States during the late 19th century.

Early clairvoyance experiments were reported in 1884 by Charles Richet. Playing cards were enclosed in envelopes and a subject put under hypnosis attempted to identify them. The subject was reported to have been successful in a series of 133 trials but the results dropped to chance level when performed before a group of scientists in Cambridge. J. M. Peirce and E. C. Pickering reported a similar experiment in which they tested 36 subjects over 23,384 trials which did not obtain above chance scores.[17]

In 1881, Eleanor Sidgwick revealed the fraudulent methods that spirit photographers such as Édouard Isidore Buguet, Frederic Hudson and William H. Mumler had utilized.[18] During the late nineteenth century many fraudulent mediums were exposed by SPR investigators.[19]

Largely due to the support of psychologist William James, the American Society for Psychical Research (ASPR) opened its doors in Boston in 1885, moving to New York City in 1905 under the leadership of James H. Hyslop. Notable cases investigated by Walter Franklin Prince of the ASPR in the early 20th century included Pierre L. O. A. Keeler, the Great Amherst Mystery and Patience Worth.[20,21]

Rhine era

In 1911, Stanford University became the first academic institution in the United States to study extrasensory perception (ESP) and psychokinesis (PK) in a laboratory setting. The effort was headed by psychologist John Edgar Coover, and was supported by funds donated by Thomas Welton Stanford, brother of the university's founder. After conducting approximately 10,000 experiments, Coover concluded "statistical treatments of the data fail to reveal any cause beyond chance."[22]

In 1930, Duke University became the second major U.S. academic institution to engage in the critical study of ESP and psychokinesis in the laboratory. Under the guidance of psychologist William McDougall, and with the help of others in the department—including psychologists Karl Zener, Joseph B. Rhine, and Louisa E. Rhine—laboratory ESP experiments using volunteer subjects from the undergraduate student body began. As opposed to the approaches of psychical research, which generally sought qualitative evidence for paranormal phenomena, the experiments at Duke University proffered a quantitative, statistical approach using cards and dice. As a consequence of the ESP experiments at Duke, standard laboratory procedures for the testing of ESP developed and came to be adopted by interested researchers throughout the world.

George Estabrooks conducted an ESP experiment using cards in 1927. Harvard students were used as the subjects. Estabrooks acted as the sender with the guesser in an adjoining room. In total 2,300 trials were conducted. When the subjects were sent to a distant room with insulation the scores dropped to chance level. Attempts to repeat the experiment also failed.

The publication of J. B. Rhine's book, *New Frontiers of the Mind* (1937) brought the laboratory's findings to the general public. In his book, Rhine popularized the word "parapsychology", which psychologist Max Dessoir had coined over 40 years earlier, to describe the research conducted at Duke. Rhine

Figure 3: *Early parapsychological research employed the use of Zener cards in experiments designed to test for the existence of telepathic communication, or clairvoyant or precognitive perception.*

also founded an autonomous Parapsychology Laboratory within Duke and started the *Journal of Parapsychology*, which he co-edited with McDougall.

Rhine, along with associate Karl Zener, had developed a statistical system of testing for ESP that involved subjects guessing what symbol, out of five possible symbols, would appear when going through a special deck of cards designed for this purpose. A percentage of correct guesses (or hits) significantly above 20% was perceived as higher than chance and indicative of psychic ability. Rhine stated in his first book, *Extrasensory Perception* (1934), that after 90,000 trials, he felt ESP is "an actual and demonstrable occurrence".[23]

Irish medium and parapsychologist, Eileen J. Garrett, was tested by Rhine at Duke University in 1933 with Zener cards. Certain symbols that were placed on the cards and sealed in an envelope, and she was asked to guess their contents. She performed poorly and later criticized the tests by claiming the cards lacked a psychic energy called "energy stimulus" and that she could not perform clairvoyance to order.[24] The parapsychologist Samuel Soal and his colleagues tested Garrett in May, 1937. Most of the experiments were carried out in the Psychological Laboratory at the University College London. A total of over 12,000 guesses were recorded but Garrett failed to produce above chance level.[25] In his report Soal wrote "In the case of Mrs. Eileen Garrett we fail to find the slightest confirmation of J. B. Rhine's remarkable claims relating to her alleged powers of extra-sensory perception. Not only did she fail when I took charge of the experiments, but she failed equally when four other carefully trained experimenters took my place."[26]

The parapsychology experiments at Duke evoked much criticism from academics and others who challenged the concepts and evidence of ESP. A number of psychological departments attempted to repeat Rhine's experiments with

Figure 4: *Hubert Pearce with J. B. Rhine*

failure. W. S. Cox (1936) from Princeton University with 132 subjects produced 25,064 trials in a playing card ESP experiment. Cox concluded "There is no evidence of extrasensory perception either in the 'average man' or of the group investigated or in any particular individual of that group. The discrepancy between these results and those obtained by Rhine is due either to uncontrollable factors in experimental procedure or to the difference in the subjects." Four other psychological departments failed to replicate Rhine's results.[27] After thousands of card runs, James Charles Crumbaugh failed to duplicate the results of Rhine.[28]

In 1938, the psychologist Joseph Jastrow wrote that much of the evidence for extrasensory perception collected by Rhine and other parapsychologists was anecdotal, biased, dubious and the result of "faulty observation and familiar human frailties".[29] Rhine's experiments were discredited due to the discovery that sensory leakage or cheating could account for all his results such as the subject being able to read the symbols from the back of the cards and being able to see and hear the experimenter to note subtle clues.[30,31,32,33]

Illusionist Milbourne Christopher wrote years later that he felt "there are at least a dozen ways a subject who wished to cheat under the conditions Rhine described could deceive the investigator". When Rhine took precautions in response to criticisms of his methods, he was unable to find any high-scoring subjects.[34] Another criticism, made by chemist Irving Langmuir, among others, was one of selective reporting. Langmuir stated that Rhine did not report

Figure 5: *Mr. Zirkle and Miss Ownbey*

scores of subjects that he suspected were intentionally guessing wrong, and that this, he felt, biased the statistical results higher than they should have been.[35]

Rhine and his colleagues attempted to address these criticisms through new experiments described in the book *Extrasensory Perception After Sixty Years* (1940).[36] Rhine described three experiments the Pearce-Pratt experiment, the Pratt-Woodruff experiment and the Ownbey-Zirkle series which he believed demonstrated ESP. However, C. E. M. Hansel wrote "it is now known that each experiment contained serious flaws that escaped notice in the examination made by the authors of *Extra-Sensory Perception After Sixty Years*". Joseph Gaither Pratt was the co-experimenter in the Pearce-Pratt and Pratt-Woodruff experiments at the Duke campus. Hansel visited the campus where the experiments took place and discovered the results could have originated through the use of a trick so could not regarded as supplying evidence for ESP.[37]

In 1957, Rhine and Joseph Gaither Pratt wrote *Parapsychology: Frontier Science of the Mind*. Because of the methodological problems, parapsychologists no longer utilize card-guessing studies.[38] Rhine's experiments into psychokinesis (PK) were also criticized. John Sladek wrote:

> *His research used dice, with subjects 'willing' them to fall a certain way. Not only can dice be drilled, shaved, falsely numbered and manipulated, but even straight dice often show bias in the long run. Casinos for this reason retire dice often, but at Duke, subjects continued to try for the same effect on the same dice over long experimental runs. Not surprisingly, PK appeared at Duke and nowhere else.*[39]

The Ownbey-Zirkle ESP experiment at Duke was criticized by parapsychologists and skeptics.[40] Ownbey would attempt to send ESP symbols to Zirkle who would guess what they were. The pair were placed in adjacent rooms unable to see each other and an electric fan was used to prevent the pair communicating by sensory cues. Ownbey tapped a telegraph key to Zirkle to inform him when she was trying to send him a symbol. The door separating the two rooms was open during the experiment, and after each guess Zirkle would call out his guess to Ownbey who recorded his choice. Critics pointed out the experiment was flawed as Ownbey acted as both the sender and the experimenter, nobody was controlling the experiment so Ownbey could have cheated by communicating with Zirkle or made recording mistakes.[41]

The Turner-Ownbey long distance telepathy experiment was discovered to contain flaws. May Frances Turner positioned herself in the Duke Parapsychology Laboratory whilst Sara Ownbey claimed to receive transmissions 250 miles away. For the experiment Turner would think of a symbol and write it down whilst Ownbey would write her guesses. The scores were highly successful and both records were supposed to be sent to J. B. Rhine, however, Ownbey sent them to Turner. Critics pointed out this invalidated the results as she could have simply written her own record to agree with the other. When the experiment was repeated and the records were sent to Rhine the scores dropped to average.[42,43]

A famous ESP experiment at the Duke University was performed by Lucien Warner and Mildred Raible. The subject was locked in a room with a switch controlling a signal light elsewhere, which she could signal to guess the card. Ten runs with ESP packs of cards were used and she achieved 93 hits (43 more than chance). Weaknesses with the experiment were later discovered. The duration of the light signal could be varied so that the subject could call for specific symbols and certain symbols in the experiment came up far more often than others which indicated either poor shuffling or card manipulation. The experiment was not repeated.[44]

The administration of Duke grew less sympathetic to parapsychology, and after Rhine's retirement in 1965 parapsychological links with the university were broken. Rhine later established the Foundation for Research on the Nature of Man (FRNM) and the Institute for Parapsychology as a successor to the Duke laboratory. In 1995, the centenary of Rhine's birth, the FRNM was renamed the Rhine Research Center. Today, the Rhine Research Center is a parapsychology research unit, stating that it "aims to improve the human condition by creating a scientific understanding of those abilities and sensitivities that appear to transcend the ordinary limits of space and time".

Establishment of the Parapsychological Association

The Parapsychological Association (PA) was created in Durham, North Carolina, on June 19, 1957. Its formation was proposed by J. B. Rhine at a workshop on parapsychology which was held at the Parapsychology Laboratory of Duke University. Rhine proposed that the group form itself into the nucleus of an international professional society in parapsychology. The aim of the organization, as stated in its Constitution, became "to advance parapsychology as a science, to disseminate knowledge of the field, and to integrate the findings with those of other branches of science".

In 1969, under the direction of anthropologist Margaret Mead, the Parapsychological Association became affiliated with the American Association for the Advancement of Science (AAAS), the largest general scientific society in the world. In 1979, physicist John A. Wheeler said that parapsychology is pseudoscientific, and that the affiliation of the PA to the AAAS needed to be reconsidered.

His challenge to parapsychology's AAAS affiliation was unsuccessful. Today, the PA consists of about three hundred full, associate, and affiliated members worldwide.

The Stargate Project

Beginning in the early 1950s, the CIA started extensive research into behavioral engineering. Various experiments were undertaken in the process of this research, including some using various hallucinogenic substances.Wikipedia:Verifiability The findings from these experiments led to the formation of the Stargate Project, which handled ESP research for the U.S. federal government.

The Stargate Project was terminated in 1995 with the conclusion that it was never useful in any intelligence operation. The information was vague and included a lot of irrelevant and erroneous data. There was also reason to suspect that the research managers had adjusted their project reports to fit the known background cues.[45]

The 1970s and 1980s

The affiliation of the Parapsychological Association (PA) with the American Association for the Advancement of Science, along with a general openness to psychic and occult phenomena in the 1970s, led to a decade of increased parapsychological research. During this period, other related organizations were also formed, including the Academy of Parapsychology and Medicine (1970), the Institute of Parascience (1971), the Academy of Religion and Psychical

Research, the Institute of Noetic Sciences (1973), the International Kirlian Research Association (1975), and the Princeton Engineering Anomalies Research Laboratory (1979). Parapsychological work was also conducted at the Stanford Research Institute (SRI) during this time.

The scope of parapsychology expanded during these years. Psychiatrist Ian Stevenson conducted much of his research into reincarnation during the 1970s, and the second edition of his *Twenty Cases Suggestive of Reincarnation* was published in 1974. Psychologist Thelma Moss devoted time to the study of Kirlian photography at UCLA's parapsychology laboratory. The influx of spiritual teachers from Asia, and their claims of abilities produced by meditation, led to research on altered states of consciousness. American Society for Psychical Research Director of Research, Karlis Osis, conducted experiments in out of body experiences. Physicist Russell Targ coined the term remote viewing for use in some of his work at SRI in 1974.

The surge in paranormal research continued into the 1980s: the Parapsychological Association reported members working in more than 30 countries. For example, research was carried out and regular conferences held in Eastern Europe and the former Soviet Union although the word parapsychology was discarded in favour of the term psychotronics. The main promoter of psychotronics was Czech scientist Zdeněk Rejdák, who described it as a physical science, organizing conferences and presiding over the International Association for Psychotronic Research.

In 1985 a Chair of Parapsychology was established within the Department of Psychology at the University of Edinburgh and was given to Robert Morris, an experimental parapsychologist from the United States. Morris and his research associates and PhD students pursued research on topics related to parapsychology.

Modern era

Since the 1980s, contemporary parapsychological research has waned considerably in the United States.[46] Early research was considered inconclusive, and parapsychologists were faced with strong opposition from their academic colleagues. Some effects thought to be paranormal, for example the effects of Kirlian photography (thought by some to represent a human aura), disappeared under more stringent controls, leaving those avenues of research at dead-ends. The bulk of parapsychology research in the US is now confined to private institutions funded by private sources. After 28 years of research, Princeton Engineering Anomalies Research Laboratory (PEAR), which studied psychokinesis, closed in 2007.

Figure 6: *Bernard Carr (astronomer) one-time president of the Society for Psychical Research*

Two universities in the United States currently have academic parapsychology laboratories. The Division of Perceptual Studies, a unit at the University of Virginia's Department of Psychiatric Medicine, studies the possibility of survival of consciousness after bodily death, near-death experiences, and out-of-body experiences. Gary Schwartz at the University of Arizona's *Veritas Laboratory* conducted laboratory investigations of mediums, criticized by scientific skeptics. Several private institutions, including the Institute of Noetic Sciences, conduct and promote parapsychological research.

Over the last two decades some new sources of funding for parapsychology in Europe have seen a "substantial increase in European parapsychological research so that the center of gravity for the field has swung from the United States to Europe". Of all nations the United Kingdom has the largest number of active parapsychologists.[47] In the UK, researchers work in conventional psychology departments, and also do studies in mainstream psychology to "boost their credibility and show that their methods are sound". It is thought that this approach could account for the relative strength of parapsychology in Britain.

As of 2007, parapsychology research is represented in some 30 different countries and a number of universities worldwide continue academic parapsychology programs. Among these are the Koestler Parapsychology Unit at the University of Edinburgh; the Parapsychology Research Group at Liverpool Hope

University (this closed in April 2011); the SOPHIA Project at the University of Arizona; the Consciousness and Transpersonal Psychology Research Unit of Liverpool John Moores University; the Center for the Study of Anomalous Psychological Processes at the University of Northampton; and the Anomalistic Psychology Research Unit at Goldsmiths, University of London.

Research and professional organizations include the Parapsychological Association; the Society for Psychical Research, publisher of the *Journal of Society for Psychical Research*; the American Society for Psychical Research, publisher of the *Journal of the American Society for Psychical Research* (last published in 2004); the Rhine Research Center and Institute for Parapsychology, publisher of the *Journal of Parapsychology*; the Parapsychology Foundation, which published the *International Journal of Parapsychology* (between 1959 and 1968 and 2000–2001) and the Australian Institute of Parapsychological Research, publisher of the *Australian Journal of Parapsychology*. The *European Journal of Parapsychology* ceased publishing in 2010.

Parapsychological research has also included other sub-disciplines of psychology. These related fields include transpersonal psychology, which studies transcendent or spiritual aspects of the human mind, and anomalistic psychology, which examines paranormal beliefs and subjective anomalous experiences in traditional psychological terms.[48]

Research

Scope

Parapsychologists study a number of ostensible paranormal phenomena, including but not limited to:

- **Telepathy**: Transfer of information on thoughts or feelings between individuals by means other than the five classical senses.
- **Precognition**: Perception of information about future places or events before they occur.
- **Clairvoyance**: Obtaining information about places or events at remote locations, by means unknown to current science.
- **Psychokinesis**: The ability of the mind to influence matter, time, space, or energy by means unknown to current science.
- **Near-death experiences**: An experience reported by a person who nearly died, or who experienced clinical death and then revived.
- **Reincarnation**: The rebirth of a soul or other non-physical aspect of human consciousness in a new physical body after death.
- **Apparitional experiences**: Phenomena often attributed to ghosts and encountered in places a deceased individual is thought to have frequented, or in association with the person's former belongings.

The definitions for the terms above may not reflect their mainstream usage, nor the opinions of all parapsychologists and their critics.

According to the Parapsychological Association, parapsychologists do not study all paranormal phenomena, nor are they concerned with astrology, UFOs, cryptozoology, paganism, vampires, alchemy, or witchcraft.

Journals dealing with parapsychology include the *Journal of Parapsychology*, *Journal of Near-Death Studies*, *Journal of Consciousness Studies*, *Journal of the Society for Psychical Research*, and *Journal of Scientific Exploration*.

Experimental research

Ganzfeld

The Ganzfeld (German for "whole field") is a technique used to test individuals for telepathy. The technique—a form of moderate sensory deprivation—was developed to quickly quiet mental "noise" by providing mild, unpatterned stimuli to the visual and auditory senses. The visual sense is usually isolated by creating a soft red glow which is diffused through half ping-pong balls placed over the recipient's eyes. The auditory sense is usually blocked by playing white noise, static, or similar sounds to the recipient. The subject is also seated in a reclined, comfortable position to minimize the sense of touch.

In the typical Ganzfeld experiment, a "sender" and a "receiver" are isolated. The receiver is put into the Ganzfeld state, or Ganzfeld effect and the sender is shown a video clip or still picture and asked to mentally send that image to the receiver. The receiver, while in the Ganzfeld, is asked to continuously speak aloud all mental processes, including images, thoughts, and feelings. At the end of the sending period, typically about 20 to 40 minutes in length, the receiver is taken out of the Ganzfeld state and shown four images or videos, one of which is the true target and three of which are non-target decoys. The receiver attempts to select the true target, using perceptions experienced during the Ganzfeld state as clues to what the mentally "sent" image might have been.

The Ganzfeld experiment studies that were examined by Ray Hyman and Charles Honorton had methodological problems that were well documented. Honorton reported only 36% of the studies used duplicate target sets of pictures to avoid handling cues.[49] Hyman discovered flaws in all of the 42 Ganzfeld experiments and to assess each experiment, he devised a set of 12 categories of flaws. Six of these concerned statistical defects, the other six covered procedural flaws such as inadequate documentation, randomization and security as well as possibilities of sensory leakage. Over half of the studies failed to safeguard against sensory leakage and all of the studies contained at least one of the 12 flaws. Because of the flaws, Honorton agreed with Hyman the 42 Ganzfeld studies could not support the claim for the existence of psi.

Figure 7: *Participant of a Ganzfeld experiment. Proponents say such experiments have shown evidence of telepathy, while critics like Ray Hyman have pointed out that they have not been independently replicated.*

Possibilities of sensory leakage in the Ganzfeld experiments included the receivers hearing what was going on in the sender's room next door as the rooms were not soundproof and the sender's fingerprints to be visible on the target object for the receiver to see.[50] Hyman reviewed the autoganzfeld experiments and discovered a pattern in the data that implied a visual cue may have taken place. Hyman wrote the autoganzfeld experiments were flawed because they did not preclude the possibility of sensory leakage.

In 2010, Lance Storm, Patrizio Tressoldi, and Lorenzo Di Risio analyzed 29 Ganzfeld studies from 1997 to 2008. Of the 1,498 trials, 483 produced hits, corresponding to a hit rate of 32.2%. This hit rate is statistically significant with $p < .001$. Participants selected for personality traits and personal characteristics thought to be psi-conducive were found to perform significantly better than unselected participants in the Ganzfeld condition. Hyman (2010) published a rebuttal to Storm *et al.* According to Hyman, "Reliance on meta-analysis as the sole basis for justifying the claim that an anomaly exists and that the evidence for it is consistent and replicable is fallacious. It distorts what scientists mean by confirmatory evidence." Hyman wrote that the Ganzfeld studies were not independently replicated and failed to produce evidence for psi. Storm *et al.* published a response to Hyman stating that the Ganzfeld experimental design has proved to be consistent and reliable, that parapsychology is a struggling discipline that has not received much attention, and that therefore further research on the subject is necessary. Rouder *et al.* 2013 wrote that critical evaluation of Storm *et al.*'s meta-analysis reveals no evidence for psi, no plausible mechanism and omitted replication failures.

Figure 8: *Russell Targ, co-founder of the Stargate Project*

Remote viewing

Remote viewing is the practice of seeking impressions about a distant or unseen target using subjective means, in particular, extrasensory perception. Typically a remote viewer is expected to give information about an object, event, person or location that is hidden from physical view and separated at some distance.[51] Several hundred such trials have been conducted by investigators over the past 25 years, including those by the Princeton Engineering Anomalies Research Laboratory (PEAR) and by scientists at SRI International and Science Applications International Corporation. Many of these were under contract by the U.S. government as part of the espionage program Stargate Project, which terminated in 1995 having failed to document any practical intelligence value.

The psychologists David Marks and Richard Kammann attempted to replicate Russell Targ and Harold Puthoff's remote viewing experiments that were carried out in the 1970s at the Stanford Research Institute. In a series of 35 studies, they were unable to replicate the results, motivating them to investigate the procedure of the original experiments. Marks and Kammann discovered that the notes given to the judges in Targ and Puthoff's experiments contained clues as to the order in which they were carried out, such as referring to yesterday's two targets, or they had the date of the session written at the top of the page.

They concluded that these clues were the reason for the experiment's high hit rates. Marks was able to achieve 100 per cent accuracy without visiting any of the sites himself but by using cues.[52] James Randi wrote controlled tests in collaboration with several other researchers, eliminating several sources of cuing and extraneous evidence present in the original tests; Randi's controlled tests produced negative results. Students were also able to solve Puthoff and Targ's locations from the cues that had inadvertently been included in the transcripts.

In 1980, Charles Tart claimed that a rejudging of the transcripts from one of Targ and Puthoff's experiments revealed an above-chance result. Targ and Puthoff again refused to provide copies of the transcripts and it was not until July 1985 that they were made available for study, when it was discovered they still contained sensory cues.[53] Marks and Christopher Scott (1986) wrote "considering the importance for the remote viewing hypothesis of adequate cue removal, Tart's failure to perform this basic task seems beyond comprehension. As previously concluded, remote viewing has not been demonstrated in the experiments conducted by Puthoff and Targ, only the repeated failure of the investigators to remove sensory cues."

PEAR closed its doors at the end of February 2007. Its founder, Robert G. Jahn, said of it that, "For 28 years, we've done what we wanted to do, and there's no reason to stay and generate more of the same data." Statistical flaws in his work have been proposed by others in the parapsychological community and within the general scientific community. The physicist Robert L. Park said of PEAR, "It's been an embarrassment to science, and I think an embarrassment for Princeton".

Psychokinesis on random number generators

The advent of powerful and inexpensive electronic and computer technologies has allowed the development of fully automated experiments studying possible interactions between mind and matter. In the most common experiment of this type, a random number generator (RNG), based on electronic or radioactive noise, produces a data stream that is recorded and analyzed by computer software. A subject attempts to mentally alter the distribution of the random numbers, usually in an experimental design that is functionally equivalent to getting more "heads" than "tails" while flipping a coin. In the RNG experiment, design flexibility can be combined with rigorous controls, while collecting a large amount of data in a very short period of time. This technique has been used both to test individuals for psychokinesis and to test the possible influence on RNGs of large groups of people.

Major meta-analyses of the RNG database have been published every few years since appearing in the journal *Foundations of Physics* in 1986. PEAR founder

Robert G. Jahn and his colleague Brenda Dunne say that the experiments produced "a very small effect" not large enough to be observed over a brief experiment but over a large number of trials resulted in a tiny statistical deviation from chance. According to Massimo Pigliucci the results from PEAR can be explained without invoking the paranormal because of two problems with the experiment "the difficulty of designing machines capable of generating truly random events and the fact that statistical "significance" is not at all a good measure of the importance or genuineness of a phenomenon."[54] Pigluicci has written the statistical analysis used by the Jahn and the PEAR group relied on a quantity called a "p-value" but a problem with p-values is that if the sample size (number of trials) is very large like PEAR then one is guaranteed to find artificially low p-values indicating a statistical "significant" result even though nothing was occurring other than small biases in the experimental apparatus.

Two German independent scientific groups have failed to replicate the PEAR results. Pigliucci has written this was "yet another indication that the simplest hypothesis is likely to be true: there was nothing to replicate." The most recent meta-analysis on psychokinesis was published in *Psychological Bulletin*, along with several critical commentaries. It analyzed the results of 380 studies; the authors reported an overall positive effect size that was statistically significant but very small relative to the sample size and could, in principle, be explained by publication bias.

Direct mental interactions with living systems

Formerly called bio-PK, "direct mental interactions with living systems" (DMILS) studies the effects of one person's intentions on a distant person's psychophysiological state. One type of DMILS experiment looks at the commonly reported "feeling of being stared at." The "starer" and the "staree" are isolated in different locations, and the starer is periodically asked to simply gaze at the staree via closed circuit video links. Meanwhile, the staree's nervous system activity is automatically and continuously monitored.

Parapsychologists have interpreted the cumulative data on this and similar DMILS experiments to suggest that one person's attention directed towards a remote, isolated person can significantly activate or calm that person's nervous system. In a meta-analysis of these experiments published in the *British Journal of Psychology* in 2004, researchers found that there was a small but significant overall DMILS effect. However, the study also found that when a small number of the highest-quality studies from one laboratory were analyzed, the effect size was not significant. The authors concluded that although the existence of some anomaly related to distant intentions cannot be ruled out, there was also a shortage of independent replications and theoretical concepts.

Dream telepathy

Parapsychological studies into dream telepathy were carried out at the Maimonides Medical Center in Brooklyn, New York led by Stanley Krippner and Montague Ullman. They concluded the results from some of their experiments supported dream telepathy. However, the results have not been independently replicated.[55,56,57]

The picture target experiments that were conducted by Krippner and Ullman were criticized by C. E. M. Hansel. According to Hansel there were weaknesses in the design of the experiments in the way in which the agent became aware of their target picture. Only the agent should have known the target and no other person until the judging of targets had been completed; however, an experimenter was with the agent when the target envelope was opened. Hansel also wrote there had been poor controls in the experiment as the main experimenter could communicate with the subject.[58] In 2002, Krippner denied Hansel's accusations, claiming the agent did not communicate with the experimenter.[59]

An attempt to replicate the experiments that used picture targets was carried out by Edward Belvedere and David Foulkes. The finding was that neither the subject nor the judges matched the targets with dreams above chance level. Results from other experiments by Belvedere and Foulkes were also negative.[60]

In 2003, Simon Sherwood and Chris Roe wrote a review that claimed support for dream telepathy at Maimonides. However, James Alcock noted that their review was based on "extreme messiness" of data. Alcock concluded the dream telepathy experiments at Maimonides have failed to provide evidence for telepathy and "lack of replication is rampant."[61]

Near-death experiences

A near-death experience (NDE) is an experience reported by a person who nearly died, or who experienced clinical death and then revived. NDEs include one or more of the following experiences: a sense of being dead; an out-of-body experience; a sensation of floating above one's body and seeing the surrounding area; a sense of overwhelming love and peace; a sensation of moving upwards through a tunnel or narrow passageway; meeting deceased relatives or spiritual figures; encountering a being of light, or a light; experiencing a life review; reaching a border or boundary; and a feeling of being returned to the body, often accompanied by reluctance.

Interest in the NDE was originally spurred by the research of psychiatrists Elisabeth Kübler-Ross, George G. Ritchie, and Raymond Moody. In 1975, Moody wrote the best-selling book *Life After Life* and in 1977 he wrote a second book,

Figure 9: *Ascent of the Blessed by Hieronymus Bosch (after 1490) depicts a tunnel of light and spiritual figures similar to those reported by near-death experiencers.*

Reflections on Life After Life.[62] In 1998 Moody was appointed chair in "consciousness studies" at the University of Nevada, Las Vegas. The International Association for Near-death Studies (IANDS) was founded in 1978 to meet the needs of early researchers and experiencers within this field of research. Later researchers, such as psychiatrist Bruce Greyson, psychologist Kenneth Ring, and cardiologist Michael Sabom, introduced the study of near-death experiences to the academic setting.

Reincarnation research

Psychiatrist Ian Stevenson, from the University of Virginia, conducted more than 2,500 case studies over a period of 40 years and published twelve books. He wrote that childhood memories ostensibly related to reincarnation normally occurred between the ages of three and seven years then fade shortly afterwards. He compared the memories with reports of people known to the deceased, attempting to do so before any contact between the child and the deceased's family had occurred, and searched for disconfirming evidence that could provide alternative explanations for the reports aside from reincarnation.

Some 35 per cent of the subjects examined by Stevenson had birthmarks or birth defects. Stevenson believed that the existence of birth marks and deformities on children, when they occurred at the location of fatal wounds in the deceased, provided the best evidence for reincarnation. However, Stevenson has never claimed that he had proved the existence of reincarnation, and cautiously referred to his cases as being "of the reincarnation type" or "suggestive of reincarnation".[63] Researchers who believe in the evidence for reincarnation have been unsuccessful in getting the scientific community to consider it a serious possibility.

Ian Wilson argued that a large number of Stevenson's cases consisted of poor children remembering wealthy lives or belonging to a higher caste. He speculated that such cases may represent a scheme to obtain money from the family of the alleged former incarnation.[64] Philosopher Keith Augustine has written "the vast majority of Stevenson's cases come from countries where a religious belief in reincarnation is strong, and rarely elsewhere, seems to indicate that cultural conditioning (rather than reincarnation) generates claims of spontaneous past-life memories." According to the research of Robert Baker many of the alleged past-life experiences investigated by Stevenson and other parapsychologists can be explained in terms of known psychological factors. Baker has written the recalling of past lives is a mixture of cryptomnesia and confabulation.[65] Philosopher Paul Edwards noted that reincarnation invokes assumptions and is inconsistent with modern science.[66]

Scientific reception

Evaluation

The scientific consensus is that there is insufficient evidence to support the existence of psi phenomena.[67,68,69,70,71,72]

Scientists critical of parapsychology state that its extraordinary claims demand extraordinary evidence if they are to be taken seriously. Scientists who have evaluated parapsychology have written the entire body of evidence is of poor quality and not adequately controlled.[73] In support of this view, critics cite instances of fraud, flawed studies, and cognitive biases (such as clustering illusion, availability error, confirmation bias, illusion of control, magical thinking, and the bias blind spot) as ways to explain parapsychological results.[74] Research has also shown that people's desire to believe in paranormal phenomena causes them to discount strong evidence that it does not exist.

The psychologists Donovan Rawcliffe (1952), C. E. M. Hansel (1980), Ray Hyman (1989) and Andrew Neher (2011) have studied the history of psi experiments from the late 19th century up until the 1980s. In every experiment investigated, flaws and weaknesses were discovered so the possibility of sensory leakage and trickery were not ruled out. The data from the Creery sister and the Soal-Goldney experiments were proven to be fraudulent, one of the

Figure 10: *James Alcock is a notable critic of parapsychology.*

subjects from the Smith-Blackburn experiments confessed to fraud, the Brug-
mans experiment, the experiments by John Edgar Coover and those conducted
by Joseph Gaither Pratt and Helmut Schmidt had flaws in the design of the experiments, did not rule out the possibility of sensory cues or trickery and have
not been replicated.[75,76,77,78]

According to critics, psi is negatively defined as any effect that cannot be currently explained in terms of chance or normal causes and this is a fallacy as it
encourages parapsychologists into using any peculiarity in the data as a characteristic of psi.[79,80] Parapsychologists have admitted it is impossible to eliminate
the possibility of non-paranormal causes in their experiments. There is no independent method to indicate the presence or absence of psi. Persi Diaconis
has written that the controls in parapsychological experiments are often loose
with possibilities of subject cheating and unconscious sensory cues.

The existence of parapsychological phenomena and the scientific validity
of parapsychological research is disputed by independent evaluators and researchers. In 1988, the U.S. National Academy of Sciences published a report
on the subject that concluded that "no scientific justification from research
conducted over a period of 130 years for the existence of parapsychological phenomena." No accepted theory of parapsychology currently exists, and
many competing and often conflicting models have been advocated by different

parapsychologists in an attempt to explain reported paranormal phenomena.[81] Terence Hines in his book *Pseudoscience and the Paranormal* (2003) wrote "Many theories have been proposed by parapsychologists to explain how psi takes place. To skeptics, such theory building seems premature, as the phenomena to be explained by the theories have yet to be demonstrated convincingly."[82] Skeptics such as Antony Flew have cited the lack of such a theory as their reason for rejecting parapsychology.[83]

In 1998, physics professor Michael W. Friedlander noted that parapsychology has "failed to produce any clear evidence for the existence of anomalous effects that require us to go beyond the known region of science."[84] Philosopher and skeptic Robert Todd Carroll has written research in parapsychology has been characterized by "deception, fraud, and incompetence in setting up properly controlled experiments and evaluating statistical data." The psychologist Ray Hyman has pointed out that some parapsychologists such as Dick Bierman, Walter Lucadou, J. E. Kennedy, and Robert Jahn have admitted the evidence for psi is "inconsistent, irreproducible, and fails to meet acceptable scientific standards."[85] Richard Wiseman has criticized the parapsychological community for widespread errors in research methods including cherry-picking new procedures which may produce preferred results, explaining away unsuccessful attempted replications with claims of an "experimenter effect", data mining, and retrospective data selection.

In a review of parapsychological reports Hyman wrote "randomization is often inadequate, multiple statistical testing without adjustment for significance levels is prevalent, possibilities for sensory leakage are not uniformly prevented, errors in use of statistical tests are much too common, and documentation is typically inadequate". Parapsychology has been criticized for making no precise predictions.[86]

In 2003, James Alcock Professor of Psychology at York University published *Give the Null Hypothesis a Chance: Reasons to Remain Doubtful about the Existence of Psi*, where he claimed that parapsychologists never seem to take seriously the possibility that psi does not exist. Because of that, they interpret null results as indicating only that they were unable to observe psi in a particular experiment, rather than taking it as support for the possibility that there is no psi. The failure to take the null hypothesis as a serious alternative to their psi hypotheses leads them to rely upon a number of arbitrary "effects" to excuse failures to find predicted effects, excuse the lack of consistency in outcomes, and to excuse failures to replicate.

Basic endemic problems in parapsychological research include amongst others: insufficient definition of the subject matter, total reliance on negative definitions of their phenomena (E.g.- psi is said to occur only when all known normal influences are ruled out); failure to produce a single phenomenon that can

Figure 11: *Ray Hyman (standing), Lee Ross, Daryl Bem and Victor Benassi at the 1983 CSICOP Conference in Buffalo, New York*

be independently replicated by neutral researchers; the invention of "effects" such as the psi-experimenter effect to explain away inconsistencies in the data and failures to achieve predicted outcomes; unfalsifiability of claims; unpredictability of effects; lack of progress in over a century of formal research; methodological weaknesses; reliance on statistical procedures to determine when psi has supposedly occurred, even though statistical analysis does not in itself justify a claim that psi has occurred; and failure to jibe with other areas of science. Overall, he argues that there is nothing in parapsychological research that would ever lead parapsychologists to conclude that psi does not exist, and so, even if it does not, the search is likely to continue for a long time to come. "I continue to believe that parapsychology is, at bottom, motivated by belief in search of data, rather than data in search of explanation."

Richard Land has written that from what is known about human biology it is highly unlikely that evolution has provided humans with ESP as research has shown the recognized five senses are adequate for the evolution and survival of the species. Michael Shermer in an article *Psychic Drift: Why most scientists do not believe in ESP and psi phenomena* for *Scientific American* wrote "the reason for skepticism is that we need replicable data and a viable theory, both of which are missing in psi research."

In January 2008 the results of a study using neuroimaging were published. To provide what are purported to be the most favorable experimental conditions, the study included appropriate emotional stimuli and had participants who are biologically or emotionally related, such as twins. The experiment was designed to produce positive results if telepathy, clairvoyance or precognition occurred, but despite this no distinguishable neuronal responses were found between psychic stimuli and non-psychic stimuli, while variations in the same stimuli showed anticipated effects on patterns of brain activation. The researchers concluded that "These findings are the strongest evidence yet obtained against the existence of paranormal mental phenomena." Other studies have attempted to test the psi hypothesis by using functional neuroimaging. A neuroscience review of the studies (Acunzo *et al.* 2013) discovered methodological weaknesses that could account for the reported psi effects.

A 2014 study discovered that schizophrenic patients have more belief in psi than healthy adults.

Some researchers have become skeptical of parapsychology such as Susan Blackmore and John Taylor after years of study and no progress in demonstrating the existence of psi by the scientific method.[87,88]

Physics

The ideas of psi (precognition, psychokinesis and telepathy) violate well-established laws of physics.[89] Psychokinesis violates the inverse-square law, the second law of thermodynamics, and the conservation of momentum.[90,91] There is no known mechanism for psi.[92]

On the subject of psychokinesis, the physicist Sean M. Carroll has written that both human brains and the spoons they try to bend are made, like all matter, of quarks and leptons; everything else they do emerges as properties of the behavior of quarks and leptons. And the quarks and leptons interact through the four forces: strong, weak, electromagnetic and gravitational. Thus either it's one of the four known forces or it's a new force, and any new force with range over 1 millimetre must be at most a billionth the strength of gravity or it will have been captured in experiments already done. This leaves no physical force that could possibly account for psychokinesis.

Physicist John G. Taylor who investigated parapsychological claims has written an unknown fifth force causing psychokinesis would have to transmit a great deal of energy. The energy would have to overcome the electromagnetic forces binding the atoms together. The atoms would need to respond more strongly to the fifth force while it is operative than to electric forces. Such an additional force between atoms should therefore exist all the time and not during only alleged paranormal occurrences. Taylor wrote there is no scientific trace of such a force in physics, down to many orders of magnitude; thus if a scientific viewpoint is to be preserved the idea of any fifth force must be discarded. Taylor concluded there is no possible physical mechanism for psychokinesis and it is in complete contradiction to established science.[93]

Felix Planer, a professor of electrical engineering, has written that if psychokinesis was real then it would be easy to demonstrate by getting subjects to depress a scale on a sensitive balance, raise the temperature of a water bath which could be measured with an accuracy of a hundredth of a degree Celsius or affect an element in an electrical circuit such as a resistor which could be monitored to better than a millionth of an ampere.[94] Planer writes that such experiments are extremely sensitive and easy to monitor but are not utilized by parapsychologists as they "do not hold out the remotest hope of demonstrating even a minute trace of PK" because the alleged phenomenon is non-existent. Planer has written parapsychologists have to fall back on studies that involve only statistics that are unrepeatable, owing their results to poor experimental methods, recording mistakes and faulty statistical mathematics.

According to Planer, "all research in medicine and other sciences would become illusionary, if the existence of PK had to be taken seriously; for no experiment could be relied upon to furnish objective results, since all measurements would become falsified to a greater or lesser degree, according to his PK ability, by the experimenter's wishes." Planer concluded the concept of psychokinesis is absurd and has no scientific basis.[95]

Philosopher and physicist Mario Bunge has written that "psychokinesis, or PK, violates the principle that mind cannot act directly on matter. (If it did, no experimenter could trust his readings of measuring instruments.) It also violates the principles of conservation of energy and momentum. The claim that quantum mechanics allows for the possibility of mental power influencing randomizers—an alleged case of micro-PK—is ludicrous since that theory respects the said conservation principles, and it deals exclusively with physical things."

The physicist Robert L. Park questioned if mind really could influence matter then it would be easy for parapsychologists to measure such a phenomenon by using the alleged psychokinetic power to deflect a microbalance which would not require any dubious statistics but "the reason, of course, is that the microbalance stubbornly refuses to budge."[96] Park has suggested the reason statistical studies are so popular in parapsychology is because they introduce opportunities for uncertainty and error which are used to support the biases of the experimenter. Park wrote "No proof of psychic phenomena is ever found. In spite of all the tests devised by parapsychologists like Jahn and Radin, and huge amounts of data collected over a period of many years, the results are no more convincing today than when they began their experiments."

Figure 12: *Mario Bunge has described parapsychology as a "pseudoscience paragon".*[97]

Pseudoscience

Parapsychological theories are viewed as pseudoscientific by the scientific community as they are incompatible with well established laws of science. As there is no repeatable evidence for psi, the field is often regarded as a pseudoscience.[98,99,100]

The philosopher Raimo Tuomela summarized why the majority of scientists consider parapsychology to be a pseudoscience in his essay "Science, Protoscience, and Pseudoscience".[101]

- Parapsychology relies on an ill-defined ontology and typically shuns exact thinking.
- The hypotheses and theories of parapsychology have not been proven and are in bad shape.
- Extremely little progress has taken place in parapsychology on the whole and parapsychology conflicts with established science.
- Parapsychology has poor research problems, being concerned with establishing the existence of its subject matter and having practically no theories to create proper research problems.
- While in parts of parapsychology there are attempts to use the methods of science there are also unscientific areas; and in any case parapsychological

research can at best qualify as prescientific because of its poor theoretical foundation.

• Parapsychology is a largely isolated research area.

The methods of parapsychologists are regarded by critics, including those who wrote the science standards for the California State Board of Education, to be pseudoscientific. Some of the more specific criticisms state that parapsychology does not have a clearly defined subject matter, an easily repeatable experiment that can demonstrate a psi effect on demand, nor an underlying theory to explain the paranormal transfer of information. James Alcock has stated that few of parapsychology's experimental results have prompted interdisciplinary research with more mainstream sciences such as physics or biology, and that parapsychology remains an isolated science to such an extent that its very legitimacy is questionable, and as a whole is not justified in being labeled "scientific". Alcock has written "Parapsychology is indistinguishable from pseudo-science, and its ideas are essentially those of magic... There is *no* evidence that would lead the cautious observer to believe that parapsychologists and paraphysicists are on the track of a real phenomenon, a real energy or power that has so far escaped the attention of those people engaged in "normal" science."[102]

The scientific community considers parapsychology a pseudoscience because it continues to explore the hypothesis that psychic abilities exist despite a century of experimental results that fail to conclusively demonstrate that hypothesis. A panel commissioned by the United States National Research Council to study paranormal claims concluded that "despite a 130-year record of scientific research on such matters, our committee could find no scientific justification for the existence of phenomena such as extrasensory perception, mental telepathy or 'mind over matter' exercises... Evaluation of a large body of the best available evidence simply does not support the contention that these phenomena exist."[103]

There is also an issue of non-falsifiability associated with psi. On this subject Terence Hines has written:

<templatestyles src="Template:Quote/styles.css"/>

The most common rationale offered by parapsychologists to explain the lack of a repeatable demonstration of ESP or other psi phenomena is to say that ESP in particular and psi phenomena in general are elusive or jealous phenomena. This means the phenomena go away when a skeptic is present or when skeptical "vibrations" are present. This argument seems nicely to explain away some of the major problems facing parapsychology until it is realized that it is nothing more than a classic nonfalsifiable hypothesis... The use of the nonfalsifiable hypothesis is permitted in parapsychology to a degree unheard of in any scientific discipline. To the extent that investigators accept this type of hypothesis, they will be immune to having their belief in psi disproved. No matter how many experiments fail to provide evidence for psi and no matter how good those experiments are, the nonfalsifiable hypothesis will always protect the belief.[104]

Mario Bunge has written that research in parapsychology for over a hundred years has produced no single firm finding and no testable predictions. All parapsychologists can do is claim alleged data is anomalous and lying beyond the reach of ordinary science. The aim of parapsychologists "is not that of finding laws and systematizing them into theories in order to understand and forecast" but to "buttress ancient spiritualist myths or to serve as a surrogate for lost religions." In response to Bunge's position, Eberhard Bauer and Walter von Lucadou have argued that "there is not one single argument used by Bunge which has not been extensively discussed in the relevant literature for decades".

The psychologist David Marks has written that parapsychologists have failed to produce a single repeatable demonstration of the paranormal and described psychical research as a pseudoscience, an "incoherent collection of belief systems steeped in fantasy, illusion and error."[105] However, Chris French who is not convinced that parapsychology has demonstrated evidence for psi, has argued that parapsychological experiments still adhere to the scientific method, and should not be completely dismissed as pseudoscience. French has noted his position is "the minority view among critics of parapsychology".[106]

Philosopher Bradley Dowden characterized parapsychology as a pseudoscience as parapsychologists have no valid theories to test and no reproducible data from their experiments.[107]

Fraud

There have been instances of fraud in the history of parapsychology research.[108] In the late 19th century the Creery Sisters (Mary, Alice, Maud, Kathleen, and Emily) were tested by the Society for Psychical Research and believed them to have genuine psychic ability; however, during a later experiment they were caught utilizing signal codes and they confessed to fraud.[109,110] George Albert Smith and Douglas Blackburn were claimed to be genuine psychics by the Society for Psychical Research but Blackburn confessed to fraud:

<tcmplatcstyles src="Template:Quote/styles.css"/>

For nearly thirty years the telepathic experiments conducted by Mr. G. A. Smith and myself have been accepted and cited as the basic evidence of the truth of thought transference...

Figure 13: *Stage magician and skeptic James Randi has demonstrated that magic tricks can simulate or duplicate some supposedly psychic phenomena.*

...the whole of those alleged experiments were bogus, and originated in the honest desire of two youths to show how easily men of scientific mind and training could be deceived when seeking for evidence in support of a theory they were wishful to establish.[111]

The experiments of Samuel Soal and K. M. Goldney of 1941–1943 (suggesting precognitive ability of a single participant) were long regarded as some of the best in the field because they relied upon independent checking and witnesses to prevent fraud. However, many years later, statistical evidence, uncovered and published by other parapsychologists in the field, suggested that Soal had cheated by altering some of the raw data.[:140–141][112]

In 1974, a number of experiments by Walter J. Levy, J. B. Rhine's successor as director of the Institute for Parapsychology, were exposed as fraudulent.[113] Levy had reported on a series of successful ESP experiments involving computer-controlled manipulation of non-human subjects, including rats. His experiments showed very high positive results. However, Levy's fellow researchers became suspicious about his methods. They found that Levy interfered with data-recording equipment, manually creating fraudulent strings of positive results. Levy confessed to the fraud and resigned.[114]

In 1974 Rhine published the paper *Security versus Deception in Parapsychology* in the Journal of Parapsychology which documented 12 cases of fraud that he had detected from 1940 to 1950 but refused to give the names of the participants in the studies.[115] Massimo Pigliucci has written:

> *Most damning of all, Rhine admitted publicly that he had uncovered at least twelve instances of dishonesty among his researchers in a single decade, from 1940 to 1950. However, he flaunted standard academic protocol by refusing to divulge the names of the fraudsters, which means that there is unknown number of published papers in the literature that claim paranormal effects while in fact they were the result of conscious deception.*[116]

Martin Gardner claimed to have inside information that files in Rhine's laboratory contain material suggesting fraud on the part of Hubert Pearce.[117] Pearce was never able to obtain above-chance results when persons other than the experimenter were present during an experiment, making it more likely that he was cheating in some way. Rhine's other subjects were only able to obtain non-chance levels when they were able to shuffle the cards, which has suggested they used tricks to arrange the order of the Zener cards before the experiments started.[118]

A researcher from Tarkio College in Missouri, James D. MacFarland, was suspected of falsifying data to achieve positive psi results. Before the fraud was discovered, MacFarland published 2 articles in the Journal of Parapsychology (1937 & 1938) supporting the existence of ESP. Presumably speaking about MacFarland, Louisa Rhine wrote that in reviewing the data submitted to the lab in 1938, the researchers at the Duke Parapsychology Lab recognized the fraud. "...before long they were all certain that Jim had consistently falsified his records... To produce extra hits, Jim had to resort to erasures and transpositions in the records of his call series."[119] MacFarland never published another article in the Journal of Parapsychology after the fraud was discovered.

Some instances of fraud amongst spiritualist mediums were exposed by early psychical researchers such as Richard Hodgson and Harry Price.[120] In the 1920s, magician and escapologist Harry Houdini said that researchers and observers had not created experimental procedures which absolutely preclude fraud.

Criticism of experimental results

Critical analysts, including some parapsychologists, are not satisfied with experimental parapsychology studies. Some reviewers, such as psychologist Ray Hyman, contend that apparently successful experimental results in psi research are more likely due to sloppy procedures, poorly trained researchers, or methodological flaws rather than to genuine psi effects. Fellow psychologist Stuart Vyse hearkens back to a time of data manipulation, now recognized as "p-hacking," as part of the issue. Within parapsychology there are disagreements over the results and methodology as well. For example, the experiments at the PEAR laboratory were criticized in a paper published by the *Journal of Parapsychology* in which parapsychologists independent from the PEAR laboratory concluded that these experiments "depart[ed] from criteria usually expected in formal scientific experimentation" due to "[p]roblems with regard to randomization, statistical baselines, application of statistical models, agent coding of descriptor lists, feedback to percipients, sensory cues, and precautions against cheating." They felt that the originally stated significance values were "meaningless".

A typical measure of psi phenomena is statistical deviation from chance expectation. However, critics point out that statistical deviation is, strictly speaking, only evidence of a statistical anomaly, and the cause of the deviation is not known. Hyman contends that even if psi experiments could be designed that would regularly reproduce similar deviations from chance, they would not necessarily prove psychic functioning. Critics have coined the term *The Psi Assumption* to describe "the assumption that any significant departure from the laws of chance in a test of psychic ability is evidence that something anomalous or paranormal has occurred...[in other words] assuming what they should be proving." These critics hold that concluding the existence of psychic phenomena based on chance deviation in inadequately designed experiments is *affirming the consequent* or *begging the question*.

In 1979, magician and debunker James Randi engineered a hoax, now referred to as Project Alpha to encourage a tightening of standards within the parapsychology community. Randi recruited two young magicians and sent them undercover to Washington University's McDonnell Laboratory where they " fooled researchers ... into believing they had paranormal powers." The aim was to expose poor experimental methods and the credulity thought to be common in parapsychology. Randi has stated that both of his recruits deceived experimenters over a period of three years with demonstrations of supposedly psychic abilities: blowing electric fuses sealed in a box, causing a lightweight paper rotor perched atop a needle to turn inside a bell jar, bending metal spoons sealed in a glass bottle, etc.[121] The hoax by Randi raised ethical concerns in the scientific and parapsychology communities, eliciting criticism even among skeptical communities such as the Committee for the Scientific Investigation of Claims of the Paranormal (CSICOP), which he helped found, but also positive responses from the President of the Parapsychological Association Stanley Krippner. Psychologist Ray Hyman, a CSICOP member, called the results "counterproductive".

Selection bias and meta-analysis

Selective reporting has been offered by critics as an explanation for the positive results reported by parapsychologists. Selective reporting is sometimes referred to as a "file drawer" problem, which arises when only positive study results are made public, while studies with negative or null results are not made public. Selective reporting has a compounded effect on meta-analysis, which is a statistical technique that aggregates the results of many studies in order to generate sufficient statistical power to demonstrate a result that the individual studies themselves could not demonstrate at a statistically significant level. For example, a recent meta-analysis combined 380 studies on psychokinesis, including data from the PEAR lab. It concluded that, although there is a statistically significant overall effect, it is not consistent and relatively few negative studies would cancel it out. Consequently, biased publication of positive results could be the cause.

The popularity of meta-analysis in parapsychology has been criticized by numerous researchers, and is often seen as troublesome even within parapsychology itself. Critics have said that parapsychologists misuse meta-analysis to create the incorrect impression that statistically significant results have been obtained that indicate the existence of psi phenomena. Physicist Robert Park states that parapsychology's reported positive results are problematic because most such findings are invariably at the margin of statistical significance and that might be explained by a number of confounding effects; Park states that such marginal results are a typical symptom of pathological science as described by Irving Langmuir.

Researcher J. E. Kennedy has said that concerns over the use of meta-analysis in science and medicine apply as well to problems present in parapsychological meta-analysis. As a post-hoc analysis, critics emphasize the opportunity the method presents to produce biased outcomes via the selection of cases chosen for study, methods employed, and other key criteria. Critics say that analogous problems with meta-analysis have been documented in medicine, where it has been shown different investigators performing meta-analyses of the same set of studies have reached contradictory conclusions.

Anomalistic psychology

In anomalistic psychology, paranormal phenomena have naturalistic explanations resulting from psychological and physical factors which have sometimes given the impression of paranormal activity to some people when, in fact, there have been none.[122] According to the psychologist Chris French:

<templatestyles src="Template:Quote/styles.css"/>

*The difference between anomalistic psychology and parapsychology is in
terms of the aims of what each discipline is about. Parapsychologists
typically are actually searching for evidence to prove the reality of paranormal forces, to prove they really do exist. So the starting assumption
is that paranormal things do happen, whereas anomalistic psychologists
tend to start from the position that paranormal forces probably don't exist
and that therefore we should be looking for other kinds of explanations, in
particular the psychological explanations for those experiences that people typically label as paranormal.*[123]

Whilst parapsychology has been said to be in decline, anomalistic psychology
has been reported to be on the rise. It is now offered as an option on many
psychology degree programmes and is also an option on the A2 psychology
syllabus in the UK.[124]

Skeptics organizations

Organizations that encourage a critical examination of parapsychology and
parapsychological research include the Committee for Skeptical Inquiry, publisher of the *Skeptical Inquirer*; the James Randi Educational Foundation,
founded by illusionist and skeptic James Randi, and the Occult Investigative
Committee of the Society of American Magicians a society for professional
magicians/illusionists that seeks "the promotion of harmony among magicians,
and the opposition of the unnecessary public exposure of magical effects."

Further reading

<templatestyles src="Template:Refbegin/styles.css" />

- Alcock, James (1981). *Parapsychology-Science Or Magic?: A Psycholog-
  ical Perspective*. Pergamon Press.
- Bunge, Mario (1987). "Why Parapsychology Cannot Become a
  Science". *Behavioral and Brain Sciences*. **10** (4): 576–577. doi:
  10.1017/s0140525x00054595[125].
- Hines, Terence (2003). *Pseudoscience and the Paranormal*. Prometheus
  Books. ISBN 1-57392-979-4
- Irwin, Harvey J.; Watt, Caroline. (2007). *An Introduction to Parapsychol-
  ogy*. McFarland & Company. p. 320. ISBN 978-0-7864-3059-8.
- Marks, David (2000). *The Psychology of the Psychic (2nd Edition)*. New
  York: Prometheus Books. p. 336. ISBN 978-1-57392-798-7.
- Moore, E. Garth (1977). *Believe It or Not: Christianity and Psychical
  Research*. London: Mowbray. ISBN 0-264-66010-2
- Neher, Andrew (2011). *Paranormal and Transcendental Experience: A
  Psychological Examination*. Dover Publications.

- Randi, James (June 1982). *Flim-Flam! Psychics, ESP, Unicorns, and Other Delusions*. Prometheus Books. p. 342. ISBN 978-0-345-40946-1.
- Randi, James; Arthur C. Clarke (1997). *An Encyclopedia of Claims, Frauds, and Hoaxes of the Occult and Supernatural*. St. Martin's Griffin. p. 336. ISBN 978-0-312-15119-5.
- Sagan, Carl; Ann Druyan (1997). *The Demon-Haunted World: Science as a Candle in the Dark*. Ballantine Books. p. 349. ISBN 978-0-345-40946-1.
- Shepard, Leslie (2000). *Encyclopedia of Occultism and Parapsychology*. Thomson Gale. p. 1939. ISBN 978-0-8103-8570-2.
- Shermer, Michael (2003). "Psychic drift. Why most scientists do not believe in ESP and psi phenomena". *Scientific American*. **288**: 2.
- Wiseman, Richard; Watt, Caroline (2005). *Parapsychology (International Library of Psychology)*. Ashgate Publishing. pp. 501 pages. ISBN 978-0-7546-2450-9.

External links

- The Division of Perceptual Studies[126] at the University of Virginia School of Medicine.
- Institute of Noetic Sciences[127] A nonprofit organization that sponsors research in parapsychology.
- Parapsychological Association[128] An organization of scientists and scholars engaged in the study of psychic phenomena, affiliated with the American Association for the Advancement of Science in 1969.
- Rhine Research Center[129] A historical parapsychological research center featuring the first building ever made for experimental work in parapsychology. The Rhine Research Center is a hub for research and education in Parapsychology.
- Society for Psychical Research[130] Founded in 1882, the SPR was the first society to conduct organised scholarly research into parapsychology and other human experiences that challenge contemporary scientific models. It continues its work today.
- Committee for Skeptical Inquiry[131] Organization formed in 1976 to promote scientific skepticism and encourage the critical investigation of paranormal claims and parapsychology.
- James Randi Educational Foundation[132] The James Randi Education Foundation(JREF) was founded to promote critical thinking in the areas of the supernatural and paranormal. The JREF has provided skeptical views in the area of parapsychology.

- FindArticles.com Index[133] Large number of articles about parapsychol-
  ogy, from publications such as the *Journal of Parapsychology* and the
  Skeptical Inquirer.
- Parapsychology[134] at Curlie (based on DMOZ)

Research Scope

Telepathy

Telepathy (from the Greek τῆλε, *tele* meaning "distant" and πάθος, *pathos* or *-patheia* meaning "feeling, perception, passion, affliction, experience")[138,139] is the purported transmission of information from one person to another without using any known human sensory channels or physical interaction. The term was coined in 1882 by the classical scholar Frederic W. H. Myers, a founder of the Society for Psychical Research, and has remained more popular than the earlier expression *thought-transference*.[140]

Telepathy experiments have historically been criticized for lack of proper controls and repeatability. There is no convincing evidence that telepathy exists, and the topic is generally considered by the scientific community to be pseudoscience.[141,142]

Origins of the concept

According to historians such as Roger Luckhurst and Janet Oppenheim the origin of the concept of telepathy in Western civilization can be tracked to the late 19th century and the formation of the Society for Psychical Research.[143,144]

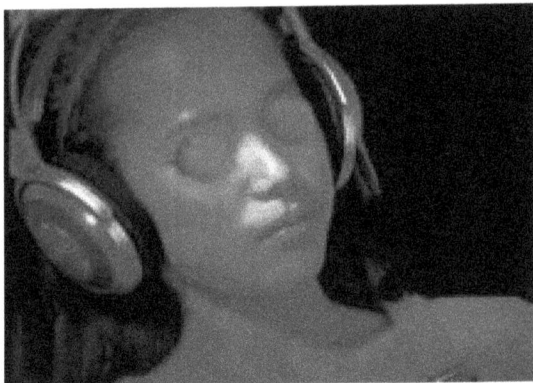

Figure 14: *The Ganzfeld experiments that aimed to demonstrate telepathy have been criticized for lack of replication and poor controls.*[136,137]

As the physical sciences made significant advances, scientific concepts were applied to mental phenomena (e.g., animal magnetism), with the hope that this would help to understand paranormal phenomena. The modern concept of telepathy emerged in this context.

Psychical researcher Eric Dingwall criticized SPR founding members Frederic W. H. Myers and William F. Barrett for trying to "prove" telepathy rather than objectively analyze whether or not it existed.[145]

Thought reading

In the late 19th century, the magician and mentalist, Washington Irving Bishop would perform "thought reading" demonstrations. Bishop claimed no supernatural powers and ascribed his powers to muscular sensitivity (reading thoughts from unconscious bodily cues).[146] Bishop was investigated by a group of scientists including the editor of the *British Medical Journal* and the psychologist Francis Galton. Bishop performed several feats successfully such as correctly identifying a selected spot on a table and locating a hidden object. During the experiment Bishop required physical contact with a subject who knew the correct answer. He would hold the hand or wrist of the helper. The scientists concluded that Bishop was not a genuine telepath but using a highly trained skill to detect ideomotor movements.[147]

Another famous thought reader was the magician Stuart Cumberland. He was famous for performing blindfolded feats such as identifying a hidden object in a room that a person had picked out or asking someone to imagine a murder scene and then attempt to read the subject's thoughts and identify the victim

Figure 15: *Gilbert Murray conducted early telepathy experiments.*

and reenact the crime. Cumberland claimed to possess no genuine psychic ability and his thought reading performances could only be demonstrated by holding the hand of his subject to read their muscular movements. He came into dispute with psychical researchers associated with the Society for Psychical Research who were searching for genuine cases of telepathy. Cumberland argued that both telepathy and communication with the dead were impossible and that the mind of man cannot be read through telepathy, but only by muscle reading.[148]

Case studies

In the late 19th century the Creery Sisters (Mary, Alice, Maud, Kathleen, and Emily) were tested by the Society for Psychical Research and believed to have genuine psychic ability. However, during a later experiment they were caught utilizing signal codes and they confessed to fraud.[149,150] George Albert Smith and Douglas Blackburn were claimed to be genuine psychics by the Society for Psychical Research but Blackburn confessed to fraud:

For nearly thirty years the telepathic experiments conducted by Mr. G. A. Smith and myself have been accepted and cited as the basic evidence of the truth of thought transference...

*...the whole of those alleged experiments were bogus, and originated in
the honest desire of two youths to show how easily men of scientific mind
and training could be deceived when seeking for evidence in support of a
theory they were wishful to establish.*[151]

Between 1916 and 1924, Gilbert Murray conducted 236 experiments into
telepathy and reported 36% as successful, however, it was suggested that the
results could be explained by hyperaesthesia as he could hear what was being
said by the sender.[152,153,154,155,156] Psychologist Leonard T. Troland had carried out experiments in telepathy at Harvard University which were reported
in 1917.[157,158,159,160] The subjects produced below chance expectations.[161]

Arthur Conan Doyle and W. T. Stead were duped into believing Julius and
Agnes Zancig had genuine psychic powers. Both Doyle and Stead wrote the
Zancigs performed telepathy. In 1924, Julius and Agnes Zancig confessed
that their mind reading act was a trick and published the secret code and all
the details of the trick method they had used under the title of *Our Secrets!!*
in a London newspaper.[162]

In 1924, Robert H. Gault of Northwestern University with Gardner Murphy
conducted the first American radio test for telepathy. The results were entirely
negative. One of their experiments involved the attempted thought transmission of a chosen number, out of 2010 replies none were correct.[163]

In February 1927, with the co-operation of the British Broadcasting Corporation (BBC), V. J. Woolley who was at the time the Research Officer for the
SPR, arranged a telepathy experiment in which radio listeners were asked to
take part. The experiment involved 'agents' thinking about five selected objects in an office at Tavistock Square, whilst listeners on the radio were asked
to identify the objects from the BBC studio at Savoy Hill. 24, 659 answers
were received. The results revealed no evidence for telepathy.[164,165]

A famous experiment in telepathy was recorded by the American author Upton
Sinclair in his book *Mental Radio* which documents Sinclair's test of psychic
abilities of Mary Craig Sinclair, his second wife. She attempted to duplicate
290 pictures which were drawn by her husband. Sinclair claimed Mary successfully duplicated 65 of them, with 155 "partial successes" and 70 failures.
However, these experiments were not conducted in a controlled scientific laboratory environment.[166] Science writer Martin Gardner suggested that the possibility of sensory leakage during the experiment had not been ruled out:

<templatestyles src="Template:Quote/styles.css"/>

*In the first place, an intuitive wife, who knows her husband intimately,
may be able to guess with a fair degree of accuracy what he is likely to
draw—particularly if the picture is related to some freshly recalled event*

Figure 16: *Frederick Marion who was investigated by the Society for Psychical Research in the late 1930-1940s.*

the two experienced in common. At first, simple pictures like chairs and tables would likely predominate, but as these are exhausted, the field of choice narrows and pictures are more likely to be suggested by recent experiences. It is also possible that Sinclair may have given conversational hints during some of the tests—hints which in his strong will to believe, he would promptly forget about. Also, one must not rule out the possibility that in many tests, made across the width of a room, Mrs. Sinclair may have seen the wiggling of the top of a pencil, or arm movements, which would convey to her unconscious a rough notion of the drawing.

The Turner-Ownbey long distance telepathy experiment was discovered to contain flaws. May Frances Turner positioned herself in the Duke Parapsychology Laboratory whilst Sara Ownbey claimed to receive transmissions 250 miles away. For the experiment Turner would think of a symbol and write it down whilst Ownbey would write her guesses.[167] The scores were highly successful and both records were supposed to be sent to J. B. Rhine; however, Ownbey sent them to Turner. Critics pointed out this invalidated the results as she could have simply written her own record to agree with the other. When the experiment was repeated and the records were sent to Rhine the scores dropped to average.[168,169]

Another example is the experiment carried out by the author Harold Sherman with the explorer Hubert Wilkins who carried out their own experiment in telepathy for five and a half months starting in October 1937. This took place when Sherman was in New York and Wilkins was in the Arctic. The experiment consisted of Sherman and Wilkins at the end of each day to relax and visualise a mental image or "thought impression" of the events or thoughts they had experienced in the day and then to record those images and thoughts on paper in a diary. The results at the end when comparing Sherman's and Wilkins' diaries were claimed to be more than 60 percent.[170]

The full results of the experiments were published in 1942 in a book by Sherman and Wilkins titled *Thoughts Through Space*. In the book both Sherman and Wilkins had written they believed they had demonstrated that it was possible to send and receive thought impressions from the mind of one person to another.[171] The magician John Booth wrote the experiment was not an example of telepathy as a high percentage of misses had occurred. Booth wrote it was more likely that the "hits" were the result of "coincidence, law of averages, subconscious expectancy, logical inference or a plain lucky guess".[172] A review of their book in the *American Journal of Orthopsychiatry* cast doubt on their experiment noting "the study was published five years after it was conducted, arouses suspicion on the validity of the conclusions.[173]

In 1948, on the BBC radio Maurice Fogel made the claim that he could demonstrate telepathy. This intrigued the journalist Arthur Helliwell who wanted to discover his methods. He found that Fogel's mind reading acts were all based on trickery, he relied on information about members of his audience before the show started. Helliwell exposed Fogel's methods in a newspaper article. Although Fogel managed to fool some people into believing he could perform genuine telepathy, the majority of his audience knew he was a showman.[174]

In a series of experiments Samuel Soal and his assistant K. M. Goldney examined 160 subjects over 128,000 trials and obtained no evidence for the existence of telepathy.[175] Soal tested Basil Shackleton and Gloria Stewart between 1941 and 1943 in over five hundred sittings and over twenty thousand guesses. Shackleton scored 2890 compared with a chance expectation of 2308 and Gloria scored 9410 compared with a chance level of 7420. It was later discovered the results had been tampered with. Gretl Albert who was present during many of the experiments said she had witnessed Soal altering the records during the sessions. Betty Marwick discovered Soal had not used the method of random selection of numbers as he had claimed. Marwick showed that there had been manipulation of the score sheets "all the experiments reported by Soal had thereby been discredited."[176,177]

In 1979 the physicists John G. Taylor and Eduardo Balanovski wrote the only scientifically feasible explanation for telepathy could be electromagnetism

(EM) involving EM fields. In a series of experiments the EM levels were many orders of magnitude lower than calculated and no paranormal effects were observed. Both Taylor and Balanovski wrote their results were a strong argument against the validity of telepathy.

Research in anomalistic psychology has discovered that in some cases telepathy can be explained by a covariation bias. In an experiment (Schienle *et al.* 1996) 22 believers and 20 skeptics were asked to judge the covariation between transmitted symbols and the corresponding feedback given by a receiver. According to the results the believers overestimated the number of successful transmissions whilst the skeptics made accurate hit judgments. The results from another telepathy experiment involving 48 undergraduate college students (Rudski, 2002) were explained by hindsight and confirmation biases.

In parapsychology

Within the field of parapsychology, telepathy is considered to be a form of extrasensory perception (ESP) or anomalous cognition in which information is transferred through Psi. It is often categorized similarly to precognition and clairvoyance.[178] Experiments have been used to test for telepathic abilities. Among the most well known are the use of Zener cards and the Ganzfeld experiment.

Types

Parapsychology describes several forms of telepathy:

- **Latent telepathy**, formerly known as "deferred telepathy",[179] is described as the transfer of information, through Psi, with an observable time-lag between transmission and reception.
- **Retrocognitive,Wikipedia:Verifiability precognitive, and intuitiveWikipedia:Verifiability telepathy** is described as being the transfer of information, through Psi, about the past, future or present state of an individual's mind to another individual.
- **Emotive telepathy**, also known as remote influence[180] or emotional transfer, is the process of transferring kinesthetic sensations through altered states.
- **Superconscious telepathy** involves tapping into the superconscious[181] to access the collective wisdom of the human species for knowledge.

Figure 17: *Zener cards*

Zener Cards

Zener cards are marked with five distinctive symbols. When using them, one individual is designated the "sender" and another the "receiver". The sender selects a random card and visualize the symbol on it, while the receiver attempts to determine that symbol using Psi. Statistically, the receiver has a 20% chance of randomly guessing the correct symbol, so to demonstrate telepathy, they must repeatedly score a success rate that is significantly higher than 20%. If not conducted properly, this method can be vulnerable to sensory leakage and card counting.

J. B. Rhine's experiments with Zener cards were discredited due to the discovery that sensory leakage or cheating could account for all his results such as the subject being able to read the symbols from the back of the cards and being able to see and hear the experimenter to note subtle clues.[182] Once Rhine took precautions in response to criticisms of his methods, he was unable to find any high-scoring subjects.[183] Due to the methodological problems, parapsychologists no longer utilize card-guessing studies.[184]

Dream telepathy

Parapsychological studies into dream telepathy were carried out at the Maimonides Medical Center in Brooklyn, New York led by Stanley Krippner and Montague Ullman. They concluded the results from some of their experiments supported dream telepathy. However, the results have not been independently replicated.[185,186,187] The psychologist James Alcock has written the dream telepathy experiments at Maimonides have failed to provide evidence for telepathy and "lack of replication is rampant."

The picture target experiments that were conducted by Krippner and Ullman were criticized by C. E. M. Hansel. According to Hansel there were weaknesses in the design of the experiments in the way in which the agent became aware of their target picture. Only the agent should have known the target and no other person until the judging of targets had been completed, however, an experimenter was with the agent when the target envelope was opened. Hansel also wrote there had been poor controls in the experiment as the main experimenter could communicate with the subject.[188]

An attempt to replicate the experiments that used picture targets was carried out by Edward Belvedere and David Foulkes. The finding was that neither the subject nor the judges matched the targets with dreams above chance level. Results from other experiments by Belvedere and Foulkes were also negative.[189]

Ganzfeld experiment

When using the Ganzfeld experiment to test for telepathy, one individual is designated the receiver and is placed inside a controlled environment where they are deprived of sensory input, and another is designated the sender and is placed in a separate location. The receiver is then required to receive information from the sender. The nature of the information may vary between experiments.[190]

The ganzfeld experiment studies that were examined by Ray Hyman and Charles Honorton had methodological problems that were well documented. Honorton reported only 36% of the studies used duplicate target sets of pictures to avoid handling cues.[191] Hyman discovered flaws in all of the 42 ganzfeld experiments and to access each experiment, he devised a set of 12 categories of flaws. Six of these concerned statistical defects, the other six covered procedural flaws such as inadequate documentation, randomization and security as well as possibilities of sensory leakage.[192] Over half of the studies failed to safeguard against sensory leakage and all of the studies contained at least one of the 12 flaws. Because of the flaws, Honorton agreed with Hyman the 42 ganzfeld studies could not support the claim for the existence of psi.

Possibilities of sensory leakage in the ganzfeld experiments included the receivers hearing what was going on in the sender's room next door as the rooms were not soundproof and the sender's fingerprints to be visible on the target object for the receiver to see.[193,194]

Hyman also reviewed the autoganzfeld experiments and discovered a pattern in the data that implied a visual cue may have taken place:

<templatestyles src=”Template:Quote/styles.css”/>

The most suspicious pattern was the fact that the hit rate for a given target increased with the frequency of occurrence of that target in the experiment. The hit rate for the targets that occurred only once was right at the chance expectation of 25%. For targets that appeared twice the hit rate crept up to 28%. For those that occurred three times it was 38%, and for those targets that occurred six or more times, the hit rate was 52%. Each time a videotape is played its quality can degrade. It is plausible then, that when a frequently used clip is the target for a given session, it may be physically distinguishable from the other three decoy clips that are presented to the subject for judging. Surprisingly, the parapsychological community has not taken this finding seriously. They still include the autoganzfeld series in their meta-analyses and treat it as convincing evidence for the reality of psi.

Hyman wrote the autoganzfeld experiments were flawed because they did not preclude the possibility of sensory leakage. In 2010, Lance Storm, Patrizio Tressoldi, and Lorenzo Di Risio analyzed 29 ganzfeld studies from 1997 to 2008. Of the 1,498 trials, 483 produced hits, corresponding to a hit rate of 32.2%. This hit rate is statistically significant with $p < .001$. Participants selected for personality traits and personal characteristics thought to be psi-conducive were found to perform significantly better than unselected participants in the ganzfeld condition. Hyman (2010) published a rebuttal to Storm *et al.* According to Hyman "reliance on meta-analysis as the sole basis for justifying the claim that an anomaly exists and that the evidence for it is consistent and replicable is fallacious. It distorts what scientists mean by confirmatory evidence." Hyman wrote the ganzfeld studies have not been independently replicated and have failed to produce evidence for telepathy.[195] Storm *et al.* published a response to Hyman claiming the ganzfeld experimental design has proved to be consistent and reliable but parapsychology is a struggling discipline that has not received much attention so further research on the subject is necessary. Rouder *et al.* 2013 wrote that critical evaluation of Storm *et al.*'s meta-analysis reveals no evidence for telepathy, no plausible mechanism and omitted replication failures.

A 2016 paper examined questionable research practices in the ganzfeld experiments.

Twin telepathy

Twin telepathy is a belief that has been described as a myth in psychological literature. Psychologists Stephen Hupp and Jeremy Jewell have noted that all experiments on the subject have failed to provide any scientific evidence for telepathy between twins.[196] According to Hupp and Jewell there are various behavioral and genetic factors that contribute to the twin telepathy myth "identical twins typically spend a lot of time together and are usually exposed to very similar environments. Thus, it's not at all surprising that they act in similar ways and are adept at anticipating and forecasting each other's reactions to events."

A 1993 study by Susan Blackmore investigated the claims of twin telepathy. In an experiment with six sets of twins one subject would act as the sender and the other the receiver. The sender was given selected objects, photographs or numbers and would attempt to psychically send the information to the receiver. The results from the experiment were negative, no evidence of telepathy was observed.[197]

The skeptical investigator Benjamin Radford has noted that "Despite decades of research trying to prove telepathy, there is no credible scientific evidence that psychic powers exist, either in the general population or among twins specifically. The idea that two people who shared their mother's womb — or even who share the same DNA — have a mysterious mental connection is an intriguing one not borne out in science."[198]

Scientific reception

A variety of tests have been performed to demonstrate telepathy, but there is no scientific evidence that the power exists.[199,200,201] A panel commissioned by the United States National Research Council to study paranormal claims concluded that "despite a 130-year record of scientific research on such matters, our committee could find no scientific justification for the existence of phenomena such as extrasensory perception, mental telepathy or 'mind over matter' exercises... Evaluation of a large body of the best available evidence simply does not support the contention that these phenomena exist."[202] The scientific community considers parapsychology a pseudoscience.[203,204,205] There is no known mechanism for telepathy.[206] Philosopher and physicist Mario Bunge has written that telepathy would contradict laws of science and the claim that "signals can be transmitted across space without fading with distance is inconsistent with physics".[207]

Physicist John Taylor has written the experiments that have been claimed by parapsychologists to support evidence for the existence of telepathy are based on the use of shaky statistical analysis and poor design, and attempts to duplicate such experiments by the scientific community have failed. Taylor also wrote the arguments used by parapsychologists for the feasibility of such phenomena are based on distortions of theoretical physics as well as "complete ignorance" of relevant areas of physics.[208]

Psychologist Stuart Sutherland wrote that cases of telepathy can be explained by people underestimating the probability of coincidences. According to Sutherland, "most stories about this phenomenon concern people who are close to one another - husband and wife or brother and sister. Since such people have much in common, it is highly probable that they will sometimes think the same thought at the same time."[209] Graham Reed, a specialist in anomalistic psychology, noted that experiments into telepathy often involve the subject relaxing and reporting the 'messages' to consist of colored geometric shapes. Reed wrote that these are a common type of hypnagogic image and not evidence for telepathic communication.[210]

Outside of parapsychology, telepathy is generally explained as the result of fraud, self-delusion and/or self-deception and not as a paranormal power.[211] Psychological research has also revealed other explanations such as confirmation bias, expectancy bias, sensory leakage, subjective validation and wishful thinking.[212] Virtually all of the instances of more popular psychic phenomena, such as mediumship, can be attributed to non-paranormal techniques such as cold reading.[213,214] Magicians such as Ian Rowland and Derren Brown have demonstrated techniques and results similar to those of popular psychics, without paranormal means. They have identified, described, and developed psychological techniques of cold reading and hot reading.

Psychiatry

The notion of telepathy is not dissimilar to two clinical concepts: delusions of thought insertion/removal. This similarity might explain how an individual might come to the conclusion that they were experiencing telepathy. Thought insertion/removal is a symptom of psychosis, particularly of schizophrenia, schizoaffective disorder or substance-induced psychosis.[215] Psychiatric patients who experience this symptom falsely believe that some of their thoughts are not their own and that others (e.g., other people, aliens, demons or fallen angels, or conspiring intelligence agencies) are putting thoughts into their minds (thought insertion). Some patients feel as if thoughts are being taken out of their minds or deleted (thought removal). Along with other symptoms of psychosis, delusions of thought insertion may be reduced by antipsychotic medication. Psychiatrists and clinical psychologists believe and empirical findings support the idea that people with schizotypy and schizotypal personality disorder are particularly likely to believe in telepathy.[216,217,218]

Use in fiction

Telepathy is a common theme in modern fiction and science fiction, with many extraterrestrials (such as the Protoss in the StarCraft franchise), superheroes, and supervillains having telepathic ability.

Further reading

- James Alcock. (1981). *Parapsychology: Science or Magic? A Psychological Perspective*. Pergamon Press. ISBN 0-08-025772-0
- Bergen Evans. (1954). *The Spoor of Spooks: And Other Nonsense*. Knopf.
- C. E. M. Hansel. (1989). *The Search for Psychic Power: ESP and Parapsychology Revisited*. Prometheus Books. ISBN 0-87975-516-4
- Walter Mann. (1919). *The Follies and Frauds of Spiritualism*[219]. Rationalist Association. London: Watts & Co. Chapter XII. pp. 131–191.
- David Marks. (2000). *The Psychology of the Psychic* (2nd Edition). Prometheus Books. ISBN 1-57392-798-8
- Kenneth Wilcox Payne. (1928). *Is Telepathy All Bunk?*[220] Popular Science.
- Felix Planer. (1980). *Superstition*. Cassell. ISBN 0-304-30691-6
- Graham Reed. (1988). *The Psychology of Anomalous Experience*. Prometheus Books. ISBN 0-87975-435-4
- Stuart Sutherland. (1994). *Irrationality: The Enemy Within*. Penguin Books. ISBN 0-14-016726-9

External links

- The Intuitive Magician[221] - Bruce Hood
- Telepathy[222] - Skeptic's Dictionary
- Soal-Goldney Experiment[223] - a critical evaluation of the Soal-Goldney Experiment, which claimed to prove the existence of telepathy
- Dream and Telepathy[224] - article in Science and Psychoanalysis

Precognition

Precognition (from the Latin *prae-*, "before" and *cognitio*, "acquiring knowledge"), also called **prescience**, **future vision**, **future sight** is an alleged psychic ability to see events in the future.

As with other forms of extrasensory perception, there is no reliable scientific evidence that precognition is a real ability possessed by anyone and it is widely considered to be pseudoscience. Specifically, precognition appears to violate the principle of causality, that an effect cannot occur before its cause.

Precognition has been widely believed in throughout history. Despite the lack of scientific evidence, many people still believe it to be real; it is still widely reported and remains a topic of research and discussion within the parapsychology community.

History

Antiquity

Since ancient times, precognition has been associated with trance and dream states involved in phenomena such as prophecy, fortune telling and second sight, as well as waking premonitions. These phenomena were widely accepted and reports have persisted throughout history, with most instances appearing in dreams.[226]

Such claims of seeing the future have never been without their sceptical critics. Aristotle carried out an inquiry into allegedly prophetic dreams in his *On Divination in Sleep*. He accepted that "it is quite conceivable that some dreams may be tokens and causes [of future events]" but also believed that "most [so-called prophetic] dreams are, however, to be classed as mere coincidences...". Where Democritus had suggested that emanations from future events could be sent back to the dreamer, Aristotle proposed that it was, rather, the dreamer's sense impressions which reached forward to the event.[227]

17th–19th centuries

The term "precognition" first appeared in the 17th century but did not come into common use among investigators until much later.

An early investigation into claims of precognition was published by the missionary Fr. P. Boilat in 1883. He claimed to have put an unspoken question to an African witch-doctor whom he mistrusted. Contrary to his expectations, the witch-doctor gave him the correct answer without ever having heard the question.

Early 20th century

In the early 20th century J. W. Dunne, a British aeronautics engineer, experienced several dreams which he regarded as precognitive. He developed techniques to record and analyse them, identifying any correspondences between his future experiences and his recorded dreams. He reported his findings in his 1927 book *An Experiment with Time*. In it he alleges that 10% of his dreams appeared to include some element of future experience. He also persuaded some friends to try the experiment on themselves, with mixed results. Dunne concluded that precognitive elements in dreams are common and that many people unknowingly have them.[228,229] He suggested also that dream precognition did not reference any kind of future event, but specifically the future experiences of the dreamer. He was led to this idea when he found that a dream of a volcanic eruption appeared to foresee not the disaster itself but his subsequent misreading of an inaccurate account in a newspaper.[230] In 1932 he helped the Society for Psychical Research to conduct a more formal experiment, but he and the Society's lead researcher failed to agree on the significance of the results.[231,232] The Philosopher C. D. Broad remarked that, "The only theory known to me which seems worth consideration is that proposed by Mr. Dunne in his Experiment with Time."[233]

In 1932 Charles Lindbergh's infant son was kidnapped, murdered and buried among trees. The psychologists Henry Murray and D. R. Wheeler tested precognitive dreams by inviting the public to report any dreams of the child. A total of 1,300 dreams were reported. Only five percent envisioned the child dead and only 4 of the 1,300 envisioned the location of the grave as amongst trees. This number was no better than chance.

The first ongoing and organized research program on precognition was instituted by Joseph Banks Rhine in the 1930s at Duke University's Parapsychology Laboratory. Rhine used a method of forced-choice matching in which participants guessed the order of a deck of 25 cards, each five of which bore one of five geometrical symbols. Although his results were positive and gained some academic acceptance, his methods were later shown to be badly flawed and subsequent researchers using more rigorous procedures were unable to reproduce his results.[234,235,236]

Samuel G. Soal was described by Rhine as one of his harshest critics, running many similar experiments with wholly negative results. However from around 1940 he ran forced-choice ESP experiments in which a subject attempted to identify which of five animal pictures a subject in another room was looking at. Their performance on this task was at chance, but when the scores were matched with the card that came *after* the target card, three of the thirteen subjects showed a very high hit rate. Rhine now described Soal's work as "a milestone in the field". However analyses of Soal's findings, conducted several years later, concluded that the positive results were more likely the result of deliberate fraud. The controversy continued for many years more. In 1978 the statistician and paragnostWikipedia:Please clarify Betty Markwick, while seeking to vindicate Soal, discovered that he had tampered with his data. The untainted experimental results showed no evidence of precognition.[237]

Late 20th century

As more modern technology became available, more automated techniques of experimentation were developed that did not rely on hand-scoring of equivalence between targets and guesses, and in which the targets could be more reliably and readily tested at random. In 1969 Helmut Schmidt introduced the use of high-speed random event generators (REG) for precognition testing, and experiments were also conducted at the Princeton Engineering Anomalies Research Lab. Once again, flaws were found in all of Schmidt's experiments, when the psychologist C. E. M. Hansel found that several necessary precautions were not taken.[238]

In 1963 the BBC television programme *Monitor* broadcast an appeal by the writer J.B. Priestley for experiences which challenged our understanding of Time. He received hundreds of letters in reply and believed that many of them described genuine precognitive dreams.[239,240] In 2014 the BBC Radio 4 broadcaster Francis Spufford revisited Priestley's work and its relation to the ideas of J.W. Dunne.[241]

David Ryback, a psychologist in Atlanta, used a questionnaire survey approach to investigate precognitive dreaming in college students. His survey of over 433 participants showed that 290 or 66.9 percent reported some form of paranormal dream. He rejected many of these reports, but claimed that 8.8 percent of the population was having actual precognitive dreams.[242]

G. W. Lambert, a former Council member of the SPR, proposed five criteria that needed to be met before an account of a precognitive dream could be regarded as credible:

1. The dream should be reported to a credible witness before the event.
2. The time interval between the dream and the event should be short.
3. The event should be unexpected at the time of the dream.
4. The description should be of an event destined literally, and not symbolically, to happen.
5. The details of dream and event should tally.

21st century

In 2011 the psychologist Daryl Bem, a Professor Emeritus at Cornell University, published findings showing statistical evidence for precognition in an upper tier journal, the *Journal of Personality and Social Psychology*. The paper was heavily criticised and the criticism widened to include the journal itself and the validity of the peer review process.[243] Public controversy over the paper continued until in 2012 the results were published of an independent attempt to reproduce Bem's results, which failed to do so.

Scientific criticism

Claims of precognition are, like any other claims, open to scientific criticism. However the nature of the criticism must adapt to the nature of the claim.

Claims of precognition are criticised on two main grounds:

• There is no known scientific mechanism which would allow precognition and it appears to break known scientific laws.[244]
• There is no accepted scientific evidence that precognition exists.

Consequently, precognition is widely considered to be pseudoscience.[245,246,247]

Violation of natural law

Precognition would violate the principle of antecedence (causality), that an effect does not happen before its cause.[248] Information passing backwards in time would need to be carried by physical particles doing the same. Experimental evidence from high-energy physics suggests that this cannot happen. There is therefore no direct justification for precognition from physics."[249]

Precognition contradicts "most of the neuroscience and psychology literature, from electrophysiology and neuroimaging to temporal effects found in psychophysical research." It is considered a delusion by mainstream psychiatry.Wikipedia:Citation needed

The relatively new discovery of evidence for quantum retrocausality is sometimes suggested as a possible mechanism for precognition.[250] However it is generally held that such "quantum weirdness", even if it is shown to exist, cannot carry information at a macroscopic level.

Lack of evidence

A great deal of evidence for precognition has been put forward, both as witnessed anecdotes and as experimental results, but none has yet been accepted as rigorous scientific proof of the phenomenon.Wikipedia:Citation needed

Alternative explanations

Various known psychological processes have been put forward to explain experiences of apparent precognition. These include:

* *Déjà vu* or *identifying paramnesia*, in which people conjure up a false memory of a vision having occurred before the actual event.
* *Unconscious perception* by which people unconsciously infer, from data they have unconsciously learned, that a certain event will probably happen in a certain context. When the event occurs, the former knowledge appears to have been acquired without the aid of recognized channels of information.
* *Self-fulfilling prophecy* and *Unconscious enactment* in which people unconsciously bring about events which they have previously imagined.
* *Memory biases* where people selectively remember or distort past experiences to match subsequent events.[251] In one experiment, subjects were asked to write down their dreams in a diary. This prevented the selective memory effect, and the dreams no longer seemed accurate about the future.[252] Another experiment gave subjects a fake diary of a student with apparently precognitive dreams. This diary described events from the person's life, as well as some predictive dreams and some non-predictive dreams. When subjects were asked to recall the dreams they had read, they remembered more of the successful predictions than unsuccessful ones.[253]
* *Coincidence* where apparent instances of precognition in fact arise from the law of large numbers.[254,255]

Cultural impact

Popular belief

Premonitions have sometimes affected the course of important historical events. Related activities such as prophecy and fortune telling have been practised throughout history and are still popular today.

Despite the lack of scientific evidence, many people still believe in precognition.[256] A 1978 poll found that 37% of Americans surveyed believed in it. According to some psychologists, belief is greater in college women than in men, and a 2007 poll found that women were more prone to superstitious beliefs in general. Some studies have been carried out on psychological reasons for such a belief. One such study suggested that greater belief in precognition was held by those who feel low in control, and the belief can act as a psychological coping mechanism.

Literary references

J. W. Dunne's main work *An Experiment with Time* was widely read and "undoubtedly helped to form something of the imaginative climate of [the interwar] years", influencing many writers of both fact and fiction both then and since.[257] Major writers whose work was significantly influenced by his ideas on dream precognition include H. G. Wells, J. B. Priestley and Vladimir Nabokov.[258,259] Philippa Pearce's 1958 childhood fantasy *Tom's Midnight Garden* won the British literary Carnegie Medal.

References

Bibliography

* Dunne, J. W. (1927). *An Experiment With Time*. A. C. Black.
* Hines, Terence (2003). *Pseudoscience and the Paranormal*. Prometheus Books. ISBN 978-1-57392-979-0.
* Inglis, Brian. (1985). *The Paranormal: An Encyclopedia of Psychic Phenomena*. Paladin.
* Priestley, J.B. *Man and Time*. Aldus 1964, 2nd Edition Bloomsbury 1989.
* Wynn, Charles M., and Wiggins, Arthur W. (2001). *Quantum Leaps in the Wrong Direction: Where Real Science Ends...and Pseudoscience Begins*. Joseph Henry Press. ISBN 978-0-309-07309-7

Further reading

Wikisourcehas the text of the 1911 *Encyclopædia Britannica*article *Premonition*.

* Chris French. (2012). "Precognition Studies and the Curse of the Failed Replications"[260]. *The Guardian*.
* David Marks. (2000). *The Psychology of the Psychic* (2nd Edition). Prometheus Books. ISBN 1-57392-798-8

Clairvoyance

Clairvoyance (/klɛərˈvɔɪəns/) (from French *clair* meaning "clear" and *voyance* meaning "vision") is the alleged ability to gain information about an object, person, location, or physical event through extrasensory perception.[262] Any person who is claimed to have such ability is said accordingly to be a **clairvoyant** (/klɛərˈvɔɪənt/) ("one who sees clearly").

Claims for the existence of paranormal and psychic abilities such as clairvoyance have not been supported by scientific evidence published in high impact factor peer reviewed journals.[263] Parapsychology explores this possibility, but the existence of the paranormal is not accepted by the scientific community.[264] Parapsychology, including the study of clairvoyance, is an example of pseudoscience.

Usage

Pertaining to the ability of clear-sightedness, clairvoyance refers to the paranormal ability to see persons and events that are distant in time or space. It can be divided into roughly three classes: precognition, the ability to perceive or predict future events, retrocognition, the ability to see past events, and remote viewing, the perception of contemporary events happening outside of the range of normal perception.[265]

In history

Throughout history, there have been numerous places and times in which people have claimed themselves or others to be clairvoyant.

A number of Christian saints were said to be able to see or know things that were far removed from their immediate sensory perception as a kind of gift from God, including Columba of Iona, Padre Pio and Anne Catherine Emmerich. Jesus Christ in the Gospels is also recorded as being able to know things that were far removed from his immediate human perception.

In other religions, similar stories of certain individuals being able to see things far removed from their immediate sensory perception are commonplace, especially within pagan religions where oracles were used. Prophecy often involved some degree of clairvoyance, especially when future events were predicted.

In most of these cases, however, the ability to see things was attributed to a higher power and not thought of as an ability that lay within the person himself.

Jainism

In Jainism, clairvoyance is regarded as one of the five kinds of knowledge. The beings of hell and heaven (devas) are said to possess clairvoyance by birth. According to Jain text Sarvārthasiddhi, "this kind of knowledge has been called *avadhi* as it ascertains matter in downward range or knows objects within limits".[266]

Parapsychology

Early research

The earliest record of somnambulistic clairvoyance is credited to the Marquis de Puységur, a follower of Franz Mesmer, who in 1784 was treating a local dull-witted peasant named Victor Race. During treatment, Race reportedly would go into trance and undergo a personality change, becoming fluent and articulate, and giving diagnosis and prescription for his own disease as well as those of others.[267] Clairvoyance was a reported ability of some mediums during the spiritualist period of the late 19th and early 20th centuries, and psychics of many descriptions have claimed clairvoyant ability up to the present day.[268]

Early researchers of clairvoyance included William Gregory, Gustav Pagenstecher, and Rudolf Tischner.[269] Clairvoyance experiments were reported in 1884 by Charles Richet. Playing cards were enclosed in envelopes and a subject put under hypnosis attempted to identify them. The subject was reported to have been successful in a series of 133 trials but the results dropped to chance level when performed before a group of scientists in Cambridge. J. M. Peirce and E. C. Pickering reported a similar experiment in which they tested 36 subjects over 23,384 trials which did not obtain above chance scores.[270]

Figure 18: *Character reader and clairvoyant in a British travelling show of the 1940s, collected by Arthur James Fenwick (1878–1957)*

Ivor Lloyd Tuckett (1911) and Joseph McCabe (1920) analyzed early cases of clairvoyance and came to the conclusion they were best explained by coincidence or fraud.[271,272] In 1919, the magician P. T. Selbit staged a séance at his own flat in Bloomsbury. The spiritualist Arthur Conan Doyle attended the séance and declared the clairvoyance manifestations to be genuine.[273,274]

A significant development in clairvoyance research came when J. B. Rhine, a parapsychologist at Duke University, introduced a standard methodology, with a standard statistical approach to analyzing data, as part of his research into extrasensory perception. A number of psychological departments attempted to repeat Rhine's experiments with failure. W. S. Cox (1936) from Princeton University with 132 subjects produced 25,064 trials in a playing card ESP experiment. Cox concluded "There is no evidence of extrasensory perception either in the 'average man' or of the group investigated or in any particular individual of that group. The discrepancy between these results and those obtained by Rhine is due either to uncontrollable factors in experimental procedure or to the difference in the subjects." Four other psychological departments failed to replicate Rhine's results.[275,276] It was revealed that Rhine's experiments contained methodological flaws and procedural errors.[277,278,279]

Eileen Garrett was tested by Rhine at Duke University in 1933 with Zener cards. Certain symbols that were placed on the cards and sealed in an envelope, and she was asked to guess their contents. She performed poorly and later criticized the tests by claiming the cards lacked a psychic energy called "energy stimulus" and that she could not perform clairvoyance to order.[280] The parapsychologist Samuel Soal and his colleagues tested Garrett in May, 1937. Most of the experiments were carried out in the Psychological Laboratory at the University College London. A total of over 12,000 guesses were recorded but Garrett failed to produce above chance level.[281] In his report Soal wrote "In the case of Mrs. Eileen Garrett we fail to find the slightest confirmation of Dr. J. B. Rhine's remarkable claims relating to her alleged powers of extra-sensory perception. Not only did she fail when I took charge of the experiments, but she failed equally when four other carefully trained experimenters took my place."[282]

Remote viewing

Remote viewing also known as remote sensing, remote perception, telesthesia and travelling clairvoyance is the alleged paranormal ability to perceive a remote or hidden target without support of the senses.[283]

A well known study of remote viewing in recent times has been the US government-funded project at the Stanford Research Institute during the 1970s through the mid-1990s. In 1972, Harold Puthoff and Russell Targ initiated a series of human subject studies to determine whether participants (the *viewers* or *percipients*) could reliably identify and accurately describe salient features of remote locations or *targets*. In the early studies, a human *sender* was typically present at the remote location, as part of the experiment protocol. A three-step process was used, the first step being to randomly select the target conditions to be experienced by the senders. Secondly, in the viewing step, participants were asked to verbally express or sketch their impressions of the remote scene. Thirdly, in the judging step, these descriptions were matched by separate judges, as closely as possible, with the intended targets. The term remote viewing was coined to describe this overall process. The first paper by Puthoff and Targ on remote viewing was published in *Nature* in March 1974; in it, the team reported some degree of remote viewing success. After the publication of these findings, other attempts to replicate the experiments were carried out with remotely linked groups using computer conferencing.

The psychologists David Marks and Richard Kammann attempted to replicate Targ and Puthoff's remote viewing experiments that were carried out in the 1970s at the Stanford Research Institute. In a series of 35 studies, they were unable to replicate the results so investigated the procedure of the original experiments. Marks and Kammann discovered that the notes given to the judges in Targ and Puthoff's experiments contained clues as to which order they were carried out, such as referring to yesterday's two targets, or they had the date of the session written at the top of the page. They concluded that these clues were the reason for the experiment's high hit rates. Marks was able to achieve 100 per cent accuracy without visiting any of the sites himself but by using cues.[284] James Randi has written controlled tests by several other researchers, eliminating several sources of cuing and extraneous evidence present in the original tests, produced negative results. Students were also able to solve Puthoff and Targ's locations from the clues that had inadvertently been included in the transcripts.

In 1980, Charles Tart claimed that a rejudging of the transcripts from one of Targ and Puthoff's experiments revealed an above-chance result. Targ and Puthoff again refused to provide copies of the transcripts and it was not until July 1985 that they were made available for study when it was discovered they still contained sensory cues.[285] Marks and Christopher Scott (1986) wrote "considering the importance for the remote viewing hypothesis of adequate cue removal, Tart's failure to perform this basic task seems beyond comprehension. As previously concluded, remote viewing has not been demonstrated in the experiments conducted by Puthoff and Targ, only the repeated failure of the investigators to remove sensory cues."

In 1982 Robert Jahn, then Dean of the School of Engineering at Princeton University wrote a comprehensive review of psychic phenomena from an engineering perspective. His paper included numerous references to remote viewing studies at the time. Statistical flaws in his work have been proposed by others in the parapsychological community and within the general scientific community.

Scientific reception

According to scientific research, clairvoyance is generally explained as the result of confirmation bias, expectancy bias, fraud, hallucination, self-delusion, sensory leakage, subjective validation, wishful thinking or failures to appreciate the base rate of chance occurrences and not as a paranormal power.[286,287,288] Parapsychology is regarded by the scientific community as a pseudoscience.[289,290] In 1988, the US National Research Council concluded "The committee finds no scientific justification from research conducted over a period of 130 years, for the existence of parapsychological phenomena."[291]

Skeptics say that if clairvoyance were a reality it would have become abundantly clear. They also contend that those who believe in paranormal phenomena do so for merely psychological reasons.[292] According to David G. Myers (*Psychology,* 8th ed.):

> *The search for a valid and reliable test of clairvoyance has resulted in thousands of experiments. One controlled procedure has invited 'senders' to telepathically transmit one of four visual images to 'receivers' deprived*

of sensation in a nearby chamber (Bem & Honorton, 1994). The result? A reported 32 percent accurate response rate, surpassing the chance rate of 25 percent. But follow-up studies have (depending on who was summarizing the results) failed to replicate the phenomenon or produced mixed results (Bem & others, 2001; Milton & Wiseman, 2002; Storm, 2000, 2003).
One skeptic, magician James Randi, has a longstanding offer—now U.S. $1 million—"to anyone who proves a genuine psychic power under proper observing conditions" (Randi, 1999). French, Australian, and Indian groups have parallel offers of up to 200,000 euros to anyone with demonstrable paranormal abilities (CFI, 2003). Large as these sums are, the scientific seal of approval would be worth far more to anyone whose claims could be authenticated. To refute those who say there is no ESP, one need only produce a single person who can demonstrate a single, reproducible ESP phenomenon. So far, no such person has emerged. Randi's offer has been publicized for three decades and dozens of people have been tested, sometimes under the scrutiny of an independent panel of judges. Still, nothing. "People's desire to believe in the paranormal is stronger than all the evidence that it does not exist." Susan Blackmore, "Blackmore's first law", 2004.[293]

Clairvoyance is considered hallucination by mainstream psychiatry.

Bibliography

- S. A. Jain (1992). *Reality*[294]. Jwalamalini Trust. Archived from the original[295] on 2015. <q>Not in Copyright.</q>

Further reading

- James Alcock (1981). *Parapsychology: Science or Magic? A Psychological Perspective.* Pergamon Press. ISBN 0-08-025772-0.
- Willis Dutcher (1922). *On the Other Side of the Footlights: An Expose of Routines, Apparatus and Deceptions Resorted to by Mediums, Clairvoyants, Fortune Tellers and Crystal Gazers in Deluding the Public*[296]. Berlin, WI: Heaney Magic.
- Thomas Gilovich (1993). *How We Know What Isn't So: Fallibility of Human Reason in Everyday Life.* Free Press. ISBN 978-0-02-911706-4.
- Henry Gordon (1988). *Extrasensory Deception: ESP, Psychics, Shirley MacLaine, Ghosts, UFOs.* Macmillan of Canada. ISBN 0-7715-9539-5.
- Donald Hebb (1980). *Extrasensory Perception: A Problem*[297]. In *Essays on Mind.* Lawrence Erlbaum Associates. ISBN 978-0-898-59017-3.

- C. E. M. Hansel (1989). *The Search for Psychic Power: ESP and Parapsychology Revisited*. Prometheus Books. ISBN 0-87975-516-4.
- Terence Hines (2003). *Pseudoscience and the Paranormal*. Prometheus Books. ISBN 1-57392-979-4.
- David Marks. (2000). *The Psychology of the Psychic* (2nd Edition). Prometheus Books. ISBN 1-57392-798-8.
- Joseph McCabe (1920). *Is Spiritualism Based On Fraud? The Evidence Given By Sir A. C. Doyle and Others Drastically Examined*[298]. Chapter "The Subtle Art of Clairvoyance". London: Watts & Co. pp. 93–108.

External links

> Look up *clairvoyance* or *clairvoyant* in Wiktionary, the free dictionary.

> Wikisource has the text of the 1911 *Encyclopædia Britannica* article *clairvoyance*.

- Springer Psychic: "A Study in 'Clairvoyance'"[299]—Joe Nickell
- "Debunking the Sixth Sense"[300]—*Science Daily*
- "Clairvoyance"[301]—*The Skeptic's Dictionary*

Psychokinesis

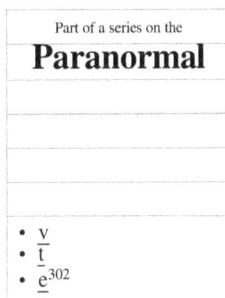

Part of a series on the
Paranormal

- $\underline{v}$
- $\underline{t}$
- $\underline{e}^{302}$

Psychokinesis (from Greek ψυχή "mind" and κίνησις "movement"), or **telekinesis** (from τηλε- "far off" and κίνηση "movement"), is an alleged psychic ability allowing a person to influence a physical system without physical interaction.

Psychokinesis experiments have historically been criticized for lack of proper controls and repeatability. There is no convincing evidence that psychokinesis is a real phenomenon, and the topic is generally regarded as pseudoscience.[303]

Etymology

The word 'psychokinesis' was coined in 1914 by American author Henry Holt in his book *On the Cosmic Relations*. The term is a linguistic blend or portmanteau of the Greek language words ψυχή ("psyche") – meaning *mind, soul, spirit*, or *breath* – and κίνησις ("kinesis") – meaning *motion, movement*.

The American parapsychologist J. B. Rhine coined the term extra-sensory perception to describe receiving information paranormally from an external source. Following this, he used the term psychokinesis in 1934 to describe mentally influencing external objects or events without the use of physical energy. His initial example of psychokinesis was experiments that were conducted to determine whether a person could influence the outcome of falling dice.

The word telekinesis, a portmanteau of the Greek τῆλε ("tēle") – meaning *distance* – and κίνησις ("kinesis") – meaning *motion* – was first used in 1890 by Russian psychical researcher Alexander N. Λksakof.

In parapsychology, fictional universes and New Age beliefs, psychokinesis refers to the mental influence of physical systems and objects without the use of any physical energy, while telekinesis refers to the movement and/or levitation of physical objects by purely mental force without any physical intervention.

Figure 19: *Artist conception of spontaneous psychokinesis from 1911 French magazine La Vie Mysterieuse.*

Reception

Evaluation

There is a broad scientific consensus that PK research, and parapsychology more generally, have not produced a reliable, repeatable demonstration.[149–161]

A panel commissioned in 1988 by the United States National Research Council to study paranormal claims concluded that "despite a 130-year record of scientific research on such matters, our committee could find no scientific justification for the existence of phenomena such as extrasensory perception, mental telepathy or 'mind over matter' exercises... Evaluation of a large body of the best available evidence simply does not support the contention that these phenomena exist."

In 1984, the United States National Academy of Sciences, at the request of the US Army Research Institute,Wikipedia:Please clarify formed a scientific panel to assess the best evidence for psychokinesis. Part of its purpose was to investigate military applications of PK, for example to remotely jam or disrupt enemy weaponry. The panel heard from a variety of military staff who believed in PK and made visits to the PEAR laboratory and two other laboratories that had claimed positive results from micro-PK experiments. The panel criticized macro-PK experiments for being open to deception by conjurors, and said that virtually all micro-PK experiments "depart from good scientific practice in a variety of ways". Their conclusion, published in a 1987 report, was that there was no scientific evidence for the existence of psychokinesis.[149–161]

Carl Sagan included telekinesis in a long list of "offerings of pseudoscience and superstition" which "it would be foolish to accept (...) without solid scientific data". Nobel Prize laureate Richard Feynman advocated a similar position.

Felix Planer, a professor of electrical engineering, has written that if psychokinesis were real then it would be easy to demonstrate by getting subjects to depress a scale on a sensitive balance, raise the temperature of a waterbath which could be measured with an accuracy of a hundredth of a degree centigrade, or affect an element in an electrical circuit such as a resistor, which could be monitored to better than a millionth of an ampere. Planer writes that such experiments are extremely sensitive and easy to monitor but are not utilized by parapsychologists as they "do not hold out the remotest hope of demonstrating even a minute trace of PK" because the alleged phenomenon is non-existent. Planer has written that parapsychologists have to fall back on studies that involve only statistics that are unrepeatable, owing their results to poor experimental methods, recording mistakes and faulty statistical mathematics.

According to Planer, "All research in medicine and other sciences would become illusionary, if the existence of PK had to be taken seriously; for no experiment could be relied upon to furnish objective results, since all measurements would become falsified to a greater or lesser degree, according to his PK ability, by the experimenter's wishes." Planer concluded that the concept of psychokinesis is absurd and has no scientific basis.

PK hypotheses have also been considered in a number of contexts outside parapsychological experiments. C. E. M. Hansel has written that a general objection against the claim for the existence of psychokinesis is that, if it were a real process, its effects would be expected to manifest in situations in everyday life; but no such effects have been observed.

Science writers Martin Gardner and Terence Hines and the philosopher Theodore Schick have written that if psychokinesis were possible, one would expect casino incomes to be affected, but the earnings are exactly as the laws of chance predict.[304:309]

Psychologist Nicholas Humphrey argues that many experiments in psychology, biology or physics assume that the intentions of the subjects or experimenter do not physically distort the apparatus. Humphrey counts them as implicit replications of PK experiments in which PK fails to appear.

Physics

The ideas of psychokinesis and telekinesis violate several well-established laws of physics, including the inverse square law, the second law of thermodynamics, and the conservation of momentum. Because of this, scientists have demanded a high standard of evidence for PK, in line with Marcello Truzzi's dictum "Extraordinary claims require extraordinary proof". The Occam's razor law of parsimony in scientific explanations of phenomena suggests that the explanation of PK in terms of ordinary ways — by trickery, special effects or by poor experimental design — is preferable to accepting that the laws of physics should be rewritten.

Philosopher and physicist Mario Bunge has written that "psychokinesis, or PK, violates the principle that mind cannot act directly on matter. (If it did, no experimenter could trust his readings of measuring instruments.) It also violates the principles of conservation of energy and momentum. The claim that quantum mechanics allows for the possibility of mental power influencing randomizers — an alleged case of micro-PK — is ludicrous since that theory respects the said conservation principles, and it deals exclusively with physical things."

Physicist John Taylor, who has investigated parapsychological claims, has written that an unknown fifth force causing psychokinesis would have to transmit a great deal of energy. The energy would have to overcome the electromagnetic forces binding the atoms together, because the atoms would need to respond more strongly to the fifth force than to electric forces. Such an additional force between atoms should therefore exist all the time and not during only alleged paranormal occurrences. Taylor wrote there is no scientific trace of such a force in physics, down to many orders of magnitude; thus, if a scientific viewpoint is to be preserved, the idea of any fifth force must be discarded. Taylor concluded that there is no possible physical mechanism for psychokinesis, and it is in complete contradiction to established science.:27–30

In 1979, Evan Harris Walker and Richard Mattuck published a parapsychology paper proposing a quantum explanation for psychokinesis. Physicist Victor J. Stenger wrote that their explanation contained assumptions not supported by any scientific evidence. According to Stenger their paper is "filled with impressive looking equations and calculations that give the appearance of placing psychokinesis on a firm scientific footing... Yet look what they have done. They have found the value of one unknown number (wavefunction steps) that gives one measured number (the supposed speed of PK-induced motion). This is numerology, not science."

Physicist Sean M. Carroll has written that spoons, like all matter, are made up of atoms and that any movement of a spoon with the mind would involve the manipulation of those atoms through the four forces of nature: the strong nuclear force, the weak nuclear force, electromagnetism, and gravitation. Psychokinesis would have to be either some form of one of these four forces, or a new force that has a billionth the strength of gravity, for otherwise it would have been captured in experiments already done. This leaves no physical force that could possibly account for psychokinesis.

Physicist Robert L. Park has found it suspicious that a phenomenon should only ever appear at the limits of detectability of questionable statistical techniques. He cites this feature as one of Irving Langmuir's indicators of pathological science. Park pointed out that if mind really could influence matter, it would be easy for parapsychologists to measure such a phenomenon by using the alleged psychokinetic power to deflect a microbalance, which would not require any dubious statistics. "[T]he reason, of course, is that the microbalance stubbornly refuses to budge." He has suggested that the reason statistical studies are so popular in parapsychology is that they introduce opportunities for uncertainty and error, which are used to support the experimenter's biases.

Explanations in terms of bias

Cognitive bias research has suggested that people are susceptible to illusions of PK. These include both the illusion that they themselves have the power, and that the events they witness are real demonstrations of PK. For example, the illusion of control is an illusory correlation between intention and external events, and believers in the paranormal have been shown to be more susceptible to this illusion than others. Psychologist Thomas Gilovich explains this as a biased interpretation of personal experience. For example, someone in a dice game wishing for a high score can interpret high numbers as "success" and low numbers as "not enough concentration." Bias towards belief in PK may be an example of the human tendency to see patterns where none exist, called the clustering illusion, which believers are also more susceptible to.

A 1952 study tested for experimenter's bias with respect to psychokinesis. Richard Kaufman of Yale University gave subjects the task of trying to influence eight dice and allowed them to record their own scores. They were secretly filmed, so their records could be checked for errors. Believers in psychokinesis made errors that favored its existence, while disbelievers made opposite errors. A similar pattern of errors was found in J. B. Rhine's dice experiments, which were considered the strongest evidence for PK at that time.:306

In 1995, Wiseman and Morris showed subjects an unedited videotape of a magician's performance in which a fork bent and eventually broke. Believers in the paranormal were significantly more likely to misinterpret the tape as a demonstration of PK, and were more likely to misremember crucial details of the presentation. This suggests that confirmation bias affects people's interpretation of PK demonstrations. Psychologist Robert Sternberg cites confirmation bias as an explanation of why belief in psychic phenomena persists, despite the lack of evidence:

> *Some of the worst examples of confirmation bias are in research on parapsychology (...) Arguably, there is a whole field here with no powerful confirming data at all. But people want to believe, and so they find ways to believe.*

Psychologist Daniel Wegner has argued that an introspection illusion contributes to belief in psychokinesis. He observes that in everyday experience, intention (such as wanting to turn on a light) is followed by action (such as flicking a light switch) in a reliable way, but the underlying neural mechanisms are outside awareness. Hence, though subjects may feel that they directly introspect their own free will, the experience of control is actually inferred from relations between the thought and the action. This theory of *apparent mental causation* acknowledges the influence of David Hume's view of the mind. This process for detecting when one is responsible for an action is not totally reliable, and when it goes wrong there can be an illusion of control. This can happen when an external event follows, and is congruent with, a thought in someone's mind, without an actual causal link. As evidence, Wegner cites a series of experiments on magical thinking in which subjects were induced to think they had influenced external events. In one experiment, subjects watched a basketball player taking a series of free throws. When they were instructed to visualize him making his shots, they felt that they had contributed to his success. Other experiments designed to create an illusion of psychokinesis have demonstrated that this depends, to some extent, on the subject's prior belief in psychokinesis.

A 2006 meta-analysis of 380 studies found a small positive effect that can be explained by publication bias.

Magic and special effects

Magicians have successfully simulated some of the specialized abilities of psychokinesis, such as object movement, spoon bending, levitation and teleportation.[305] According to Robert Todd Carroll, there are many impressive magic tricks available to amateurs and professionals to simulate psychokinetic powers. Metal objects such as keys or cutlery can be bent using a number of different techniques, even if the performer has not had access to the items beforehand.[:127–131]

According to Richard Wiseman there are a number of ways for faking psychokinetic metal bending (PKMB). These include switching straight objects

Figure 20: *An advertising poster depicting magician Harry Kellar performing the "Levitation of Princess Karnac" illusion, 1894, U.S. Library of Congress.*

for pre-bent duplicates, the concealed application of force, and secretly inducing metallic fractures. Research has also suggested that (PKMB) effects can be created by verbal suggestion. On this subject the magician Ben Harris wrote:

> *If you are doing a really convincing job, then you should be able to put a bent key on the table and comment, 'Look, it is still bending', and have your spectators really believe that it is. This may sound the height of boldness; however, the effect is astounding – and combined with suggestion, it does work.*

Between 1979 and 1981, the McDonnell Laboratory for Psychical Research at Washington University reported a series of experiments they named Project Alpha, in which two teenaged male subjects had demonstrated PK phenomena (including metal-bending and causing images to appear on film) under less than stringent laboratory conditions. James Randi eventually revealed that the subjects were two of his associates, amateur conjurers Steve Shaw and Michael Edwards. The pair had created the effects by standard trickery, but the researchers, being unfamiliar with magic techniques, interpreted them as proof of PK.

A 2014 study that utilized a magic trick to investigate paranormal belief on eyewitness testimony revealed that believers in psychokinesis were more likely to report a key continued to bend than non-believers.

Prize money for proof of psychokinesis

Internationally there are individual skeptics of the paranormal and skeptics' organizations who offer cash prize money for demonstration of the existence of an extraordinary psychic power, such as psychokinesis. Prizes have been offered specifically for PK demonstrations: for example, businessman Gerald Fleming's offer of £250,000 to Uri Geller if he can bend a spoon under controlled conditions. The James Randi Educational Foundation offered the One Million Dollar Paranormal Challenge to any accepted candidate who managed to produce a paranormal event in a controlled, mutually agreed upon experiment.Wikipedia:Verifiability

Belief

In September 2006, a survey about belief in various religious and paranormal topics conducted by phone and mail-in questionnaire polled 1,721 Americans on their belief in telekinesis. Of these participants, 28% of male participants and 31% of female participants selected "agree" or "strongly agree" with the statement, "*It is possible to influence the world through the mind alone.*"[306]

Subsets of psychokinesis

Parapsychologists divide psychokinetic phenomena into two categories: macro-psychokinesis - large-scale psychokinetic effects that can be seen with the naked eye, and micro-psychokinesis - small-scale psychokinetic effects that require the use of statistics to be detected. Some phenomena – such as apports, levitation, materialization, psychic healing, pyrokinesis, retrocausality, telekinesis, and thoughtography – are considered to be examples of psychokinesis.

In 2016, Caroline Watt stated "Overall, the majority of academic parapsychologists do not find the evidence compelling in favour of macro-PK".

Figure 21: *Eusapia Palladino "levitates" a table while researcher Alexander Aksakof (right) monitors for fraud, Milan, 1892.*

Figure 22: *Spirit photography hoaxer Édouard Isidore Buguet. (1840-1901) of France fakes telekinesis in this 1875 cabinet card photograph titled Fluidic Effect.*

Notable claimants of psychokinetic ability

There have been claimants of psychokinetic ability throughout history. Angelique Cottin (ca. 1846) known as the "Electric Girl" of France was an alleged generator of PK activity. Cottin and her family claimed that she produced electric emanations that allowed her to move pieces of furniture and scissors across a room. Frank Podmore wrote there were many observations which were "suggestive of fraud" such as the contact of the girl's garments to produce any of the alleged phenomena and the observations from several witnesses that noticed there was a double movement on the part of Cottin, a movement in the direction of the object thrown and afterwards away from it, but the movements so rapid they were not usually detected.

Spiritualist mediums have also claimed psychokinetic abilities. Eusapia Palladino, an Italian medium, could allegedly cause objects to move during séances. However, she was caught levitating a table with her foot by the magician Joseph Rinn and using tricks to move objects by the psychologist Hugo Münsterberg. Other alleged PK mediums that were exposed as frauds, include Anna Rasmussen and Maria Silbert.

The Polish medium Stanisława Tomczyk active in the early 20th century claimed to be able to perform various acts of telekinesis, such as levitating objects, by way of an entity she called "Little Stasia".[307] A photograph of her taken in 1909, which shows a pair of scissors "floating" in between her hands, is often found in books and other publications as an example of telekinesis.[308] Scientists suspected Tomczyk performed her feats by the use of a fine thread or hair, running between her hands to lift and suspend the objects in the air. This was confirmed when psychical researchers who tested Tomczyk occasionally observed the thread.

Many of India's "godmen" have claimed macro-PK abilities and demonstrated apparently miraculous phenomena in public, although as more controls are put in place to prevent trickery, fewer phenomena are produced.

Annemarie Schaberl, a 19-year-old secretary, was said to have telekinetic powers by the parapsychologist Hans Bender in the Rosenheim Poltergeist case in the 1960s. Magicians and scientists who investigated the case suspected the phenomena were produced by trickery.:[107–108]

Swami Rama, a yogi skilled in controlling his heart functions, was studied at the Menninger Foundation in the spring and fall of 1970 and was alleged by some observers at the foundation to have telekinetically moved a knitting needle twice from a distance of five feet. Although Swami Rama wore a face-mask and gown to prevent allegations that he moved the needle with his breath or body movements, and air vents in the room had been covered, at least one physician observer who was present at the time was not convinced and expressed the opinion that air movement was somehow the cause.[309]

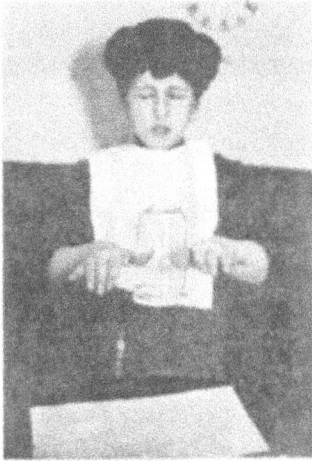

Figure 23: *Magician William Marriott reveals the trick of the medium Stanisława Tomczyk's levitation of a glass tumbler. Pearson's Magazine, June 1910*

Psychics

The Russian psychic Nina Kulagina came to wide public attention following the publication of Sheila Ostrander and Lynn Schroeder's best seller, *Psychic Discoveries Behind The Iron Curtain*. The alleged Soviet psychic of the late 1960s and early 1970s was filmed apparently performing telekinesis while seated in numerous black-and-white short films. She was also mentioned in the *U.S. Defense Intelligence Agency* report from 1978.Wikipedia:Citing sources Magicians and skeptics have argued that Kulagina's feats could easily be performed by one practiced in sleight of hand, through means such as cleverly concealed or disguised threads, small pieces of magnetic metal, or mirrors.

James Hydrick, an American martial arts expert and psychic, was famous for his alleged psychokinetic ability to turn the pages of books and make pencils spin around while placed on the edge of a desk. It was later revealed by magicians that he achieved his feats by air currents. The psychologist Richard Wiseman has written Hydrick learnt to move objects by blowing in a "highly deceptive" and skillful way. Hydrick confessed to Dan Korem that all of his feats were tricks "My whole idea behind this in the first place was to see how dumb America was. How dumb the world is." The British psychic Matthew

Manning was the subject of laboratory research in the United States and England involving PK in the late 1970s and today claims healing powers. Magicians John Booth and Henry Gordon have suspected Manning used trickery to perform his feats.

In 1971, an American psychic named Felicia Parise allegedly moved a pill bottle across a kitchen counter by psychokinesis. Her feats were endorsed by the parapsychologist Charles Honorton. Science writer Martin Gardner wrote Parise had "bamboozled" Honorton by moving the bottle by an invisible thread stretched between her hands.[:163]

Boris Ermolaev, a Russian psychic, was known for levitating small objects. His methods were exposed on the World of Discovery documentary *Secrets of the Russian Psychics* (1992). Ermolaev would sit on a chair and allegedly move the objects between his knees but due to the lighting conditions a fine thread fixed between his knees suspending the objects was observed by the camera crew.

The Russian psychic Alla Vinogradova was said to be able to move objects without touching them on transparent acrylic plastic or a plexiglass sheet. The parapsychologist Stanley Krippner had observed Vinogradova rub an aluminum tube before moving it allegedly by psychokinesis. Krippner suggested no psychokinesis was involved; the effect was produced by an electrostatic charge. Vinogradova was featured in the Nova documentary *Secrets of the Psychics* (1993) which followed the debunking work of James Randi. Vinogradova demonstrated her alleged psychokinetic abilities on camera for Randi and other investigators. Before the experiments she was observed combing her hair and rubbing the surface of the acrylic plastic. Massimo Polidoro has replicated the feats of Vinogradova by using an acrylic plastic surface and showing how easy it is to move any kind of object on top of it due to the charges of static electricity. The effect is easily achieved if the surface is electrically charged by rubbing a towel or a hand on it. The physicist John Taylor has written "It is very likely that electrostatics is all that is needed to explain Alla Vinogradova's apparently paranormal feats."[:103]

Metal bending

Psychics have also claimed the psychokinetic ability to bend metal. Uri Geller was famous for his spoon bending demonstrations, allegedly by PK. Geller has been caught many times using sleight of hand and according to science writer Terence Hines, all his effects have been recreated using conjuring tricks.[:126–130]

The French psychic Jean-Pierre Girard has claimed he can bend metal bars by PK. Girard was tested in the 1970s but failed to produce any paranormal

Figure 24: *Uri Geller was famous for his spoon bending demonstrations.*

effects in scientifically controlled conditions. He was tested on January 19, 1977 during a two-hour experiment in a Paris laboratory. The experiment was directed by the physicist Yves Farge with a magician also present. All of the experiments were negative as Girard failed to make any of the objects move paranormally. He failed two tests in Grenoble in June 1977 with the magician James Randi. He was also tested on September 24, 1977 at a laboratory at the Nuclear Research Centre. Girard failed to bend any bars or change the structure of the metals. Other experiments into spoon bending were also negative and witnesses described his feats as fraudulent. Girard later admitted that he would sometimes cheat to avoid disappointing the public but insisted he still had genuine psychic power. Magicians and scientists have written that he produced all his alleged psychokinetic feats through fraudulent means.

Stephen North, a British psychic in the late 1970s, was known for his alleged psychokinetic ability to bend spoons and teleport objects in and out of sealed containers. The British physicist John Hasted tested North in a series of experiments which he claimed had demonstrated psychokinesis, though his experiments were criticized for lack of scientific controls.Wikipedia:Citing sources North was tested in Grenoble on 19 December 1977 in scientific conditions and the results were negative. According to James Randi, during a test at Birkbeck College North was observed to have bent a metal sample with his bare hands. Randi wrote "I find it unfortunate that [Hasted] never had an epiphany in which he was able to recognize just how thoughtless, cruel, and predatory were the acts perpetrated on him by fakers who took advantage of his naivety and trust."

"PK Parties" were a cultural fad in the 1980s, begun by Jack Houck, where groups of people were guided through rituals and chants to awaken metal-bending powers. They were encouraged to shout at the items of cutlery they had brought and to jump and scream to create an atmosphere of pandemonium (or what scientific investigators called heightened suggestibility). Critics were excluded and participants were told to avoid looking at their hands. Thousands of people attended these emotionally charged parties, and many became convinced that they had bent silverware by paranormal means.[149–161]

PK parties have been described as a campaign by paranormal believers to convince people of the existence of psychokinesis, on the basis of nonscientific data from personal experience and testimony. The United States National Academy of Sciences has criticized PK parties on the grounds that conditions are not reliable for obtaining scientific results and "are just those which psychologists and others have described as creating states of heightened suggestibility.":[149–161]

Ronnie Marcus, an Israeli psychic and claimant of psychokinetic metal bending, was tested in 1994 in scientifically controlled conditions and failed to produce any paranormal phenomena. According to magicians, his alleged psychokinetic feats were sleight of hand tricks. Marcus bent a letter opener by the concealed application of force and a frame-by-frame analysis of video showed that he bent a spoon from pressure from his thumb by ordinary, physical means.

In popular culture

Psychokinesis and telekinesis have commonly been used as superpowers in comic books, movies, television, computer games, literature, and other forms of popular culture.

Notable portrayals of psychokinetic and/or telekinetic characters include the Teleks in the 1952 novella *Telek*; Carrie White in the Stephen King novel *Carrie*; Ellen Burstyn in the 1980 healer-themed film *Resurrection*; the Jedi and Sith in the *Star Wars* franchise; the Scanners in the 1981 film *Scanners*; Matilda Wormwood in the 1988 children's novel *Matilda*; three high school seniors in the 2012 film *Chronicle*; and Eleven from the Netflix series *Stranger Things*.

Further reading

- Henry Gordon (1988). *Extrasensory Deception: ESP, Psychics, Shirley MacLaine, Ghosts, UFOs* (Canadian ed.). Toronto: Macmillan of Canada. ISBN 0771595395.
- David F. Marks (2000). *The Psychology of the Psychic* (2nd ed.). Amherst, New York: Prometheus Books. ISBN 1573927988.
- Richard Wiseman (1997). *Deception & Self-Seception: Investigating Psychics*. Amherst, New York: Prometheus Books. ISBN 9781573921213.

External links

- Psychokinesis[310] at Curlie (based on DMOZ)

Near-death experience

A **near-death experience** (**NDE**) is a personal experience associated with death or impending death. Such experiences may encompass a variety of sensations including detachment from the body, feelings of levitation, total serenity, security, warmth, the experience of absolute dissolution, and the presence of a light. NDEs are a recognized part of some transcendental and religious beliefs in an afterlife.

Different models have been described to explain NDEs. Neuroscience research suggests that an NDE is a subjective phenomenon resulting from "disturbed bodily multisensory integration" that occurs during life-threatening events.

Etymology

The equivalent French term *expérience de mort imminente* (experience of imminent death) was proposed by the French psychologist and epistemologist Victor Egger as a result of discussions in the 1890s among philosophers and psychologists concerning climbers' stories of the panoramic life review during falls.[311] In 1892 a series of subjective observations by workers falling from scaffolds, war soldiers who suffered injuries, climbers who had fallen from heights or other individuals who had come close to death (near drownings, accidents) was reported by Albert Heim. This was also the first time the phenomenon was described as clinical syndrome. In 1968 Celia Green published an analysis of 400 first-hand accounts of out-of-body experiences.[312] This represented the first attempt to provide a taxonomy of such experiences, viewed simply as anomalous perceptual experiences, or hallucinations. In

Figure 25: *Ascent of the Blessed by Hieronymus Bosch is associated by some NDE researchers with aspects of the NDE.*

1969, Swiss-American psychiatrist and pioneer in near-death studies Elisabeth Kubler-Ross published her groundbreaking book *On Death and Dying: What the dying have to teach doctors, nurses, clergy, and their own families.* These experiences were also popularized by the work of psychiatrist Raymond Moody, who in 1975 coined the term "near-death experience" (NDE).

Characteristics

Common elements

Researchers have identified the common elements that define near-death experiences.[313] Bruce Greyson argues that the general features of the experience include impressions of being outside one's physical body, visions of deceased relatives and religious figures, and transcendence of egotic and spatiotemporal boundaries.[314] Many common elements have been reported, although the person's interpretation of these events often corresponds with the cultural, philosophical, or religious beliefs of the person experiencing it. For example, in the USA, where 46% of the population believes in guardian angels, they will often be identified as angels or deceased loved ones (or will be unidentified), while Hindus will often identify them as messengers of the god of death.[315]

Common traits that have been reported by NDErs are as follows:

- A sense/awareness of being dead.
- A sense of peace, well-being and painlessness. Positive emotions. A sense of removal from the world.
- An out-of-body experience. A perception of one's body from an outside position, sometimes observing medical professionals performing resuscitation efforts.
- A "tunnel experience" or entering a darkness. A sense of moving up, or through, a passageway or staircase.
- A rapid movement toward and/or sudden immersion in a powerful light (or "Being of Light") which communicates with the person.
- An intense feeling of unconditional love and acceptance.
- Encountering "Beings of Light", "Beings dressed in white", or similar. Also, the possibility of being reunited with deceased loved ones.
- Receiving a life review, commonly referred to as "seeing one's life flash before one's eyes".
- Approaching a border or a decision by oneself or others to return to one's body, often accompanied by a reluctance to return.
- Suddenly finding oneself back inside one's body.
- Connection to the cultural beliefs held by the individual, which seem to dictate some of the phenomena experienced in the NDE and particularly the later interpretation thereof.Wikipedia:Citing sources

Stages

Kenneth Ring (1980) subdivided the NDE on a five-stage continuum. The subdivisions were:[316]

1. Peace
2. Body separation
3. Entering darkness
4. Seeing the light
5. Entering the light

He stated that 60% experienced stage 1 (feelings of peace and contentment), but only 10% experienced stage 5 ("entering the light").[317] According to Alana Karran, the NDE stages resemble the so-called hero's journey.[318]

Clinical circumstances

Clinical circumstances associated with near-death experiences include cardiac arrest in myocardial infarction (clinical death); shock in postpartum loss of blood or in perioperative complications; septic or anaphylactic shock; electrocution; coma resulting from traumatic brain damage; intracerebral hemorrhage or cerebral infarction; attempted suicide; near-drowning or asphyxia; apnea; and serious depression.Wikipedia:Citation needed In contrast to common belief, Kenneth Ring argues that attempted suicides do not lead more often to unpleasant NDEs than unintended near-death situations.[319]

NDE variants

Some NDEs have elements that bear little resemblance to the "typical" near-death experience. Anywhere from one percent (according to a 1982 Gallup poll) to 20 percent of subjects may have distressing experiences and feel terrified or uneasy as various parts of the NDE occur. For instance, they may visit or view dark and depressing areas or are accosted by what seem to be hostile or oppositional forces or presences.[320]

Persons having bad experiences were not marked by more religiosity or suicidal background. According to one study (Greyson 2006) there is little association between NDEs and prior psychiatric treatment, prior suicidal behavior, or family history of suicidal behavior. There was also little association between NDEs and religiosity, or prior brushes with death, suggesting the occurrence of NDEs is not influenced by psychopathology, by religious denomination or religiosity, or by experiencers' prior expectations of a pleasant dying process or continued postmortem existence. Greyson (2007) also found that the long term recall of NDE incidents was stable and did not change due to embellishment over time.

Greyson Bush, former Executive Director to the International Association for Near-Death Studies, holds that not all negative NDE accounts are reported by people with a religious background. Suicide attempters, who should be expected to have a higher rate of psychopathology according to Greyson (1991) did not show much difference from non-suicides in the frequency of NDEs.

After-effects

NDEs are associated with changes in personality and outlook on life. Kenneth Ring (professor of psychology) has identified a consistent set of value and belief changes associated with people who have had a near-death experience. Among these changes, one finds a greater appreciation for life, higher self-esteem, greater compassion for others, less concern for acquiring material wealth, a heightened sense of purpose and self-understanding, desire to learn, elevated spirituality, greater ecological sensitivity and planetary concern, and a feeling of being more intuitive. Changes may also include a need for being alone more often, increased physical sensitivity; diminished tolerance of light, sound, alcohol, or drugs; a feeling that the brain has been "altered" to encompass more; and a feeling that one is now using the "whole brain" rather than a small part. However, not all after-effects are beneficial and Greyson describes circumstances where changes in attitudes and behavior can lead to psychosocial and psychospiritual problems.

Historical reports, incidence and prevalence

NDEs have been recorded since ancient times. In the 19th century a few studies moved beyond individual cases - one privately done by the Mormons and one in Switzerland. Up to 2005, 95% of world cultures are known to have made some mention of NDEs.

A number of more contemporary sources report incidences of near death experiences of:

* 17% amongst critically ill patients, in nine prospective studies from 4 different countries.
* 10-20% of people who have come close to death.

Research

Near-death studies

Contemporary interest in this field of study was originally spurred by the writings of Raymond Moody such as his book *Life After Life*, which was released in 1975, brought public attention to the topic of NDEs. This was soon to be followed by the establishment of the International Association for Near-Death Studies (IANDS) in 1981. IANDS is an international organization that encourages scientific research and education on the physical, psychological, social, and spiritual nature and ramifications of near-death experiences. Among its publications are the peer-reviewed *Journal of Near-Death Studies* and the quarterly newsletter *Vital Signs*.

Bruce Greyson (psychiatrist), Kenneth Ring (psychologist), and Michael Sabom (cardiologist), helped to launch the field of near-death studies and introduced the study of near-death experiences to the academic setting. From 1975 to 2005, some 2,500 self-reported individuals in the US had been reviewed in retrospective studies of the phenomena with an additional 600 outside the US in the West, and 70 in Asia. Additionally, prospective studies had identified 270 individuals. Prospective studies review groups of individuals (e.g., selected emergency room patients) and then find who had an NDE during the study's time; such studies cost more to perform. In all, close to 3,500 individual cases between 1975 and 2005 had been reviewed in one or another study. All these studies were carried out by some 55 researchers or teams of researchers.

Melvin Morse, head of the Institute for the Scientific Study of Consciousness, and colleagues[321] have investigated near-death experiences in a pediatric population.

Research scales used to classify a near-death experience

Major contributions to the field include Ring's construction of a "Weighted Core Experience Index"[322] to measure the depth of the near-death experience, and Greyson's construction of the "Near-death experience scale" to differentiate between subjects that are more or less likely to have experienced an NDE.

The latter scale is also, according to its author, clinically useful in differentiating NDEs from organic brain syndromes and non-specific stress responses. The NDE-scale was later found to fit the Rasch rating scale model.

Research in animals

Heightened brain activity has been recorded in experimental rats directly following cardiac arrest, though there has been no similar research in humans.[323,324,325,326]

Clinical research in cardiac arrest patients

Parnia 2001 study

In 2001, Sam Parnia and colleagues published the results of a year-long study of cardiac arrest survivors that was conducted at Southampton General Hospital. 63 survivors were interviewed. They had been resuscitated after being clinically dead with no pulse, no respiration, and fixed dilated pupils. Parnia and colleagues investigated out-of-body experience claims by placing figures on suspended boards facing the ceiling, not visible from the floor. Four had experiences that, according to the study criteria, were NDEs but none of them experienced the out-of-body experience. Thus, they were not able to identify the figures.

Psychologist Chris French wrote regarding the study "unfortunately, and somewhat atypically, none of the survivors in this sample experienced an OBE".

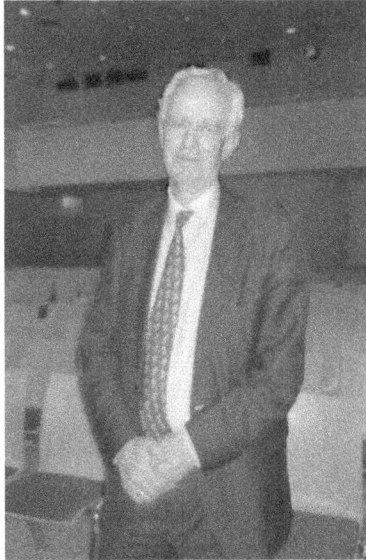

Figure 26: *Pim van Lommel*

Van Lommel's study

In 2001 Pim van Lommel, a cardiologist from the Netherlands, and his team conducted a study on NDEs including 344 cardiac arrest patients who had been successfully resuscitated in 10 Dutch hospitals. Patients not reporting NDEs were used as controls for patients who did, and psychological (e.g. fear before cardiac arrest), demographic (e.g. age, sex), medical (e.g. more than one cardiopulmonary resuscitation (CPR)) and pharmacological data were compared between the 2 groups. The work also included a longitudinal study where the 2 groups (those who had had an NDE and those who had not had one) were compared at 2 and 8 years, for life changes. One patient had a conventional out of body experience. He reported being able to watch and recall events during the time of his cardiac arrest. His claims were confirmed by hospital personnel. "This did not appear consistent with hallucinatory or illusory experiences, as the recollections were compatible with real and verifiable rather than imagined events".

Awareness during Resuscitation (AWARE) study

While at University of Southampton, Parnia was the principal investigator of the AWARE Study, which was launched in 2008.[13] This study which concluded in 2012 included 33 investigators across 15 medical centers in the UK, Austria and the USA and tested consciousness, memories and awareness during cardiac arrest. The accuracy of claims of visual and auditory awareness was examined using specific tests. One such test consisted in installing shelves, bearing a variety of images and facing the ceiling, hence not visible by hospital staff, in rooms where cardiac-arrest patients were more likely to occur. The results of the study were published in October 2014; both the launch and the study results were widely discussed in the media.

A review article analyzing the results reports that, out of 2060 cardiac arrest events, 101 of 140 cardiac arrest survivors could complete the questionnaires. Of these 101 patients 9% could be classified as near death experiences. 2 more patients (2% of those completing the questionnaires) described "seeing and hearing actual events related to the period of cardiac arrest". These two patients' cardiac arrests did not occur in areas equipped with ceiling shelves hence no images could be used to objectively test for visual awareness claims. One of the two patients was too sick and the accuracy of her recount could not be verified. For the second patient instead, it was possible to verify the accuracy of the experience and to show that awareness occurred paradoxically some minutes after the heart stopped, at a time when "the brain ordinarily stops functioning and cortical activity becomes isoelectric." The experience was not compatible with an illusion, imaginary event or hallucination since visual (other than of ceiling shelves' images) and auditory awareness could be corroborated.

AWARE II

As of May 2016[327], a posting at the UK Clinical Trials Gateway website described plans for AWARE II, a two-year multicenter observational study of 900-1500 patients experiencing cardiac arrest, which said that subject recruitment had started on 1 August 2014 and that the scheduled end date was 31 May 2017.[328]

Explanatory models

In a review article, psychologist Chris French has grouped approaches to explain NDEs in three broad groups which "are not distinct and independent, but instead show considerable overlap": spiritual theories (also called transcendental), psychological theories, and physiological theories that provide a physical explanation for NDEs.

Spiritual or transcendental theories

French summarizes this model by saying : "the most popular interpretation is that the NDE is exactly what it appears to be to the person having the experience". The NDE would then represent evidence of the supposedly immaterial existence of a soul or mind, which would leave the body upon death. An NDE would then provide information about an immaterial world where the soul would journey upon ending its physical existence on earth.

According to Greyson some NDE phenomena cannot be easily explained with our current knowledge of human physiology and psychology. For instance, at a time when they were unconscious patients could accurately describe events as well as report being able to view their bodies "from an out-of-body spatial perspective". In two different studies of patients who had survived a cardiac arrest, those who had reported leaving their bodies could describe accurately their resuscitation procedures or unexpected events, whereas others "described incorrect equipment and procedures". Sam Parnia also refers to two cardiac arrest studies and one deep hypothermic circulatory arrest study where patients reported visual and/or auditory awareness occurring when their brain function had ceased. These reports "were corroborated with actual and real events".

Five prospective studies have been carried out, to test the accuracy of out of body perceptions by placing "unusual targets in locations likely to be seen by persons having NDEs, such as in an upper corner of a room in the emergency department, the coronary care unit, or the intensive care unit of a hospital." Twelve patients reported leaving their bodies, but unfortunately none could describe the hidden visual targets. Although this is a small sample, the failure of purported out-of-body experiencers to describe the hidden targets raises questions about the accuracy of the anecdotal reports described above.

Psychologist James Alcock has described the afterlife claims of NDE researchers as pseudoscientific. Alcock has written the spiritual or transcendental interpretation "is based on belief in search of data rather than observation in search of explanation." Chris French has noted that "the survivalist approach does not appear to generate clear and testable hypotheses. Because of the vagueness and imprecision of the survivalist account, it can be made to explain any possible set of findings and is therefore unfalsifiable and unscientific."[329]

Psychological explanations

French summarises the main psychological explanations which include: the depersonalization, the expectancy and the dissociation models.

Depersonalization model

A depersonalization model was proposed in the 1970s by professor of psychiatry Russell Noyes and clinical psychologist Roy Kletti, which suggested that the NDE is a form of depersonalization experienced under emotional conditions such as life-threatening danger, potentially inescapable danger, and that the NDE can best be understood as an hallucination.[330] According to this model, those who face their impending death become detached from the surroundings and their own bodies, no longer feel emotions, and experience time distortions.

This model suffers from a number of limitations to explain NDEs for subjects who do not experience a sensation of being out of their bodies; unlike NDEs, experiences are dreamlike, unpleasant and characterized by "anxiety, panic and emptiness". Also, during NDEs subjects remain very lucid of their identities, their sense of identify is not changed unlike those experiencing depersonalization.

Expectancy model

Another psychological theory is called the expectancy model. It has been suggested that although these experiences could appear very real, they had actually been constructed in the mind, either consciously or subconsciously, in response to the stress of an encounter with death (or perceived encounter with death), and did not correspond to a real event. In a way, they are similar to wish-fulfillment: because someone thought they were about to die, they experienced certain things in accordance with what they expected or wanted to occur. Imagining a heavenly place was in effect a way for them to soothe themselves through the stress of knowing that they were close to death. Subjects use their own personal and cultural expectations to imagine a scenario that would protect them against an imminent threat to their lives.

Subjects' accounts often differed from their own "religious and personal expectations regarding death" which contradicts the hypothesis they may have imagined a scenario based on their cultural and personal background.

Although the term NDE was first coined in 1975 and the experience first described then, recent descriptions of NDEs do not differ from those reported earlier than 1975. The only exception is the more frequent description of a tunnel. Hence, the fact that information about these experiences could be more easily obtained after 1975, did not influence people's reports of the experiences.

Another flaw of this model can be found in children's accounts of NDEs. These are similar to adults', and this despite children being less affected by religious or cultural influences about death.

Dissociation model

The dissociation model proposes that NDE is a form of withdrawal to protect an individual from a stressful event. Under extreme circumstances some people may detach from certain unwanted feelings in order to avoid experiencing their emotional impact and suffering associated with them. The person also detaches from one's immediate surroundings.

Birth model

The birth model suggests that near death experiences could be a form of reliving the trauma of birth. Since a baby travels from the darkness of the womb to light and is greeted by the love and warmth of the nursing and medical staff, and so, it was proposed, the dying brain could be recreating the passage through a tunnel to light, warmth and affection.

Reports of leaving the body through a tunnel are equally frequent among subjects who were born by cesarean section and natural birth. Also, newborns do not possess "the visual acuity, spatial stability of their visual images, mental alertness, and cortical coding capacity to register memories of the birth experience".

Physiological explanations (organic theories)

A wide range of physiological theories of the NDE have been put forward including those based upon cerebral hypoxia, anoxia, and hypercapnia; endorphins and other neurotransmitters; and abnormal activity in the temporal lobes.

Neurobiological factors in the experience have been investigated by researchers in the field of medical science and psychiatry.[331] Among the researchers and commentators who tend to emphasize a naturalistic and neurological base for the experience are the British psychologist Susan Blackmore (1993), with her "dying brain hypothesis".

Neuroanatomical models

Neuroscientists Olaf Blanke and Sebastian Dieguez (2009),[332] from the *Ecole Polytechnique Fédérale de Lausanne*, Switzerland, propose a brain based model with two types of NDEs :

- "type 1 NDEs are due to bilateral frontal and occipital, but predominantly right hemispheric brain damage affecting the right temporal parietal junction and characterized by out of body experiences, altered sense of time, sensations of flying, lightness vection and flying"

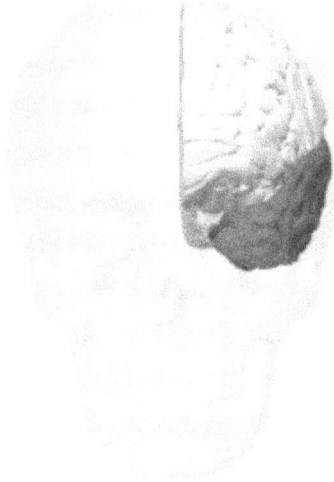

Figure 27: *Animation of the human left temporal lobe*

- "type 2 NDEs are also due to bilateral frontal and occipital, but predominantly left hemispheric brain damage affecting the left temporal parietal junction and characterized by feeling of a presence, meeting and communication with spirits, seeing of glowing bodies, as well as voices, sounds, and music without vection"

They suggest that damage to the bilateral occipital cortex may lead to visual features of NDEs such as seeing a tunnel or lights, and "damage to unilateral or bilateral temporal lobe structures such as the hippocampus and amygdala" may lead to emotional experiences, memory flashbacks or a life review. They concluded that future neuroscientific studies are likely to reveal the neuroanatomical basis of the NDE which will lead to the demystification of the subject without needing paranormal explanations.

French has written that the "temporal lobe is almost certain to be involved in NDEs, given that both damage to and direct cortical stimulation of this area are known to produce a number of experiences corresponding to those of the NDE, including OBEs, hallucinations, and memory flashbacks".

Vanhaudenhuyse *et al.* 2009 reported that recent studies employing deep brain stimulation and neuroimaging have demonstrated that out-of-body experiences result from a deficient multisensory integration at the temporoparietal junction and that ongoing studies aim to further identify the functional neuroanatomy of near-death experiences by means of standardized EEG recordings.

According to Greyson multiple neuroanatomical models have been proposed where NDEs have been hypothesized to originate from different anatomical areas of the brain, namely: the limbic system, the hippocampus, the left temporal lobe, Reissen's fiber in the central canal of the spinal cord, the prefrontal cortex, the right temporal lobe.

Blanke et al. admit that their model remains speculative to the lack of data. Likewise Greyson writes that although some or any of the neuroanatomical models proposed may serve to explain NDEs and pathways through which they are expressed, they remain speculative at this stage since they have not been tested in empirical studies.

Neurochemical models

Some theories hypothesize that drugs used during resuscitation induced NDEs, for example, ketamine or as resulting from endogeneous chemicals that transmit signals between brain cells, neurotransmitters:

• In the early eighties, Daniel Carr wrote that NDE has characteristics are suggestive of a limbic lobe syndrome and that the NDE can be explained by the release of endorphins and enkephalins in the brain. Endorphins are endogenous molecules "released in times of stress and lead to a reduction in pain perception and a pleasant, even blissful, emotional state."

• Judson and Wiltshaw (1983) noted how the administration of endorphin-blocking agents such as naloxone had been occasionally reported to produce "hellish" NDEs. This would be coherent with endorphins' role in causing a "positive emotional tone of most NDEs".

• Morse *et al.* 1989 proposed a model arguing that serotonin played a more important role than endorphins in generating NDEs "at least with respect to mystical hallucinations and OBEs".

According to Parnia, neurochemical models are not backed by data. This is true for "NMDA receptor activation, serotonin, and endorphin release" models. Parnia writes that no data has been collected via thorough and careful experimentation to back "a possible causal relationship or even an association" between neurochemical agents and NDE experiences.

Multi-factorial models

The first formal neurobiological model for NDE, included endorphins, neu-rotransmitters of the limbic system, the temporal lobe and other parts of the brain. Extensions and variations of their model came from other scientists such as Louis Appleby (1989).

Other authors suggest that all components of near-death experiences can be explained in their entirety via psychological or neurophysiological mechanisms, although the authors admit that these hypotheses have to be tested by science.

Low oxygen levels (and G-LOC) model

Low oxygen levels in the blood (hypoxia or anoxia) have been hypothesized to induce hallucinations and hence possibly explain NDEs. This is because low oxygen levels characterize life-threatening situations and also by the ap-parent similarities between NDEs and G-force induced loss of consciousness (G-LOC) episodes.

These episodes are observed with fighter pilots experiencing very rapid and intense acceleration that result in lack of sufficient blood supply to the brain. Whinnery[333] studied almost 1000 cases and noted how the experiences of-ten involved "tunnel vision and bright lights, floating sensations, automatic movement, autoscopy, OBEs, not wanting to be disturbed, paralysis, vivid dreamlets of beautiful places, pleasurable sensations, psychological alterations of euphoria and dissociation, inclusion of friends and family, inclusion of prior memories and thoughts, the experience being very memorable (when it can be remembered), confabulation, and a strong urge to understand the experience."

However, hypoxia-induced acceleration's primary characteristics are "rythmic jerking of the limbs, compromised memory of events just prior to the onset of unconsciousness, tingling of extremities ..." that are not observed during NDEs. Also G-LOC episodes do not feature life reviews, mystical experiences and "long-lasting transformational aftereffects", although this may be due to the fact that subjects have no expectation of dying.

Also, hypoxic hallucinations are characterized by "distress and agitation" and this is very different from near death experiences which subjects report as being pleasant.

Altered blood gas levels models

Some investigators have studied whether hypercarbia or higher than normal carbon dioxide levels, could explain the occurrence of NDEs. However, studies are difficult to interpret since NDEs have been observed both with increased levels as well as decreased levels of carbon dioxide, and finally some other studies have observed NDEs when levels had not changed, and there is little data.

Other models

French said that at least some reports of NDEs might be based upon false memories.

According to Engmann (2008) near-death experiences of people who are clinically dead are psychopathological symptoms caused by a severe malfunction of the brain resulting from the cessation of cerebral blood circulation.[334] An important question is whether it is possible to "translate" the bloomy experiences of the reanimated survivors into psychopathologically basic phenomena, e.g., acoasms (nonverbal auditory hallucinations), central narrowing of the visual field, autoscopia, visual hallucinations, activation of limbic and memory structures according to Moody's stages. The symptoms suppose a primary affliction of the occipital and temporal cortices under clinical death. This basis could be congruent with the thesis of pathoclisis—the inclination of special parts of the brain to be the first to be damaged in case of disease, lack of oxygen, or malnutrition—established eighty years ago by Cécile and Oskar Vogt.[335]

Professor of neurology Terence Hines (2003) claimed that near-death experiences are hallucinations caused by cerebral anoxia, drugs, or brain damage.

Cross-cultural aspects

Gregory Shushan published an analysis of the afterlife beliefs of five ancient civilizations (Old and Middle Kingdom Egypt, Sumerian and Old Babylonian Mesopotamia, Vedic India, pre-Buddhist China, and pre-Columbian Mesoamerica) and compared them with historical and contemporary reports of near-death experiences, and shamanic afterlife "journeys". Shushan found similarities across time, place, and culture that he found could not be explained by coincidence; he also found elements that were specific to cultures; Shushan concludes that some form of mutual influence between experiences of an afterlife and culture probably influence one another and that this inheritance in turn influences individual NDEs.

According to Parnia, near death experiences' interpretations are influenced by religious, social, cultural backgrounds. However, the core elements appear to transcend borders and can be considered universal. In fact, some of these core elements have even been reported by children <3 years old (this occurred over many months, whilst playing and communicated using children's language). In other words, at an age where they should not have been influenced by culture or tradition.

Also, according to Greyson, the central features of NDEs are universal and have not been influenced by time. These have been observed throughout history and in different cultures. This notwithstanding, cultural influences have probably played a role in some NDEs' reported descriptions.

External links

Wikimedia Commons has media related to *Near-death experiences*.

Wikimedia Commons has media related to *Near-death experiences*.

- "International Association for Near-Death Studies (IANDS)"[336]

Further reading

- James Alcock. (1979). *Psychology and Near-Death Experiences*. Skeptical Inquirer 3: 25–41.
- Lee Worth Bailey; Jenny Yates. (1996). *The Near-Death Experience: A Reader*. Routledge. ISBN 0-415-91431-0
- Blackmore, Susan (2002). "Near-Death Experiences". In Shermer, Ed. M. *The Skeptic Encyclopedia of Pseudoscience*[337]. Santa Barbara, CA.: ABC-Clio,. pp. 152–157. ISBN 9781576076538.
- Choi, Charles Q. (September 12, 2011). "Peace of Mind: Near-Death Experiences Now Found to Have Scientific Explanations"[338]. *Scientific American*.
- Carroll, Robert T. (12 September 2014). "Near-death experience (NDE)"[339]. The Skeptic's Dictionary. Retrieved 21 August 2017.
- Engmann, Birk (2014). *Near-death experiences : heavenly insight or human illusion?*. Imprint: Springer. ISBN 978-3-319-03727-1.
- Bruce Greyson, Charles Flynn. (1984). *The Near-Death Experience: Problems, Prospects, Perspectives*. Springfield. ISBN 0-398-05008-2
- Perera, Mahendra; Jagadheesan, Karuppiah; Peake, Anthony, eds. (2012). *Making sense of near-death experiences : a handbook for clinicians*. London: Jessica Kingsley Publishers. ISBN 978-1-84905-149-1.
- Roberts, Glenn; Owen, John (1988). "The Near-Death Experience". *British Journal of Psychiatry*. **153** (5): 607–617. doi: 10.1192/bjp.153.5.607[340]. PMID 3076496[341].

- Shermer, Michael (April 1, 2013). "Proof of Hallucination"[342]. *Scientific American*. **308** (4): 86. doi: 10.1038/scientificamerican0413-86[343]. PMID 23539795[344].
- Woerlee, G.M. (May 2004). "Darkness, Tunnels, and Light"[345]. *Skeptical Inquirer*. **28** (3).
- Woerlee, G.M. (2005). *Mortal minds : the biology of near-death experiences*. Amherst, NY: Prometheus Books. ISBN 978-1-59102-283-1.
- Lommel, Pim van (2010). *After life : a scientific approach to near-death experiences* (1st ed.). New York: HarperOne. ISBN 978-0-06-177725-7.
- Zaleski, Carol (1987). *Otherworld journeys : accounts of near-death experience in medieval and modern times* (Paperback ed.). New York: Oxford University Press. ISBN 978-0-19-503915-3.

Reincarnation

Part of a series on the

Paranormal

- v
- t
- e[346]

Reincarnation is the philosophical or religious concept that an aspect of a living being starts a new life in a different physical body or form after each biological death. It is also called rebirth or transmigration, and is a part of the Saṃsāra doctrine of cyclic existence.[347,348] It is a central tenet of all major Indian religions, namely Jainism, Hinduism, Buddhism, and Sikhism.[348,349] The idea of reincarnation is found in many ancient cultures,[350] and a belief in rebirth/metempsychosis was held by Greek historic figures, such as Pythagoras, Socrates, and Plato.[351] It is also a common belief of various ancient and modern religions such as Spiritism, Theosophy, and Eckankar, and as an esoteric belief in many streams of Orthodox Judaism. It is found as well in many tribal societies around the world, in places such as Australia, East Asia, Siberia, and South America.[352]

Although the majority of denominations within Christianity and Islam do not believe that individuals reincarnate, particular groups within these religions do refer to reincarnation; these groups include the mainstream historical and

Figure 28: *The drawing illustrates how the soul travels to any one of the four states of existence after death depending on its karmas, according to Jainism.*

contemporary followers of Cathars, Alawites, the Druze,[353] and the Rosicrucians.[354] The historical relations between these sects and the beliefs about reincarnation that were characteristic of Neoplatonism, Orphism, Hermeticism, Manicheanism, and Gnosticism of the Roman era as well as the Indian religions have been the subject of recent scholarly research.[355] Unity Church and its founder Charles Fillmore teaches reincarnation.

In recent decades, many Europeans and North Americans have developed an interest in reincarnation, and many contemporary works mention it.

Conceptual definitions

The word "reincarnation" derives from Latin, literally meaning, "entering the flesh again". The Greek equivalent *metempsychosis* (μετεμψύχωσις) derives from *meta* (change) and *empsykhoun* (to put a soul into),[356] a term attributed to Pythagoras.[357] An alternate term is transmigration implying migration from one life (body) to another. Reincarnation refers to the belief that an aspect of every human being (or all living beings in some cultures) continues to exist after death, this aspect may be the soul or mind or consciousness or something transcendent which is reborn in an interconnected cycle of existence; the transmigration belief varies by culture, and is envisioned to be in the form of a newly born human being, or animal, or plant, or spirit, or as a being in some other non-human realm of existence.[358] The term has been used by modern philosophers such as Kurt Gödel and has entered the English language. Another Greek term sometimes used synonymously is *palingenesis*, "being born again".

Rebirth is a key concept found in major Indian religions, and discussed with various terms. *Punarjanman* (Sanskrit: पुनर्जन्मन्) means "rebirth, transmigration". Reincarnation is discussed in the ancient Sanskrit texts of Hinduism, Buddhism, and Jainism, with many alternate terms such as *punarāvṛtti* (पुनरावृत्ति), *punarājāti* (पुनराजाति), *punarjīvātu* (पुनर्जीवातु), *punarbhava* (पुनर्भव), *āgati-gati* (आगति-गति, common in Buddhist Pali text), *nibbattin* (निब्बत्तिन्), *upapatti* (उपपत्ति), and *uppajjana* (उप्पज्जन). These religions believe that this reincarnation is cyclic and an endless Saṃsāra, unless one gains spiritual insights that ends this cycle leading to liberation.[348,349] The reincarnation concept is considered in Indian religions as a step that starts each "cycle of aimless drifting, wandering or mundane existence",[348] but one that is an opportunity to seek spiritual liberation through ethical living and a variety of meditative, yogic (*marga*), or other spiritual practices.[359,360] They consider the release from the cycle of reincarnations as the ultimate spiritual goal, and call the liberation by terms such as moksha, nirvana, *mukti* and *kaivalya*.[361,362] However, the Buddhist, Hindu and Jain traditions have differed, since ancient times, in their assumptions and in their details on what reincarnates, how reincarnation occurs and what leads to liberation.[363,364]

Gilgul, *Gilgul neshamot* or *Gilgulei Ha Neshamot* (Heb. גלגול (הנשמות) refers to the concept of reincarnation in Kabbalistic Judaism, found in much Yiddish literature among Ashkenazi Jews. *Gilgul* means "cycle" and *neshamot* is "souls". Kabbalistic reincarnation says that humans reincarnate only to humans and to the same sex only: men to men, women to women.Wikipedia:Citation needed

History

Origins

The origins of the notion of reincarnation are obscure. Discussion of the subject appears in the philosophical traditions of India. The Greek Pre-Socratics discussed reincarnation, and the Celtic Druids are also reported to have taught a doctrine of reincarnation.[365]

The ideas associated with reincarnation may have arisen independently in different regions, or they might have spread as a result of cultural

contact. Proponents of cultural transmission have looked for links between Iron Age Celtic, Greek and Vedic philosophy and religion,[366]
someWikipedia:Manual of Style/Words to watch#Unsupported attributions
even suggesting that belief in reincarnation was present in Proto-Indo-
European religion.Wikipedia:Accuracy dispute#Disputed statement[367] In ancient European, Iranian and Indian agricultural cultures, the life cycles of birth,
death, and rebirth were recognized as a replica of natural agricultural cycles.[368]

Early Hinduism, Jainism and Buddhism

The idea of reincarnation has early roots in the Vedic period (c. 1500 – c. 500
BCE), predating the Buddha and the Mahavira. The concepts of the cycle of
birth and death, samsara, and liberation partly derive from ascetic traditions
that arose in India around the middle of the first millennium BCE.[369] Though
no direct evidence of this has been found, the tribes of the Ganges valley or
the Dravidian traditions of South India have been proposed as another early
source of reincarnation beliefs.[370]

Hinduism's Rigveda makes references to reincarnation in the Brahmanas layer.
Though these early textual layers of the Vedas, from 2nd millennium BCE,
mention and anticipate the doctrine of Karma and rebirth, the idea is not fully
developed.[371,372] It is in the early Upanishads, which are pre-Buddha and pre-
Mahavira, where these ideas are more explicitly developed in a general way.[371]
Detailed descriptions first appear around the mid 1st millennium BCE in di-
verse traditions, including Buddhism, Jainism and various schools of Hindu
philosophy, each of which gave unique expression to the general principle.[349]

The texts of ancient Jainism that have survived into the modern era are post-
Mahavira, likely from the last centuries of the 1st millennium BCE, and extensively mention rebirth and karma doctrines.[373] The Jaina philosophy assumes
that the soul (*Jiva* in Jainism, *Atman* in Hinduism) exists and is eternal, passing through cycles of transmigration and rebirth.[374] After death, reincarnation
into a new body is asserted to be instantaneous in early Jaina texts. Depending
upon the accumulated karma, rebirth occurs into a higher or lower bodily form,
either in heaven or hell or earthly realm.[375] No bodily form is permanent: ev-
eryone dies and reincarnates further. Liberation (*kevalya*) from reincarnation
is possible, however, through removing and ending karmic accumulations to
one's soul. From the early stages of Jainism on, a human being was considered
the highest mortal being, with the potential to achieve liberation, particularly
through asceticism.

The early Buddhist texts discuss rebirth as part of the doctrine of *Saṃsāra*.
This asserts that the nature of existence is a "suffering-laden cycle of life, death,
and rebirth, without beginning or end".[376] Also referred to as the wheel of existence (*Bhavacakra*), it is often mentioned in Buddhist texts with the term

punarbhava (rebirth, re-becoming). Liberation from this cycle of existence, *Nirvana*, is the foundation and the most important purpose of Buddhism.[377] Buddhist texts also assert that an enlightened person knows his previous births, a knowledge achieved through high levels of meditative concentration.[378] Tibetan Buddhism discusses death, bardo (an intermediate state), and rebirth in texts such as the *Tibetan Book of the Dead*. While Nirvana is taught as the ultimate goal in the Theravadin Buddhism, and is essential to Mahayana Buddhism, the vast majority of contemporary lay Buddhists focus on accumulating good karma and acquiring merit to achieve a better reincarnation in the next life.[379]

In early Buddhist traditions, *Saṃsāra* cosmology consisted of five realms through which the wheel of existence cycled. This included hells (*niraya*), hungry ghosts (*pretas*), animals (*tiryak*), humans (*manushya*), and gods (*devas*, heavenly). In latter Buddhist traditions, this list grew to a list of six realms of rebirth, adding demi-gods (*asuras*).

Rationale

The earliest layers of Vedic text incorporate the concept of life, followed by an afterlife in heaven and hell based on cumulative virtues (merit) or vices (demerit). However, the ancient Vedic Rishis challenged this idea of afterlife as simplistic, because people do not live an equally moral or immoral life. Between generally virtuous lives, some are more virtuous; while evil too has degrees, and the texts assert that it would be unfair for people, with varying degrees of virtue or vices, to end up in heaven or hell, in "either or" and disproportionate manner irrespective of how virtuous or vicious their lives were.[380] They introduced the idea of an afterlife in heaven or hell in proportion to one's merit, and when this runs out, one returns and is reborn. This idea appears in ancient and medieval texts, as the cycle of life, death, rebirth and redeath, such as section 6:31 of the Mahabharata and section 6.10 of Devi Bhagavata Purana.[380,381]

Comparison

Early texts of Hinduism, Buddhism and Jainism share the concepts and terminology related to reincarnation.[382] They also emphasize similar virtuous practices and karma as necessary for liberation and what influences future rebirths. For example, all three discuss various virtues – sometimes grouped as Yamas and Niyamas – such as non-violence, truthfulness, non-stealing, non-possessiveness, compassion for all living beings, charity and many others.

Hinduism, Buddhism and Jainism disagree in their assumptions and theories about rebirth. Hinduism relies on its foundational assumption that "soul, Self exists" (Atman, attā), in contrast to Buddhist assumption that there is "no soul,

Figure 29: *A 2nd-century Roman sarcophagus shows the mythology and symbolism of the Orphic and Dionysiac Mystery schools. Orpheus plays his lyre to the left.*

no Self" (Anatta, anatman).[383,384,385] Hindu traditions consider soul to be the unchanging eternal essence of a living being, and what journeys across reincarnations until it attains self-knowledge.[386] Buddhism, in contrast, asserts a rebirth theory without a Self, and considers realization of non-Self or Emptiness as Nirvana (nibbana). Thus Buddhism and Hinduism have a very different view on whether a self or soul exists, which impacts the details of their respective rebirth theories.

The reincarnation doctrine in Jainism differs from those in Buddhism, even though both are non-theistic Sramana traditions. Jainism, in contrast to Buddhism, accepts the foundational assumption that soul exists (*Jiva*) and asserts this soul is involved in the rebirth mechanism. Further, Jainism considers asceticism as an important means to spiritual liberation that ends all reincarnation, while Buddhism does not.

Early Greece

Early Greek discussion of the concept likewise dates to the 6th century BCE. An early Greek thinker known to have considered rebirth is Pherecydes of Syros (fl. 540 BCE).[387] His younger contemporary Pythagoras (c. 570–c. 495 BCE[388]), its first famous exponent, instituted societies for its diffusion. Plato (428/427–348/347 BCE) presented accounts of reincarnation in his works, particularly the *Myth of Er*.

Authorities have not agreed on how the notion arose in Greece: sometimes Pythagoras is said to have been Pherecydes' pupil, sometimes to have introduced it with the doctrine of Orphism, a Thracian religion that was to be important in the diffusion of reincarnation, or else to have brought the teaching from India. In *Phaedo*, Plato makes his teacher Socrates, prior to his death, state: "I am confident that there truly is such a thing as living again, and that the living spring from the dead." However Xenophon does not mention Socrates as believing in reincarnation and Plato may have systematised Socrates' thought with concepts he took directly from Pythagoreanism or Orphism.

Classical Antiquity

The Orphic religion, which taught reincarnation, about the 6th century BC, organized itself into mystery schools at Eleusis and elsewhere, and produced a copious literature.[389,390,391] Orpheus, its legendary founder, is said to have taught that the immortal soul aspires to freedom while the body holds it prisoner. The wheel of birth revolves, the soul alternates between freedom and captivity round the wide circle of necessity. Orpheus proclaimed the need of the grace of the gods, Dionysus in particular, and of self-purification until the soul has completed the spiral ascent of destiny to live for ever.

An association between Pythagorean philosophy and reincarnation was routinely accepted throughout antiquity. In the *Republic* Plato makes Socrates tell how Er, the son of Armenius, miraculously returned to life on the twelfth day after death and recounted the secrets of the other world. There are myths and theories to the same effect in other dialogues, in the Chariot allegory of the Phaedrus, in the Meno, Timaeus and Laws. The soul, once separated from the body, spends an indeterminate amount of time in "formland" (see The Allegory of the Cave in *The Republic*) and then assumes another body.

In later Greek literature the doctrine is mentioned in a fragment of Menander[392] and satirized by Lucian.[393] In Roman literature it is found as early as Ennius,[394] who, in a lost passage of his *Annals*, told how he had seen Homer in a dream, who had assured him that the same soul which had animated both the poets had once belonged to a peacock. Persius in his satires (vi. 9) laughs at this, it is referred to also by Lucretius[395] and Horace.[396]

Virgil works the idea into his account of the Underworld in the sixth book of the Aeneid.[397] It persists down to the late classic thinkers, Plotinus and the other Neoplatonists. In the Hermetica, a Graeco-Egyptian series of writings on cosmology and spirituality attributed to Hermes Trismcgistus/Thoth, the doctrine of reincarnation is central.

In Greco-Roman thought, the concept of metempsychosis disappeared with the rise of Early Christianity, reincarnation being incompatible with the Christian core doctrine of salvation of the faithful after death. It has been suggested that some of the early Church Fathers, especially Origen, still entertained a belief in the possibility of reincarnation, but evidence is tenuous, and the writings of Origen as they have come down to us speak explicitly against it.[398]

Some early Christian Gnostic sects professed reincarnation. The Sethians and followers of Valentinus believed in it.[399] The followers of Bardaisan of Mesopotamia, a sect of the 2nd century deemed heretical by the Catholic Church, drew upon Chaldean astrology, to which Bardaisan's son Harmonius, educated in Athens, added Greek ideas including a sort of metempsychosis. Another such teacher was Basilides (132–? CE/AD), known to us through the criticisms of Irenaeus and the work of Clement of Alexandria (see also Neoplatonism and Gnosticism and Buddhism and Gnosticism).

In the third Christian century Manichaeism spread both east and west from Babylonia, then within the Sassanid Empire, where its founder Mani lived about 216–276. Manichaean monasteries existed in Rome in 312 AD. Noting Mani's early travels to the Kushan Empire and other Buddhist influences in Manichaeism, Richard Foltz[400] attributes Mani's teaching of reincarnation to Buddhist influence. However the inter-relation of Manicheanism, Orphism, Gnosticism and neo-Platonism is far from clear.

The Celts

In the 1st century BCE Alexander Cornelius Polyhistor wrote:

<templatestyles src="Template:Quote/styles.css"/>

The Pythagorean doctrine prevails among the Gauls' teaching that the souls of men are immortal, and that after a fixed number of years they will enter into another body.

Julius Caesar recorded that the druids of Gaul, Britain and Ireland had metempsychosis as one of their core doctrines:[401]

<templatestyles src="Template:Quote/styles.css"/>

The principal point of their doctrine is that the soul does not die and that after death it passes from one body into another... the main object of all education is, in their opinion, to imbue their scholars with a firm belief in the indestructibility of the human soul, which, according to their belief, merely passes at death from one tenement to another; for by such doctrine alone, they say, which robs death of all its terrors, can the highest form of human courage be developed.

Judaism

The belief in reincarnation had first existed amongst Jewish mystics in the Ancient World, among whom differing explanation given of the after-life, although with a universal belief in an immortal soul.[402] Today, reincarnation is an esoteric belief within many streams of modern Judaism. Kabbalah (Jewish mysticism), teaches a belief in gilgul, transmigration of souls, and hence the belief in reincarnation is universal in Hasidic Judaism, which regards the Kabbalah as sacred and authoritative, and is also held as an esoteric belief within Modern Orthodox Judaism. In Judaism, the Zohar, first published in the 13th century, discusses reincarnation at length, especially in the Torah portion "Balak." The most comprehensive kabbalistic work on reincarnation, *Shaar HaGilgulim*,[403,404] was written by Chaim Vital, based on the teachings of his mentor, the 16th century kabbalist Isaac Luria, who was said to know the past lives of each person through his semi-prophetic abilities. The 18th century Lithuanian master scholar and kabbalist, Rabbi Elijah, known as the Vilna Gaon (Elijah of Vilna), authored a commentary on the biblical Book of Jonah as an allegory of reincarnation.

The practice of conversion to Judaism is sometimes understood within Orthodox Judaism in terms of reincarnation. According to this school of thought in Judaism, when non-Jews are drawn to Judaism, it is because they had been Jews in a former life. Such souls may "wander among nations" through multiple lives, until they find their way back to Judaism, including through finding themselves born in a gentile family with a "lost" Jewish ancestor.[405]

There is an extensive literature of Jewish folk and traditional stories that refer to reincarnation.[406]

Taoism

Taoist documents from as early as the Han Dynasty claimed that Lao Tzu appeared on earth as different persons in different times beginning in the legendary era of Three Sovereigns and Five Emperors. The (ca. 3rd century BC) *Chuang Tzu* states: "Birth is not a beginning; death is not an end. There is existence without limitation; there is continuity without a starting-point. Existence without limitation is Space. Continuity without a starting point is Time. There is birth, there is death, there is issuing forth, there is entering in."

European Middle Ages

Around the 11–12th century in Europe, several reincarnationist movements were persecuted as heresies, through the establishment of the Inquisition in the Latin west. These included the Cathar, Paterene or Albigensian church of

Figure 30: *Sváfa holding the dying Helgi in their first incarnation of three*

western Europe, the Paulician movement, which arose in Armenia, and the Bogomils in Bulgaria.[407]

Christian sects such as the Bogomils and the Cathars, who professed reincarnation and other gnostic beliefs, were referred to as "Manichean", and are today sometimes described by scholars as "Neo-Manichean".[408] As there is no known Manichaean mythology or terminology in the writings of these groups there has been some dispute among historians as to whether these groups truly were descendants of Manichaeism.

Norse mythology

Reincarnation also appears in Norse mythology, in the *Poetic Edda*. The editor of the *Poetic Edda* says that Helgi Hjörvarðsson and his mistress, the valkyrie Sváfa, whose love story is told in the poem *Helgakviða Hjörvarðssonar*, were reborn as Helgi Hundingsbane and the valkyrie Sigrún. Helgi and Sigrún's love story is the matter of a part of the *Völsunga saga* and the lays *Helgakviða Hundingsbana I and II*. They were reborn a second time as Helgi Haddingjaskati and the valkyrie Kára, but unfortunately their story, *Káruljóð*, only survives in a probably modified form in the *Hrómundar saga Gripssonar*.

The belief in reincarnation may have been commonplace among the Norse since the annotator of the *Poetic Edda* wrote that people formerly used to believe in it:

<templatestyles src=":"Template:Quote/styles.css"/>

> *Sigrun was early dead of sorrow and grief. It was believed in olden times that people were born again, but that is now called old wives' folly. Of Helgi and Sigrun it is said that they were born again; he became Helgi Haddingjaskati, and she Kara the daughter of Halfdan, as is told in the Lay of Kara, and she was a Valkyrie.*

Renaissance and Early Modern period

While reincarnation has been a matter of faith in some communities from an early date it has also frequently been argued for on principle, as Plato does when he argues that the number of souls must be finite because souls are indestructible,[409] Benjamin Franklin held a similar view.[410] Sometimes such convictions, as in Socrates' case, arise from a more general personal faith, at other times from anecdotal evidence such as Plato makes Socrates offer in the *Myth of Er*.

During the Renaissance translations of Plato, the Hermetica and other works fostered new European interest in reincarnation. Marsilio Ficino[411] argued that Plato's references to reincarnation were intended allegorically, Shakespeare alluded to the doctrine of reincarnation[412] but Giordano Bruno was burned at the stake by authorities after being found guilty of heresy by the Roman Inquisition for his teachings.[413] But the Greek philosophical works remained available and, particularly in north Europe, were discussed by groups such as the Cambridge Platonists.

19th to 20th centuries

By the 19th century the philosophers Schopenhauer[414] and Nietzsche[415] could access the Indian scriptures for discussion of the doctrine of reincarnation, which recommended itself to the American Transcendentalists Henry David Thoreau, Walt Whitman and Ralph Waldo Emerson and was adapted by Francis Bowen into *Christian Metempsychosis*.

By the early 20th century, interest in reincarnation had been introduced into the nascent discipline of psychology, largely due to the influence of William James, who raised aspects of the philosophy of mind, comparative religion, the psychology of religious experience and the nature of empiricism.[416] James was influential in the founding of the American Society for Psychical Research (ASPR) in New York City in 1885, three years after the British Society for Psychical Research (SPR) was inaugurated in London, leading to systematic, critical investigation of paranormal phenomena.

At this time popular awareness of the idea of reincarnation was boosted by the Theosophical Society's dissemination of systematised and universalised Indian

Figure 31: *American psychologist and philosopher William James (1842–1910) was an early psychical researcher.*

concepts and also by the influence of magical societies like The Golden Dawn. Notable personalities like Annie Besant, W. B. Yeats and Dion Fortune made the subject almost as familiar an element of the popular culture of the west as of the east. By 1924 the subject could be satirised in popular children's books.[417]

Théodore Flournoy was among the first to study a claim of past-life recall in the course of his investigation of the medium Hélène Smith, published in 1900, in which he defined the possibility of cryptomnesia in such accounts.[418] Carl Gustav Jung, like Flournoy based in Switzerland, also emulated him in his thesis based on a study of cryptomnesia in psychism. Later Jung would emphasise the importance of the persistence of memory and ego in psycho-logical study of reincarnation: "This concept of rebirth necessarily implies the continuity of personality... (that) one is able, at least potentially, to remember that one has lived through previous existences, and that these existences were one's own...." Hypnosis, used in psychoanalysis for retrieving forgotten mem-ories, was eventually tried as a means of studying the phenomenon of past life recall.

Figure 32: *Hindus believe the self or soul (atman) repeatedly takes on a physical body, until moksha.*

Religions and philosophies

Hinduism

The body dies, assert the Hindu traditions, but not the soul, which they assume to be the eternal reality, indestructible and bliss.[419] Everything and all existence is believed to be connected and cyclical in Hinduism, all living beings composed of two things, the soul and the body or matter.[420] Atman does not change and cannot change by its innate nature in the Hindu belief.[420] In contrast, the body and personality, can change, constantly changes, is born and dies.[420] Current Karma impacts the future circumstances in this life, as well as the future forms and realms of lives.[421] Good intent and actions lead to good future, bad intent and actions lead to bad future, impacting how one reincarnates, in the Hindu view of existence.[422]

There is no permanent heaven or hell in Hinduism. In the afterlife, based on one's karma, the soul is reborn as another being in heaven, hell, or a living being on earth (human, animal). Gods too die once their past karmic merit runs out, as do those in hell, and they return getting another chance on earth. This reincarnation continues, endlessly in cycles, until one embarks on a spiritual pursuit, realizes self-knowledge, and thereby gains *mokṣa*, the final release out of the reincarnation cycles.[423] This release is believed to be a state of utter bliss, which Hindu traditions believe is either related or identical to Brahman, the unchanging reality that existed before the creation of universe, continues to exist, and shall exist after the universe ends.

The Upanishads, part of the scriptures of the Hindu traditions, primarily focus on the liberation from reincarnation.[424] The Bhagavad Gita discusses various paths to liberation.[419] The Upanishads, states Harold Coward, offer a "very optimistic view regarding the perfectibility of human nature", and the goal of human effort in these texts is a continuous journey to self-perfection and self-knowledge so as to end *Saṃsāra* – the endless cycle of rebirth and redeath.[425] The aim of spiritual quest in the Upanishadic traditions is find the true self within and to know one's soul, a state that it believes leads to blissful state of freedom, moksha.[426]

The Bhagavad Gita states:

<templatestyles src="Template:Quote/styles.css"/>

Just as in the body childhood, adulthood and old age happen to an embodied being. So also he (the embodied being) acquires another body. The wise one is not deluded about this. – (2:13)[427]

As, after casting away worn out garments, a man later takes new ones. So after casting away worn out bodies, the embodied Self encounters other new ones. – (2:22)[428]

When an embodied being transcends, these three qualities which are the source of the body. Released from birth, death, old age and pain, he attains immortality. – (14:20)[429]

There are internal differences within Hindu traditions on reincarnation and the state of moksha. For example, the dualistic devotional traditions such as Madhvacharya's Dvaita Vedanta tradition of Hinduism champion a theistic premise, assert that human soul and Brahman are different, loving devotion to Brahman (god Vishnu in Madhvacharya's theology) is the means to release from Samsara, it is the grace of God which leads to moksha, and spiritual liberation is achievable only in after-life (*videhamukti*). The nondualistic traditions such as Adi Shankara's Advaita Vedanta tradition of Hinduism champion a monistic premise, asserting that the individual human soul and Brahman are identical, only ignorance, impulsiveness and inertia leads to suffering through Saṃsāra, in reality they are no dualities, meditation and self-knowledge is the path to liberation, the realization that one's soul is identical to Brahman is moksha, and spiritual liberation is achievable in this life (*jivanmukti*).

Figure 33: *In this 8-meter (25-foot) tall Buddhist relief, made between 1177 and 1249, Mara, Lord of Death and Desire, clutches a Wheel of Reincarnation which outlines the Buddhist cycle of reincarnation.*

Buddhism

According to various Buddhist scriptures, Gautama Buddha believed in the existence of an afterlife in another world and in reincarnation,

<templatestyles src="Template:Quote/styles.css"/>

Since there actually is another world (any world other than the present human one, i.e. different rebirth realms), one who holds the view 'there is no other world' has wrong view...

—*Buddha, Majjhima Nikaya i.402, Apannaka Sutta, Translated by Peter Harvey*

The Buddha also asserted that karma influences rebirth, and that the cycles of repeated births and deaths are endless. Before the birth of Buddha, ancient Indian scholars had developed competing theories of afterlife, including the materialistic school such as Charvaka, which posited that death is the end, there is no afterlife, no soul, no rebirth, no karma, and they described death to be a state where a living being is completely annihilated, dissolved. Buddha rejected this theory, adopted the alternate existing theories on rebirth, criticizing the materialistic schools that denied rebirth and karma, states Damien Keown. Such beliefs are inappropriate and dangerous, stated Buddha, because such annihilationism views encourage moral irresponsibility and material hedonism; he tied moral responsibility to rebirth.

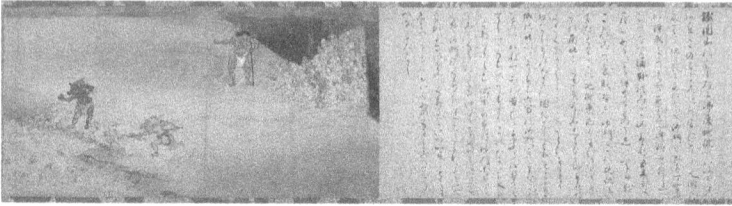

Figure 34: *A 12th-century Japanese painting showing one of the six Buddhist realms of reincarnation (rokudō, 六道)*

The Buddha introduced the concept that there is no permanent self (soul), and this central concept in Buddhism is called *anattā*. Major contemporary Buddhist traditions such as Theravada, Mahayana and Vajrayana traditions accept the teachings of Buddha. These teachings assert there is rebirth, there is no permanent self and no irreducible ātman (soul) moving from life to another and tying these lives together, there is impermanence, that all compounded things such as living beings are aggregates dissolve at death, but every being reincarnates. The rebirth cycles continue endlessly, states Buddhism, and it is a source of *Dukkha* (suffering, pain), but this reincarnation and *Dukkha* cycle can be stopped through nirvana. The *anattā* doctrine of Buddhism is a contrast to Hinduism, the latter asserting that "soul exists, it is involved in rebirth, and it is through this soul that everything is connected".[430]

Different traditions within Buddhism have offered different theories on what reincarnates and how reincarnation happens. One theory suggests that it occurs through consciousness (Pali: *samvattanika-viññana*)[431,432] or stream of consciousness (Pali: *viññana-sotam*,[433] Sanskrit: *vijñāna-srotām, vijñāna-santāna*, or *citta-santāna*) upon death, which reincarnates into a new aggregation. This process, states this theory, is similar to the flame of a dying candle lighting up another. The consciousness in the newly born being is neither identical to nor entirely different from that in the deceased but the two form a causal continuum or stream in this Buddhist theory. Transmigration is influenced by a being's past *karma* (*kamma*).[434,435] The root cause of rebirth, states Buddhism, is the abiding of consciousness in ignorance (Pali: *avijja*, Sanskrit: *avidya*) about the nature of reality, and when this ignorance is uprooted, rebirth ceases.[436]

Buddhist traditions also vary in their mechanistic details on rebirth. Theravada Buddhists assert that rebirth is immediate while the Tibetan schools hold to the notion of a *bardo* (intermediate state) that can last up to 49 days.[437] The *bardo* rebirth concept of Tibetan Buddhism, along with *yidam*, developed independently in Tibet without Indian influence, and involves 42 peaceful deities, and 58 wrathful deities. These ideas led to mechanistic maps on karma and what

Figure 35: *17th-century cloth painting depicting seven levels of Jain hell according to Jain cosmology. Left panel depicts the demi-god and his animal vehicle presiding over each hell.*

form of rebirth one takes after death, discussed in texts such as *The Tibetan Book of the Dead*.[438] The major Buddhist traditions accept that the reincarnation of a being depends on the past karma and merit (demerit) accumulated, and that there are six realms of existence in which the rebirth may occur after each death.[439,358]

Within Japanese Zen, reincarnation is accepted by some, but rejected by others. A distinction can be drawn between "folk Zen", as in the Zen practiced by devotional lay people, and "philosophical Zen". Folk Zen generally accepts the various supernatural elements of Buddhism such as rebirth. Philosophical Zen, however, places more emphasis on the present moment.

Some schools conclude that karma continues to exist and adhere to the person until it works out its consequences. For the Sautrantika school, each act "perfumes" the individual or "plants a seed" that later germinates. Tibetan Buddhism stresses the state of mind at the time of death. To die with a peaceful mind will stimulate a virtuous seed and a fortunate rebirth; a disturbed mind will stimulate a non-virtuous seed and an unfortunate rebirth.[440]

Jainism

In Jainism, the reincarnation doctrine, along with its theories of *Saṃsāra* and Karma, are central to its theological foundations, as evidenced by the extensive literature on it in the major sects of Jainism, and their pioneering ideas on these topics from the earliest times of the Jaina tradition.[373] Reincarnation in contemporary Jainism traditions is the belief that the worldly life is characterized by continuous rebirths and suffering in various realms of existence.[441]

Karma forms a central and fundamental part of Jain faith, being intricately connected to other of its philosophical concepts like transmigration, reincarnation, liberation, non-violence (*ahiṃsā*) and non-attachment, among others. Actions are seen to have consequences: some immediate, some delayed, even into future incarnations. So the doctrine of karma is not considered simply in relation to one life-time, but also in relation to both future incarnations and past lives.[442] *Uttarādhyayana-sūtra* 3.3–4 states: "The *jīva* or the soul is sometimes born in the world of gods, sometimes in hell. Sometimes it acquires the body of a demon; all this happens on account of its karma. This *jīva* sometimes takes birth as a worm, as an insect or as an ant."[443] The text further states (32.7): "Karma is the root of birth and death. The souls bound by karma go round and round in the cycle of existence."

Actions and emotions in the current lifetime affect future incarnations depending on the nature of the particular karma. For example, a good and virtuous life indicates a latent desire to experience good and virtuous themes of life. Therefore, such a person attracts karma that ensures that his future births will allow him to experience and manifest his virtues and good feelings unhindered.[444] In this case, he may take birth in heaven or in a prosperous and virtuous human family. On the other hand, a person who has indulged in immoral deeds, or with a cruel disposition, indicates a latent desire to experience cruel themes of life.[445] As a natural consequence, he will attract karma which will ensure that he is reincarnated in hell, or in lower life forms, to enable his soul to experience the cruel themes of life.

There is no retribution, judgment or reward involved but a natural consequences of the choices in life made either knowingly or unknowingly. Hence, whatever suffering or pleasure that a soul may be experiencing in its present life is on account of choices that it has made in the past.[446] As a result of this doctrine, Jainism attributes supreme importance to pure thinking and moral behavior.[447]

The Jain texts postulate four *gatis*, that is states-of-existence or birth-categories, within which the soul transmigrates. The four *gatis* are: *deva* (demi-gods), *manuṣya* (humans), *nāraki* (hell beings) and *tiryañca* (animals, plants and micro-organisms).[448]   The four *gatis* have four corresponding realms or habitation levels in the vertically tiered Jain universe: demi-gods occupy the higher levels where the heavens are situated; humans, plants and animals occupy the middle levels; and hellish beings occupy the lower levels where seven hells are situated.

Single-sensed souls, however, called *nigoda*,[449] and element-bodied souls pervade all tiers of this universe. *Nigodas* are souls at the bottom end of the existential hierarchy. They are so tiny and undifferentiated, that they lack even individual bodies, living in colonies. According to Jain texts, this infinity of *nigodas* can also be found in plant tissues, root vegetables and animal bodies.[450] Depending on its karma, a soul transmigrates and reincarnates within the scope of this cosmology of destinies. The four main destinies are further divided into sub-categories and still smaller sub-sub-categories. In all, Jain texts speak of a cycle of 8.4 million birth destinies in which souls find themselves again and again as they cycle within *samsara*.[451]

In Jainism, God has no role to play in an individual's destiny; one's personal destiny is not seen as a consequence of any system of reward or punishment, but rather as a result of its own personal karma. A text from a volume of the ancient Jain canon, *Bhagvati sūtra* 8.9.9, links specific states of existence to specific karmas. Violent deeds, killing of creatures having five sense organs, eating fish, and so on, lead to rebirth in hell. Deception, fraud and falsehood lead to rebirth in the animal and vegetable world. Kindness, compassion and humble character result in human birth; while austerities and the making and keeping of vows lead to rebirth in heaven.[452]

Each soul is thus responsible for its own predicament, as well as its own salvation. Accumulated karma represent a sum total of all unfulfilled desires, attachments and aspirations of a soul.[453,454] It enables the soul to experience the various themes of the lives that it desires to experience. Hence a soul may transmigrate from one life form to another for countless of years, taking with it the karma that it has earned, until it finds conditions that bring about the required fruits. In certain philosophies, heavens and hells are often viewed as places for eternal salvation or eternal damnation for good and bad deeds. But according to Jainism, such places, including the earth are simply the places which allow the soul to experience its unfulfilled karma.[455]

Judaism

Part of a series on

Kabbalah

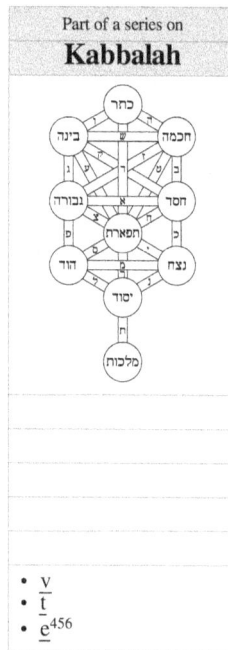

- v
- t
- e[456]

Jewish mystical texts (the Kabbalah), from their classic Medieval canon on-ward, teach a belief in *Gilgul Neshamot* (Hebrew for metempsychosis of souls: literally "soul cycle", plural *"gilgulim"*). The Zohar and the Sefer HaBahir specifically discuss reincarnation. It is a common belief in contemporary Ha-sidic Judaism, which regards the Kabbalah as sacred and authoritative, though understood in light of a more innate psychological mysticism. Kabbalah also teaches that "The soul of Moses is reincarnated in every generation."[457] Other, Non-Hasidic, Orthodox Jewish groups while not placing a heavy emphasis on reincarnation, do acknowledge it as a valid teaching. Its popularization entered modern secular Yiddish literature and folk motif.

The 16th century mystical renaissance in communal Safed replaced scholastic Rationalism as mainstream traditional Jewish theology, both in scholarly cir-cles and in the popular imagination. References to *gilgul* in former Kabbalah became systematized as part of the metaphysical purpose of creation. Isaac Luria (the Ari) brought the issue to the centre of his new mystical articula-tion, for the first time, and advocated identification of the reincarnations of historic Jewish figures that were compiled by Haim Vital in his Shaar HaG-ilgulim.[458] *Gilgul* is contrasted with the other processes in Kabbalah of Ibbur ("pregnancy"), the attachment of a second soul to an individual for (or by) good means, and Dybuk ("possession"), the attachment of a spirit, demon, etc. to an individual for (or by) "bad" means.

In Lurianic Kabbalah, reincarnation is not retributive or fatalistic, but an expression of Divine compassion, the microcosm of the doctrine of cosmic rectification of creation. *Gilgul* is a heavenly agreement with the individual soul, conditional upon circumstances. Luria's radical system focused on rectification of the Divine soul, played out through Creation. The true essence of anything is the divine spark within that gives it existence. Even a stone or leaf possesses such a soul that "came into this world to receive a rectification". A human soul may occasionally be exiled into lower inanimate, vegetative or animal creations. The most basic component of the soul, the nefesh, must leave at the cessation of blood production. There are four other soul components and different nations of the world possess different forms of souls with different purposes. Each Jewish soul is reincarnated in order to fulfill each of the 613 Mosaic commandments that elevate a particular spark of holiness associated with each commandment. Once all the Sparks are redeemed to their spiritual source, the Messianic Era begins. Non-Jewish observance of the 7 Laws of Noah assists the Jewish people, though Biblical adversaries of Israel reincarnate to oppose.

Among the many rabbis who accepted reincarnation are Nahmanides (the Ramban) and Rabbenu Bahya ben Asher, Levi ibn Habib (the Ralbah), Shelomoh Alkabez, Moses Cordovero, Moses Chaim Luzzatto; early Hasidic masters such as the Baal Shem Tov, Schneur Zalman of Liadi and Nachman of Breslov, as well as virtually all later Hasidic masters; contemporary Hasidic teachers such as DovBer Pinson and Moshe Weinberger; and key Mitnagdic leaders, such as the Vilna Gaon and Chaim Volozhin and their school, as well as Rabbi Shalom Sharabi (known at the RaShaSH), the Ben Ish Chai of Baghdad, Baba Sali and Rabbi Joel Landau. Rabbis who have rejected the idea include Saadia Gaon, David Kimhi, Hasdai Crescas, Joseph Albo, Abraham ibn Daud, Leon de Modena, Solomon ben Aderet, Maimonides and Asher ben Jehiel. Among the Geonim, Hai Gaon argued in favour of *gilgulim*.

Sikhism

Founded in the 15th century, Sikhism's founder Guru Nanak had a choice between the cyclical reincarnation concept of ancient Indian religions and the linear concept of early 7th-century Islam, and he chose the cyclical concept of time. Sikhism teaches reincarnation theory similar to those in Hinduism, but with some differences from its traditional doctrines. Sikh rebirth theories about the nature of existence are similar to ideas that developed during the devotional Bhakti movement particularly within some Vaishnavism traditions,

Figure 36: *An Egungun masquerade dance garment in the permanent collection of The Children's Museum of Indianapolis*

which define liberation as a state of union with God attained through the grace of God.

The doctrines of Sikhism teach that the soul exists, and is passed from one body to another in endless cycles of Saṃsāra, until liberation. Each birth begins with karma (*karam*), and these actions leave a *karni* (karmic signature) on one's soul which influences future rebirths, but it is God whose grace that liberates. The way out of the reincarnation cycle, asserts Sikhism, is to live an ethical life, devote oneself to God and constantly remember God's name. The precepts of Sikhism encourage the bhakti of One Lord for *mukti* (liberation).

Yoruba religion

The Yoruba believe in reincarnation within the family. The names Babatunde (Father returns), Yetunde (Mother returns), Babatunji (Father wakes once again) and Sotunde (The wise man returns) all offer vivid evidence of the Ifa concept of familial or lineal rebirth. There is no simple guarantee that your grandfather or great uncle will "come back" in the birth of your child, however.

Whenever the time arrives for a spirit to return to Earth (otherwise known as The Marketplace) through the conception of a new life in the direct bloodline of the family, one of the component entities of a person's being returns, while the other remains in Heaven (Ikole Orun). The spirit that returns does so in the form of a Guardian Ori. One's Guardian Ori, which is represented and contained in the crown of the head, represents not only the spirit and energy of one's previous blood relative, but the accumulated wisdom he or she has acquired through a myriad of lifetimes. This is not to be confused with one's spiritual Ori, which contains personal destiny, but instead refers to the coming back to The Marketplace of one's personal blood Ori through one's new life and experiences.

Native American nations

Reincarnation is an intrinsic part of many Native American and Inuit traditions. In the now heavily Christian Polar North (now mainly parts of Greenland and Nunavut), the concept of reincarnation is enshrined in the Inuit language.

The following is a story of human-to-human reincarnation as told by Thunder Cloud, a Winnebago (Ho-Chunk tribe) shaman referred to as T. C. in the narrative. Here T. C. talks about his two previous lives and how he died and came back again to this his third lifetime. He describes his time between lives, when he was "blessed" by Earth Maker and all the abiding spirits and given special powers, including the ability to heal the sick.

T. C.'s Account of His Two Reincarnations:

<templatestyles src="Template:Quote/styles.css"/>

> *I (my ghost) was taken to the place where the sun sets (the west). ... While at that place, I thought I would come back to earth again, and the old man with whom I was staying said to me, "My son, did you not speak about wanting to go to the earth again?" I had, as a matter of fact, only thought of it, yet he knew what I wanted. Then he said to me, "You can go, but you must ask the chief first." Then I went and told the chief of the village of my desire, and he said to me, "You may go and obtain your revenge upon the people who killed your relatives and you." Then I was brought down to earth. ... There I lived until I died of old age. ... As I was lying [in my grave], someone said to me, "Come, let us go away." So then we went toward the setting of the sun. There we came to a village where we met all the dead. ... From that place I came to this earth again for the third time, and here I am. (Radin, 1923)*

Christianity

Though the major Christian denominations reject the concept of reincarnation, a large number of Christians profess the belief. In a survey by the Pew Forum in 2009, 24% of American Christians expressed a belief in reincarnation. In a 1981 Survey in Europe 31% of regular churchgoing Catholics expressed a belief in reincarnation.

Geddes MacGregor, an Episcopalian priest and professor of Philosophy, makes a case for the compatibility of Christian doctrine and reincarnation.

There is evidence[459] that the writing of Origen, a Church father in early Christian times, was mistranslated into Latin due to religious bias and that he taught reincarnation in his lifetime. One of the epistles written by St. Jerome, "To Avitus" (Letter 124 ; Ad Avitum. Epistula CXXIV), asserts that Origen's *On First Principles* (Latin: *De Principiis*; Greek: Περὶ Ἀρχῶν[460]) was mistranscribed from Greek into Latin:

<templatestyles src="Template:Quote/styles.css"/>

About ten years ago that saintly man Pammachius sent me a copy of a certain person's [Rufinus's] rendering, or rather misrendering, of Origen's First Principles; with a request that in a Latin version I should give the true sense of the Greek and should set down the writer's words for good or for evil without bias in either direction. When I did as he wished and sent him the book, he was shocked to read it and locked it up in his desk lest being circulated it might wound the souls of many.

Under the impression that Origen was a heretic like Arius, St. Jerome criticizes ideas described in *On First Principles*. Further in "To Avitus" (Letter 124), St. Jerome writes about "convincing proof" that Origen teaches reincarnation in the original version of the book:

<templatestyles src="Template:Quote/styles.css"/>

The following passage is a convincing proof that he holds the transmigration of the souls and annihilation of bodies. 'If it can be shown that an incorporeal and reasonable being has life in itself independently of the body and that it is worse off in the body than out of it; then beyond a doubt bodies are only of secondary importance and arise from time to time to meet the varying conditions of reasonable creatures. Those who require bodies are clothed with them, and contrariwise, when fallen souls have lifted themselves up to better things, their bodies are once more annihilated. They are thus ever vanishing and ever reappearing.'

The original text of *On First Principles* has almost completely disappeared. It remains extant as *De Principiis* in fragments faithfully translated into Latin by St. Jerome and in "the not very reliable Latin translation of Rufinus."

Islam

Islamic scriptures reject any idea of reincarnation of human beings or God.[461] It teaches a linear concept of life, wherein a human being has only one life and upon death he or she is judged by God, then rewarded in heaven or punished in hell. Islam teaches final resurrection and Judgement Day,[462] but there is no prospect for the reincarnation of a human being into a different body or being. During the early history of Islam, some of the Caliphs persecuted all reincarnation-believing people to the point of extinction (Manichaeism) in Mesopotamia and Persia (modern day Iraq and Iran).[461] However, some Muslim minority sects such as those found among Sufis, and some Muslims in South Asia and Indonesia have retained their pre-Islamic Hindu and Buddhist beliefs in reincarnation.[461] For instance, historically, South Asian Isma'ilis performed chantas yearly, one of which is for seeking forgiveness of sins committed in past lives.

Ghulat sects

بِسْمِ اللَّهِ الرَّحْمَنِ الرَّحِيمِ

Part of a series on
Shia Islam

Shia Islam portal

- v
- t
- e[463]

The idea of reincarnation is accepted by a few Muslim sects, particularly of the Ghulat,[464] and by other sects in the Muslim world. Alawis belonging to Shia denomination of Islam hold that they were originally stars or divine lights that were cast out of heaven through disobedience and must undergo repeated reincarnation (or metempsychosis) before returning to heaven. They can be reincarnated as Christians or others through sin and as animals if they become infidels.[465]

Reincarnation was also accepted by some streams of Sufism. Modern Sufis who embrace the idea include Bawa Muhaiyadeen.[466] However Inayat Khan has criticized the idea as unhelpful to the spiritual seeker.[467]

Druze

Part of a series on
Druze
• 🏛 **Religion portal**
• v
• t
• e[468]

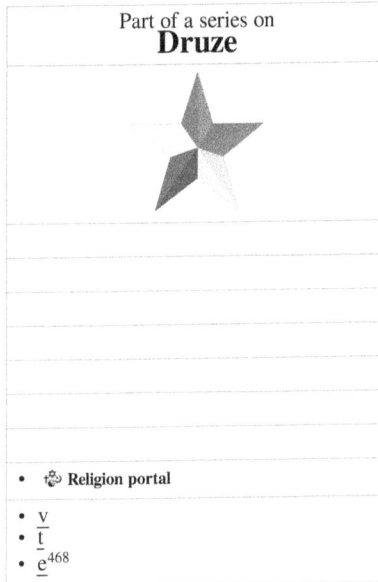

Reincarnation is a paramount tenet in the Druze faith.[469] There is an eternal duality of the body and the soul and it is impossible for the soul to exist without the body. Therefore, reincarnations occur instantly at one's death. While in the Hindu and Buddhist belief system a soul can be transmitted to any living creature, in the Druze belief system this is not possible and a human soul will only transfer to a human body. Furthermore, a male Druze can only be reincarnated as another male Druze and a female Druze can only be reincarnated as another female Druze. Additionally, souls cannot be divided and the number of souls existing is finite.[470]

Very few Druzes are able to recall their past but, if they are able to they are called a *Nateq*. Typically souls who have died violent deaths in their previous incarnation will be able to recall memories. Since death is seen as a quick transient state, mourning is discouraged. Unlike other Abrahamic faiths, heaven and hell are spiritual. Heaven is the ultimate happiness received when soul escapes the cycle of rebirths and reunites with the Creator, while hell is conceptualized as the bitterness of being unable to reunite with the Creator and escape from the cycle of rebirth.

New religious and spiritual movements

Part of a series on the
Paranormal

- v
- t
- e[346]

Theosophy

The Theosophical Society draws much of its inspiration from India. The idea is, according to a recent Theosophical writer, "the master-key to modern problems", including heredity. In the Theosophical world-view reincarnation is the vast rhythmic process by which the soul, the part of a person which belongs to the formless non-material and timeless worlds, unfolds its spiritual powers in the world and comes to know itself. It descends from sublime, free, spiritual realms and gathers experience through its effort to express itself in the world. Afterwards there is a withdrawal from the physical plane to successively higher levels of reality, in death, a purification and assimilation of the past life. Having cast off all instruments of personal experience it stands again in its spiritual and formless nature, ready to begin its next rhythmic manifestation, every lifetime bringing it closer to complete self-knowledge and self-expression. However it may attract old mental, emotional, and energetic *karma* patterns to form the new personality.Wikipedia:Citation needed

Modern astrology

Inspired by Helena Blavatsky's major works, including *Isis Unveiled* and *The Secret Doctrine*, astrologers in the early twentieth-century integrated the concepts of karma and reincarnation into the practice of Western astrology. Notable astrologers who advanced this development included Alan Leo, Charles E. O. Carter, Marc Edmund Jones, and Dane Rudhyar. A new synthesis of East and West resulted as Hindu and Buddhist concepts of reincarnation were fused with Western astrology's deep roots in Hermeticism and Neoplatonism.

In the case of Rudhyar, this synthesis was enhanced with the addition of Jungian depth psychology.[471] This dynamic integration of astrology, reincarnation and depth psychology has continued into the modern era with the work of astrologers Steven Forrest and Jeffrey Wolf Green. Their respective schools of Evolutionary Astrology are based on "an acceptance of the fact that human beings incarnate in a succession of lifetimes."

Anthroposophy

Anthroposophy describes reincarnation from the point of view of Western philosophy and culture. The ego is believed to transmute transient soul experiences into universals that form the basis for an individuality that can endure after death. These universals include ideas, which are intersubjective and thus transcend the purely personal (spiritual consciousness), intentionally formed human character (spiritual life), and becoming a fully conscious human being (spiritual humanity). Rudolf Steiner described both the general principles he believed to be operative in reincarnation, such as that one's will activity in one life forms the basis for the thinking of the next,[472] and a number of successive lives of various individualities.[473]

Scientology

Past reincarnation, usually termed "past lives", is a key part of the principles and practices of the Church of Scientology. Scientologists believe that the human individual is actually a *thetan*, an immortal spiritual entity, that has fallen into a degraded state as a result of past-life experiences. Scientology auditing is intended to free the person of these past-life traumas and recover past-life memory, leading to a higher state of spiritual awareness. This idea is echoed in their highest fraternal religious order, the Sea Organization, whose motto is "Revenimus" or "We Come Back", and whose members sign a "billion-year contract" as a sign of commitment to that ideal. L. Ron Hubbard, the founder of Scientology, does not use the word "reincarnation" to describe its beliefs, noting that: "The common definition of reincarnation has been altered from its original meaning. The word has come to mean 'to be born again in different life forms' whereas its actual definition is 'to be born again into the flesh of another body.' Scientology ascribes to this latter, original definition of reincarnation."

The first writings in Scientology regarding past lives date from around 1951 and slightly earlier. In 1960, Hubbard published a book on past lives entitled *Have You Lived Before This Life*. In 1968 he wrote *Mission into Time*, a report on a five-week sailing expedition to Sardinia, Sicily and Carthage to see if specific evidence could be found to substantiate L. Ron Hubbard's recall of incidents in his own past, centuries ago.

Figure 37: *Tomb of Allan Kardec, founder of spiritism.*
The inscription says in French "To be born, die, again
be reborn, and so progress unceasingly, such is the law".

Meher Baba

The Indian spiritual teacher Meher Baba stated that reincarnation occurs due
to desires and once those desires are extinguished the ego-mind ceases to reincarnate.[474]

Spiritism

Spiritism is a Christian philosophy codified in the 19th century by the French
educator Allan Kardec. Spiritism teaches reincarnation or rebirth into human
life after death. This basically distinguishes Spiritism from Spiritualism. According to the Spiritist doctrine, free will and cause and effect are the corollar-
ies of reincarnation, and reincarnation provides a mechanism for man's spiritual evolution in successive lives.

Wicca

Wicca is a neo-pagan religion focused on nature, guided by the philosophy
of Wiccan Rede that advocates Harm None, Do As Ye Will. The concept
of karmic return in Wicca states that our deeds return to us threefold, or

multiple times to teach us lessons (The Threefold Law), whether in this life-time or the next. Reincarnation therefore is an accepted part of the Wiccan faith.[475] Wikipedia:Citing sources#What information to include Wiccans also believe in death and afterlife as important experiences for the soul to transform and prepare for future lifetimes. Wikipedia:Citation needed

Reincarnation research

Psychiatrist Ian Stevenson, from the University of Virginia, investigated many reports of young children who claimed to remember a past life. He conducted more than 2,500 case studies over a period of 40 years and published twelve books, including *Twenty Cases Suggestive of Reincarnation* and *Where Reincarnation and Biology Intersect*. Stevenson methodically documented each child's statements and then identified the deceased person the child identified with, and verified the facts of the deceased person's life that matched the child's memory. He also matched birthmarks and birth defects to wounds and scars on the deceased, verified by medical records such as autopsy photographs, in *Reincarnation and Biology*.[476]

Stevenson searched for disconfirming evidence and alternative explanations for the reports, and believed that his strict methods ruled out all possible "normal" explanations for the child's memories. However, a significant majority of Stevenson's reported cases of reincarnation originated in Eastern societies, where dominant religions often permit the concept of reincarnation. Following this type of criticism, Stevenson published a book on *European Cases of the Reincarnation Type*. Other people who have undertaken reincarnation research include Jim B. Tucker, Antonia Mills, Satwant Pasricha, Godwin Samararatne, and Erlendur Haraldsson.

Skeptics such as Paul Edwards have analyzed many of these accounts, and called them anecdotal,[477] while also suggesting that claims of evidence for reincarnation originate from selective thinking and from the false memories that often result from one's own belief system and basic fears, and thus cannot be counted as empirical evidence.[478] Carl Sagan referred to examples apparently from Stevenson's investigations in his book *The Demon-Haunted World* as an example of carefully collected empirical data, though he rejected reincarnation as a parsimonious explanation for the stories. Sam Harris cited Stevenson's works in his book *The End of Faith* as part of a body of data that seems to attest to the reality of psychic phenomena.

Stevenson claimed there were a handful of cases that suggested evidence of xenoglossy. These included two where a subject under hypnosis could allegedly converse with people speaking the foreign language, instead of merely being able to recite foreign words. Sarah Thomason, a linguist at the University of

Michigan, reanalyzed these cases, concluding that "the linguistic evidence is too weak to provide support for the claims of xenoglossy."[479]

Ian Wilson argued that a large number of Stevenson's cases consisted of poor children remembering wealthy lives or belonging to a higher caste. He speculated that such cases may represent a scheme to obtain money from the family of the alleged former incarnation.[480] The philosopher Keith Augustine has written "the vast majority of Stevenson's cases come from countries where a religious belief in reincarnation is strong, and rarely elsewhere, seems to indicate that cultural conditioning (rather than reincarnation) generates claims of spontaneous past-life memories." According to the research of Robert Baker many of the alleged past-life experiences investigated by Stevenson and other parapsychologists can be explained in terms of known psychological factors. Baker has written that recalling past lives is a mixture of cryptomnesia and confabulation.[481] The philosopher Paul Edwards noted that reincarnation invokes assumptions and is inconsistent with modern science.[482]

Objections to claims of reincarnation include the facts that the vast majority of people do not remember previous lives and there is no mechanism known to modern science that would enable a personality to survive death and travel to another body. Researchers such as Stevenson have acknowledged these limitations.

Reincarnation in the Western world

During recent decades, many people in the West have developed an interest in reincarnation. Recent studies have indicated that some Westerners accept the idea of reincarnation including certain contemporary people who were from Catholic families,[483] modern Neopagans, followers of Spiritism, Theosophists and students of esoteric philosophies such as Kabbalah, and Gnostic and Esoteric Christianity as well as followers of Indian religions. Demographic survey data from 1999–2002 shows a significant minority of people from Europe and America, where there is reasonable freedom of thought and access to ideas but no outstanding recent reincarnationist tradition, believe we had a life before we were born, will survive death and be born again physically. The mean for the Nordic countries is 22%. The belief in reincarnation is particularly high in the Baltic countries, with Lithuania having the highest figure for the whole of Europe, 44%. The lowest figure is in East Germany, 12%. In Russia, about one-third believes in reincarnation. The effect of communist anti-religious ideas on the beliefs of the populations of Eastern Europe seems to have been rather slight, if any, except apparently in East Germany. Overall, 22% of respondents in Western Europe believe in reincarnation. According to a 2005 Gallup poll 20 percent of U.S. adults believe in reincarnation. Recent surveys

Figure 38: *The 14th Dalai Lama has stated his belief that it would be difficult for science to disprove reincarnation.*

by the Barna Group, a Christian research nonprofit organization, have found that a quarter of U.S. Christians, including 10 percent of all born again Christians, embrace the idea.

Skeptic Carl Sagan asked the Dalai Lama what he would do if a fundamental tenet of his religion (reincarnation) were definitively disproved by science. The Dalai Lama answered, "If science can disprove reincarnation, Tibetan Buddhism would abandon reincarnation... but it's going to be mighty hard to disprove reincarnation."[484]

Ian Stevenson reported that belief in reincarnation is held (with variations in details) by adherents of almost all major religions except Christianity and Islam. In addition, between 20 and 30 percent of persons in western countries who may be nominal Christians also believe in reincarnation.[485]

One 1999 study by Walter and Waterhouse reviewed the previous data on the level of reincarnation belief and performed a set of thirty in-depth interviews in Britain among people who did not belong to a religion advocating reincarnation. The authors reported that surveys have found about one fifth to one quarter of Europeans have some level of belief in reincarnation, with similar results found in the USA. In the interviewed group, the belief in the existence of this phenomenon appeared independent of their age, or the type of religion that these people belonged to, with most being Christians. The beliefs of this group also did not appear to contain any more than usual of "new age" ideas (broadly defined) and the authors interpreted their ideas on reincarnation as "one way of tackling issues of suffering", but noted that this seemed to have little effect on their private lives.

Waterhouse also published a detailed discussion of beliefs expressed in the interviews. She noted that although most people "hold their belief in reincarnation quite lightly" and were unclear on the details of their ideas, personal experiences such as past-life memories and near-death experiences had influenced most believers, although only a few had direct experience of these phenomena. Waterhouse analyzed the influences of second-hand accounts of reincarnation, writing that most of the people in the survey had heard other people's accounts of past-lives from regression hypnosis and dreams and found these fascinating, feeling that there "must be something in it" if other people were having such experiences.

References

Bibliography

- John Bowker (2014). *God: A Very Short Introduction*[486]. Oxford University Press. ISBN 978-0-19-870895-7.
- Chapple, Christopher Key, W Sargeant (Translator) (2010). *The Bhagavad Gita: Twenty-fifth–Anniversary Edition*[487]. State University of New York Press. ISBN 978-1-4384-2840-6.
- Harold Coward (2008). *The Perfectibility of Human Nature in Eastern and Western Thought: The Central Story*[488]. State University of New York Press. ISBN 978-0-7914-7336-8.
- Jeaneane D. Fowler (1997). *Hinduism: Beliefs and Practices*[489]. Sussex Academic Press. ISBN 978-1-898723-60-8.
- Padmanabh Jaini (1980). Wendy Doniger, ed. *Karma and Rebirth in Classical Indian Traditions*[490]. University of California Press. ISBN 978-0-520-03923-0.
- Kalupahana, David J. (1992), *A history of Buddhist philosophy*, Motilal Banarsidass
- Keown, Damien (2013). *Buddhism: A Very Short Introduction*[491]. Oxford University Press. ISBN 978-0-19-966383-5.
- Mark Juergensmeyer; Wade Clark Roof (2011). *Encyclopedia of Global Religion*[492]. SAGE Publications. ISBN 978-1-4522-6656-5.
- Stephen J. Laumakis (2008). *An Introduction to Buddhist Philosophy*[493]. Cambridge University Press. ISBN 978-1-139-46966-1.

- Norman C. McClelland (2010), *Encyclopedia of Reincarnation and Karma*[494], McFarland, ISBN 978-0-7864-5675-8
- Giannis Stamatellos (2013), *"Plotinus on Transmigration: a Reconsideration"*[495], Journal of Ancient Philosophy 7,1
- Obeyesekere, Gananath (2005). Wendy Doniger, ed. *Karma and Rebirth: A Cross Cultural Study*. Motilal Banarsidass. ISBN 978-8120826090.
- Trainor, Kevin (2004). *Buddhism: The Illustrated Guide*[496]. Oxford University Press. ISBN 978-0-19-517398-7.
- Paul Williams; Anthony Tribe; Alexander Wynne (2012), *Buddhist Thought*[497], Routledge, ISBN 978-1-136-52088-4

Further reading

- Alegretti, Wagner, *Retrocognitions: An Investigation into Memories of Past Lives and the Period Between Lives*. ISBN 0-9702131-6-6, 2004.
- Archiati, Pietro, *Reincarnation in Modern Life: Toward a new Christian Awareness*. ISBN 0-904693-88-0.
- Atkinson, William Walker, *Reincarnation and the Law of Karma: A Study of the Old-new World-doctrine of Rebirth and Spiritual Cause and Effect*, Kessinger Publishing, 1997. ISBN 0-7661-0079-0.
- Baba, Meher, *Discourses*[498], Sufism Reoriented, 1967, ISBN 1-880619-09-1.
- Bache, Christopher M., *Lifecycles, Reincarnation and the Web of Life*, 1991, ISBN 1-55778-645-3.
- Besant, A.W., *Reincarnation*, Published by Theosophical Pub. Society, 1892.
- Boulting, W. *Giordano Bruno, His Life, Thought, and Martyrdom*, London: Kegan Paul, 1914.
- Bowman, Carol, *Children's Past Lives*, 1998, ISBN 0-553-57485-X.
- Bowman, Carol, *Return from Heaven*, 2003, ISBN 0-06-103044-9.
- Cerminara, Gina, *Many Mansions: The Edgar Cayce Story on Reincarnation*, 1990, ISBN 0-451-03307-8.
- Childs, Gilbert and Sylvia, *Your Reincarnating Child: Welcoming a soul to the world*. ISBN 1-85584-126-6.
- Doniger O'Flaherty, Wendy (1980). *Karma and Rebirth in Classical Indian Traditions*[490]. University of California Press. ISBN 0-520-03923-8.
- Doore, Gary, *What Survives?*, 1990, ISBN 0-87477-583-3.
- Edwards, Paul, *Reincarnation: A Critical Examination* ISBN 1-57392-921-2.
- Foltz, Richard, *Religions of the Silk Road*, New York: Palgrave Macmillan, 2010, ISBN 978-0-230-62125-1.

- Gyatso, Geshe Kelsang, *Joyful Path of Good Fortune*, pp 336–47, Tharpa Publications (2nd. ed., 1995) ISBN 978-0-948006-46-3.
- Gyatso, Geshe Kelsang, *Living Meaningfully, Dying Joyfully*: The Profound Practice of Transference of Consciousness, Tharpa Publications (1999) ISBN 978-0-948006-63-0.
- Head, Joseph and Cranston, S.L., editors, *Reincarnation: The Phoenix Fire Mystery*, 1994, ISBN 0-517-56101-8.
- Jefferson, Warren. 2009. "Reincarnation Beliefs of North American Indians: Soul Journeys, Metamorphoses, and Near-Death Experiences." Summertown, TN: Native Voices. ISBN 978-1-57067-212-5.
- Heindel, Max, *The Rosicrucian Cosmo-Conception* (Part I, Chapter IV: Rebirth and the Law of Consequence[499]), 1909, ISBN 0-911274-34-0.
- Leland, Kurt. *The Unanswered Question: Death, Near-Death, and the Afterlife*. Hampton Roads Publishing (2002). ISBN 978-1-57174-299-5.
- Emily Williams Kelly, *Science, the Self, and Survival after Death*, Rowman, 2012.
- Klemp, H. (2003). Past lives, dreams, and soul travel. Minneapolis, MN: Eckankar. ISBN 1-57043-182-5.
- Luchte, James, *Pythagoras and the Doctrine of Transmigration: Wandering Souls*, Bloomsbury Publishing, 2009, ISBN 978-1441131027.
- Newton, Michael, *Life Between Lives: Hypnotherapy for Spiritual Regression*, 2004, ISBN 0-7387-0465-2.
- Newton, Michael, *Destiny of Souls: New Case Studies of Life Between Lives*, 2000, ISBN 1-56718-499-5.
- Nikhilananda, Swami. *Gospel of Sri Ramakrishna*, (8th Ed. 1992) ISBN 0-911206-01-9.
- Prophet, Elizabeth Clare, Erin L. Prophet, *Reincarnation: The Missing Link in Christianity*, 1997, ISBN 0-922729-27-1.
- Palamidessi Tommaso, The Memory of Past Lives and Its Technique, ed. Archeosofica, 1977.
- Ramster, Peter, *In Search of Lives Past*, ISBN 0-646-00021-7.
- Rinehart, Robin, ed., *Contemporary Hinduism*, (2004).
- Roberts, Jane. *Seth Speaks: The Eternal Validity of the Soul*, (1972). ISBN 1-878424-07-6.
- Semkiw, Walter, *Return of the Revolutionaries: The Case for Reincarnation and Soul Groups Reunited*, 2003, ISBN 1-57174-342-1.
- Steiner, Rudolf, *Karmic Relationships: Esoteric studies[500]*, 8 volumes, various dates, Rudolf Steiner Press. ISBN 0-85440-260-8 and others.
- Steiner, Rudolf, *A Western Approach to Reincarnation and Karma: selected lectures and writings*; ed. and intr. by René Querido. Hudson, NY: Anthroposophic Press, c1997, ISBN 0-88010-399-X.

- Steinpach, Richard, *Hidden Connections Determine Our Earth-Life*[501], 1988, ISBN 1-57461-013-9.
- Stevenson, Ian (1980). *Twenty Cases Suggestive of Reincarnation,* second (revised and enlarged) edition, University of Virginia Press. ISBN 978-0-8139-0872-4.
- Taylor, Michael, "Master of the Rose", Comstar Media LLC, 1997–2007, ISBN 1-933866-07-1.
- Tucker, Jim (2005). *Life Before Life: A Scientific Investigation of Children's Memories of Previous Lives*, ISBN 0-312-32137-6.
- Weiss, Brian L., *Only Love is real: the story of soulmates reunited*, 1996, ISBN 0-446-51945-6.

External links

Wikimedia Commonshas media related to:
Reincarnation (category)

Wikiquote has quotations related to: *Reincarnation*

Wikiversity has learning resources about *Reincarnation and Christianity*

- The Columbia Encyclopedia: Transmigration of Souls or Metempsychosis[502]
- The Catholic Encyclopedia: Metempsychosis[503]
- Jewish View of Reincarnation[504]
- Philosophy of Incarnation[505] - series of ebooks "The New Cosmic Philosophy"

Apparitional experience

In parapsychology, an **apparitional experience** is an anomalous experience characterized by the apparent perception of either a living being or an inanimate object without there being any material stimulus for such a perception. The person experiencing the apparition is awake, excluding dream visions from consideration.

In academic discussion, the term "apparitional experience" is to be preferred to the term "ghost" in respect of the following points:

1. The term ghost implies that some element of the human being survives death and, at least under certain circumstances, can make itself perceptible to living human beings. There are other competing explanations of apparitional experiences.
2. Firsthand accounts of apparitional experiences differ in many respects from their fictional counterparts in literary or traditional ghost stories and films (see below).
3. The content of apparitional experiences includes living beings, both human and animal, and even inanimate objects.[506]

History of the concept

Attempts to apply modern scientific or investigative standards to the study of apparitional experiences began with the work of Edmund Gurney, Frederic W. H. Myers and Frank Podmore,[507] who were leading figures in the early years of the Society for Psychical Research (founded in 1882). Their motive, as with most of the early work of the Society,[508] was to provide evidence for human survival after death. For this reason they had a particular interest in what are known as 'crisis cases'. These are cases in which a person reports having a hallucinatory experience, visual or otherwise, which apparently represents someone at a distance, this experience subsequently being considered to have coincided with that person's death, or a significant life event of some kind. If the temporal coincidence of the crisis and the distant apparitional experience cannot be explained by any conventional means, then in parapsychology the presumption is made that some as yet unknown form of communication, such as telepathy (a term coined by Myers[509]) has taken place.

While it may be said that the work of Gurney and his colleagues failed to provide convincing evidence for either telepathy or survival of death, the large collection of firsthand written accounts which resulted from their methods may nevertheless be regarded as providing a valuable body of data concerning the phenomenology of hallucinations in the sane.

A notable later discussion of apparitional experiences was that of G. N. M. Tyrrell,[510] also a leading member of the Society for Psychical Research of his day. Tyrrell accepted the hallucinatory character of the experience, pointing out that it is virtually unknown for firsthand accounts to claim that apparitional figures leave any of the normal physical effects, such as footprints in snow, that one would expect of a real person.[511] However, Tyrrell develops the idea that the apparition may be a way for the unconscious part of the mind to bring to consciousness information that has been paranormally acquired – in crisis cases, for example. He introduces an evocative metaphor of a mental 'stage-carpenter',[512] behind the scenes in the unconscious part of the mind, and constructing the quasi-perceptual experience that eventually appears on the stage of consciousness, so that it embodies paranormal information in a symbolic way, a person drowning at a distance appearing soaked in water, for example.

The study and discussion of apparitions developed in a different direction in the 1970s, with the work of Celia Green and Charles McCreery.[513] They were not primarily interested in the question of whether apparitions could shed any light on the existence or otherwise of telepathy, or in the survival question; instead they were concerned to analyse a large number of cases with a view to providing a taxonomy of the different types of experience, viewed simply as a type of anomalous perceptual experience or hallucination.

One of the points that was highlighted by their work was point (2) listed above, namely that 'real-life' accounts of apparitional experiences differ markedly from the traditional or literary ghost story. These are some of the more notable differences, at least as indicated by their own collection of 1800 firsthand accounts:

- Subjects of apparitional experiences are by no means always frightened by the experience; indeed they may find them soothing or reassuring at times of crisis or ongoing stress in their lives.[514]
- Spontaneous apparitional experiences tend to happen in humdrum or everyday surroundings, and under conditions of low central nervous system arousal, most often in the subject's own home - while doing housework, for example. By contrast, subjects who visit reputedly haunted locations in hopes of 'seeing a ghost' are more often than not disappointed.[515]
- Apparitions tend to be reported as appearing solid and not transparent; indeed they may be so realistic in a variety of ways as to deceive the percipient as to their hallucinatory nature; in some cases the subject only achieves insight after the experience has ended.[516]
- It is unusual for an apparitional figure to engage in any verbal interaction with the percipient; this is consistent with the finding that the majority of such experiences only involve one sense (most commonly the visual).[517]

Psychological implications

Psychological theories of perception

Apparitional experiences have relevance to psychological theories of perception, and in particular to the distinction between top-down and bottom-up approaches (cf. article on Top-down and bottom-up design). Top-down theories, such as that of Richard Langton Gregory, who conceives of perception as a process whereby the brain makes a series of hypotheses about the external world, stress the importance of central factors such as memory and expectation in determining the phenomenological content of perception; while the bottom-up approach, exemplified by the work of James J. Gibson, emphasises the role of the external sensory stimulus.[518]

Apparitional experiences would seem to lend support to the importance of central factors, since they represent a form of quasi-perceptual experience in which the role of external stimuli is minimal or possibly non-existent, while the experience nevertheless continues to be phenomenologically indistinguishable from normal perception, at least in some cases.[519]

The concept of schizotypy

The interest of apparitional experiences to psychology has acquired an added dimension in recent years with the development of the concept of schizotypy or psychosis-proneness. This is conceived of as a dimension of personality,[520] continuously distributed throughout the normal population, and analogous to the dimensions of extraversion or neuroticism. As long as mental illness is regarded under the disease model, according to which a person either does or does not 'have' schizophrenia or manic depression, just as a person either does or does not have syphilis or tuberculosis, then to talk of the occurrence of an apparitional or hallucinatory experience in a normal person is either an oxymoron, or to be taken as an indication of latent or incipient psychosis. If, on the contrary, a dimensional view of the matter is taken, it becomes easier to conceive of how normal people, more or less high on the putative schizotypy dimension, might be more or less prone to anomalous perceptual experiences, without their ever tipping over into psychosis.

Green and McCreery's identification of a class of what they called 'reassuring apparitions'[514] is of particular interest in this regard, as it suggests that the experiencing of hallucinations may even have an adaptive effect in certain subjects, making them better able to cope with adverse life events. This would fit with the model of schizotypy as essentially a normal dimension of personality, and might help to explain why the proneness to anomalous perceptual experiences has apparently not been 'weeded out' by the process of natural selection.

Philosophical implications

Direct realism

Apparitional experiences also have implications for the philosophy of perception. The occurrence of hallucinations, that is, perceptual experiences 'having the character of sense perception, but without relevant or adequate sensory stimulation [...]',[521] have long been one of the standard objections to the philosophical theory of direct realism. According to this theory we are in some sense in direct contact with the external world when we seem to be perceiving it, and not merely in direct contact with some mediating representation in our mind, such as a sense-datum or an image, which may or may not correspond to external reality. The psychologist J.J. Gibson, referred to above, became an advocate of the philosophical theory of direct realism.[522]

Hallucinatory experiences reported by sane people do not pose any new problem in principle for the theory of direct realism, other than that posed already by the more widely discussed hallucinations reported by people in a state of psychosis or under other abnormal conditions such as sensory deprivation. However, they do pose the problem in a particularly stark way, for the following reasons:

- *Scepticism about the status of verbal reports:*

In the case of hallucinations reported to have occurred in pathological or abnormal states there is some scope for uncertainty about the accuracy, or even the meaning, of the percipient's verbal report. Horowitz,[523] for example, summarising his experience of questioning chronic schizophrenic patients about their visual experiences during painting sessions, wrote:

'It was necessary to persist beyond initial verbal descriptions of their hallucinations, and insist that the patient describe and draw what he had seen. Initial descriptions of "vicious snakes" might then be drawn and redescribed as wavy lines. "Two armies struggling over my soul" arose from the subjective experience of seeing moving sets of dots. "Spiders" might be reduced, when the patient stated and drew what he actually saw, to a few radiating lines. In drawings of their hallucinations patients could often distinguish between those forms which duplicated what they saw with their eyes from those forms which were what they "made out of it".'[524]

Such difficulties of interpretation are much less obvious in the case of written reports by ostensibly normal subjects, in good health and not medicated at the time of the experience.

- *Extreme realism of the experience:*

As mentioned above, at least some of the apparitional experiences reported by normal subjects appear to mimic normal perception to such a degree that the subject is deceived into thinking that what they are experiencing actually is normal perception. Similar close mimicking of normal perception is reported by some of the subjects of a lucid dream[525] and out-of-body experiences,[526] which therefore pose similar problems for the theory of direct realism.

Representationalism

Apparitional experiences appear *prima facie* more compatible with the philosophical theory of representationalism. According to this theory, the immediate objects of experience when we are perceiving the world normally are representations of the world, rather than the world itself. These representations have been variously called sense-data or images. In the case of an apparitional experience one might say that the subject is aware of sense-data or images which happen not to correspond to, or represent, the external world in the normal way.

The philosophical implications of hallucinatory experiences in the sane are discussed by McCreery.[527] He argues that they provide empirical support for the theory of representationalism rather than direct realism.

Sources

- Bennett, Sir Ernest (1939). *Apparitions and Haunted Houses: A Survey of Evidence*. London: Faber and Faber.
- Tyrell, G. N. M.; Price, H. H. (1943). *Apparitions*. London: Gerald Duckworth. ISBN 978-1169829879.
- Horowitz, M. J. (1964). "The imagery of visual hallucinations". *Journal of Nervous and Mental Disease*. **138**. doi: 10.1097/00005053-196406000-00002[528].
- Green, Celia Elizabeth; McCreery, Charles (1975). *Apparitions*. London: Hamish Hamilton. ISBN 9780241891827.

Ganzfeld experiment

Ganzfeld experiment

A **ganzfeld experiment** (from the German for "entire field") is a technique used in parapsychology which is used to test individuals for extrasensory perception (ESP). The ganzfeld experiments are among the most recent in parapsychology for testing telepathy.

Consistent, independent replication of ganzfeld experiments has not been achieved.[529,530,531,532,533]

Historical context

The ganzfeld was originally introduced into experimental psychology due to the experiments of the German psychologist Wolfgang Metzger (1899–1979) on the perception of a homogenous visual field.[534] In the early 1970s, Charles Honorton had been investigating ESP and dreams at the Maimonides Medical Center and began using the ganzfeld technique to achieve a state of sensory deprivation in which he hypothesised that psi could work. Honorton believed that by reducing the ordinary sensory input, psi conductive states may be enhanced and psi-mediated information could be transmitted.

Since the first full experiment was published by Honorton and Sharon Harper in the *Journal of the American Society for Psychical Research* in 1974, the Ganzfeld has remained a mainstay of parapsychological research.

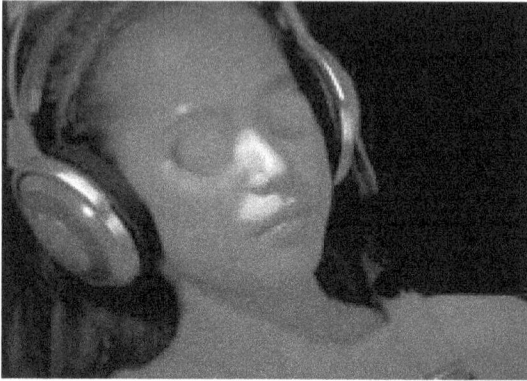

Figure 39: *Participant in a ganzfeld telepathy experiment*

Experimental procedure

In a typical ganzfeld experiment, a "receiver" is placed in a room relaxing in a comfortable chair with halved ping-pong balls over the eyes, having a red light shone on them. The receiver also wears a set of headphones through which white or pink noise (static) is played. The receiver is in this state of mild sensory deprivation for half an hour. During this time, a "sender" observes a randomly chosen target and tries to mentally send this information to the receiver. The receiver speaks out loud during the thirty minutes, describing what he or she can see. This is recorded by the experimenter (who is blind to the target) either by recording onto tape or by taking notes, and is used to help the receiver during the judging procedure.

In the judging procedure, the receiver is taken out of the Ganzfeld state and given a set of possible targets, from which they select one which most resembled the images they witnessed. Most commonly there are three decoys along with the target, giving an expected rate of 25%, by chance, over several dozens of trials.

Analysis of results

Early experiments

Between 1974 and 1982, 42 ganzfeld experiments were performed. In 1982, Charles Honorton presented a paper at the annual convention of the Parapsychological Association that summarized the results of the ganzfeld experiments up to that date, and concluded that they represented sufficient evidence to demonstrate the existence of psi. Ray Hyman, a psychologist, disagreed. The two men later independently analyzed the same studies, and both presented meta-analyses of them in 1985.

Hyman criticized the ganzfeld papers for not describing optimal protocols, nor including the appropriate statistical analysis. He presented a factor analysis that he said demonstrated a link between success and three flaws, namely: flaws in randomization for choice of target; flaws in randomization in judging procedure; and insufficient documentation. Honorton asked a statistician, David Saunders, to look at Hyman's factor analysis and he concluded that the number of experiments was too small to complete a factor analysis.

The ganzfeld studies examined by Hyman and Honorton had methodological problems that were well documented. Honorton reported only 36% of the studies used duplicate target sets of pictures to avoid handling cues.[535] Hyman discovered flaws in all of the 42 ganzfeld experiments and to assess each experiment, he devised a set of 12 categories of flaws. Six of these concerned statistical defects, the other six covered procedural flaws such as inadequate documentation, randomization and security as well as possibilities of sensory leakage.."[536] Over half of the studies failed to safeguard against sensory leakage and all of the studies contained at least one of the 12 flaws. Because of the flaws, Honorton agreed with Hyman the 42 ganzfeld studies could not support the claim for the existence of psi.

In 1986, Hyman and Honorton published *A Joint Communiqué* which agreed on the methodological problems and on ways to fix them. They suggested a computer-automated control, where randomization and the other methodological problems identified were eliminated. Hyman and Honorton agreed that replication of the studies was necessary before final conclusions could be drawn. They also agreed that more stringent standards were necessary for ganzfeld experiments, and they jointly specified what those standards should be.[537,538]

Figure 40: *Ray Hyman in 1983 with Lee Ross, Daryl Bem and Victor Benassi.*

Autoganzfeld

In 1982 Honorton had started a series of autoganzfeld experiments at his Psychophysical Research Laboratories (PRL). These studies were specifically designed to avoid the same potential problems as those identified in the 1986 joint communiqué issued by Hyman and Honorton. The PRL trials continued until September 1989. In 1990 Honorton *et al.* published the results of 11 autoganzfeld experiments they claimed met the standards specified by Hyman and Honorton (1986).[539] In these experiments, 240 participants contributed 329 sessions.

Hyman analyzed these experiments and wrote they met most, but not all of the "stringent standards" of the joint communiqué. He expressed concerns with the randomization procedure, the reliability of which he was not able to confirm based on the data provided by Bem. Hyman further noted that although the overall hit rate of 32% was significant, the hit rate for static targets (pictures) was in fact insignificant (inconsistently with previous ganzfeld research). The overall significance of the experiments was solely due to dynamic targets (videos). In the hit rates regarding these dynamic targets, however, some interesting patterns were found that implied visual cues may have been leaked:

<templatestyles src="Template:Quote/styles.css"/>

The most suspicious pattern was the fact that the hit rate for a given target increased with the frequency of occurrence of that target in the experiment. The hit rate for the targets that occurred only once was right at the chance expectation of 25%. For targets that appeared twice the hit rate crept up to 28%. For those that occurred three times it was 38%, and for those targets that occurred six or more times, the hit rate was 52%. Each time a videotape is played its quality can degrade. It is plausible then, that when a frequently used clip is the target for a given session, it may be physically distinguishable from the other three decoy clips that are presented to the subject for judging.

Hyman wrote these studies were an improvement over their older counterparts, but were not a successful replication of the ganzfeld experiments, nor a confirmation of psi. He concluded the autoganzfeld experiments were flawed because they did not preclude the possibility of sensory leakage.

Richard Wiseman published a paper discussing a non-psi hypothesis based on possible sender to experimenter acoustic leakage in the autoganzfeld to account for the results.[540,541] David Marks has written "Wiseman and his colleagues identified various different ways in which knowledge of the target could have been leaked to the experimenter. These included cues from the videocassette recorder and sounds from the sender who, of course, knew the target's identity... their conclusions provide little reassurance that sensory cueing of the experimenter was in any way substantially blocked."

Milton and Wiseman (1999) carried out a meta-analysis of ganzfeld experiments in other laboratories. They found no psi effect; the results showed no effect greater than chance from a database of 30 experiments and a non-significant Stouffer Z of 0.70.

Lance Storm and Suitbert Ertel (2001) published a meta-analysis of 79 studies published between 1974 and 1996 and concluded the positive statistically significant overall outcome indicates a psi effect.[542] In response, Milton and Wiseman (2001) wrote the meta-analysis of Storm and Ertel was not an accurate quantitative summary of ganzfeld research as they had included early studies which had been widely recognized as having methodological problems which make it impossible to interpret the results as evidence of a psi effect.[543]

Another meta-analysis was conducted by Daryl Bem, John Palmer, and Richard Broughton in which the experiments were sorted according to how closely they adhered to a pre-existing description of the ganzfeld procedure. Additionally, ten experiments that had been published in the time since Milton and Wiseman's deadline were introduced. Now the results were significant again with a Stouffer Z of 2.59.[544]

Contemporary research

The ganzfeld procedure has continued to be refined over the years. In its current incarnation, an automated computer system is used to select and display the targets ("digital autoganzfeld"). This overcomes many of the shortcomings of earlier experimental setups, such as randomization and experimenter blindness with respect to the targets.

In 2010, Lance Storm, Patrizio Tressoldi, and Lorenzo Di Risio analyzed 29 ganzfeld studies from 1997 to 2008. Of the 1,498 trials, 483 produced hits, corresponding to a hit rate of 32.2%. This hit rate is statistically significant with p < .001. Participants selected for personality traits and personal characteristics thought to be psi-conducive were found to perform significantly better than unselected participants in the ganzfeld condition. Hyman (2010) published a rebuttal to Storm *et al*. According to Hyman "reliance on meta-analysis as the sole basis for justifying the claim that an anomaly exists and that the evidence for it is consistent and replicable is fallacious. It distorts what scientists mean by confirmatory evidence." Hyman wrote the ganzfeld studies have not been independently replicated and have failed to produce evidence for psi. Storm *et al*. published a response to Hyman claiming the ganzfeld experimental design has proved to be consistent and reliable but parapsychology is a struggling discipline that has not received much attention so further research on the subject is necessary. Rouder *et al*. in 2013 wrote that critical evaluation of Storm *et al*.'s meta-analysis reveals no evidence for psi, no plausible mechanism and omitted replication failures.

A 2016 paper examined questionable research practices in the ganzfeld experiments.

Psi-conducive variables

Bem and Honorton (1994) investigated certain personality traits and characteristics as potential psi-conducive variables which they suggested play an important role in claimed ESP performance. According to parapsychologists these factors are thought to be positively correlated with increased scores in ganzfeld experiments, as compared to unselected participants. Traits and characteristics of subjects thought to increase the chance of obtaining a successful hit rate in a psi experiment include:

- Positive belief in psi; ESP
- Prior psi experiences
- Practicing a mental discipline such as meditation
- Creativity
- Artistic ability

Figure 41: *Richard Wiseman has suggested various sensory leakage problems with the autoganzfeld experiments.*

- Emotional closeness with the sender

While there are a number of reasons that researchers avoid special participants and sample only normal populations, these factors are important considerations in future replications of ganzfeld experiment, and may be useful in predicting the outcome of these studies.

Criticism

There are several common criticisms of some or all of the ganzfeld experiments·

- *Isolation* — Richard Wiseman and others argue that not all of the studies used soundproof rooms, so it is possible that when videos were playing, the experimenter could have heard it, and later given involuntary cues to the receiver during the selection process. It could even have been possible that the receiver themselves could hear the video.
- *Randomization* — When subjects are asked to choose from a variety of selections, there is an inherent bias to choose the first selection they are shown. If the order in which they are shown the selections is randomized each time, this bias will be averaged out. The randomization procedures

used in the experiment have been criticized for not randomizing satisfactorily.

• *The psi assumption* — The assumption that any statistical deviation from chance is evidence for telepathy is highly controversial. Strictly speaking, a deviation from chance is only evidence that either this was a rare, statistically unlikely occurrence that happened by chance, or *something* was causing a deviation from chance. Flaws in the experimental design are a common cause of this, and so the assumption that it must be telepathy is fallacious.

Writing in 1985, C. E. M. Hansel discovered weaknesses in the design and possibilities of sensory leakage in the ganzfeld experiments reported by Carl Sargent and other parapsychologists. Hansel concluded the ganzfeld studies had not been independently replicated and that "ESP is no nearer to being established than it was a hundred years ago."[545]

David Marks in his book *The Psychology of the Psychic* (2000) has noted that during the autoganzfeld experiments the experimenter sat only fourteen feet from the sender's room. Soundproofing tiles were eventually added but they were designed to "absorb sound not to prevent transmission." According to Marks this was inadequate and no different than using any standard internal wall. The door and door frame were also a possible source of sensory leakage and none of these problems were ever eliminated.

Terence Hines wrote in 2003 that the ganzfeld studies could not be said to provide evidence for psi as the alleged evidence disappears as the tightness of experimental controls is increased. As research progresses variables in science become clearer as more studies are published that describe under what specific condition the particular effect can be demonstrated. This is in opposition to the ganzfeld studies. According to Hines, there was "no clear way to obtain results showing any psychic phenomenon reliably" and that "the most reasonable conclusion" was that the effect did not exist and had never existed.[546]

In a 2007 review, Ray Hyman wrote that parapsychologists agree they have no positive theory of psi as it is negatively defined as any effect that cannot be currently explained in terms of chance or normal causes. Hyman saw this as a fallacy, as it encouraged parapsychologists to use any peculiarity in the data as a characteristic of psi. Hyman also wrote that parapsychologists have admitted it is impossible to eliminate the possibility of non-paranormal causes in the ganzfeld experiment. There is no independent method to indicate the presence or absence of psi.

<templatestyles src="Template:Quote/styles.css"/>

Until parapsychologists can provide a positive way to indicate the presence of psi, the different effect sizes that occur in experiments are just as likely to result from many different things rather than one thing called psi. Indeed given the obvious instability and elusiveness of the findings, the best guess might very well be that we are dealing with a variety of Murphy's Law rather than a revolutionary anomaly called psi.

—*Ray Hyman, Evaluating Parapsychological Claims, 2007*

In their book *50 Great Myths of Popular Psychology* (2011), Scott O. Lilienfeld and colleagues have written that the ganzfeld being a reliable technique is far from being resolved. They concluded that ESP has not been successfully demonstrated in experiments for over 150 years so this is hardly encouraging.[547]

In a 2013 podcast, Brian Dunning reviewed the flaws of the ganzfeld studies and came to the conclusion the technique had failed as evidence for psi and interest in ganzfeld has declined.

Controversy

In 1979, Susan Blackmore visited the laboratories of Carl Sargent in Cambridge. She noticed a number of irregularities in the procedure and wrote about them for the *Journal of the Society for Psychical Research*.

<templatestyles src="Template:Quote/styles.css"/>

It now appeared that in one session – number 9 – the following events had taken place.

1. *Sargent did the randomization when he should not have.*
2. *A 'B' went missing from the drawer during the session, instead of afterwards.*
3. *Sargent came into the judging and "pushed" the subject towards 'B'.*
4. *An error of addition was made in favour of 'B' and 'B' was chosen.*
5. *'B' was the target and the session a direct hit.*

This article, along with further criticisms of Sargent's work from Adrian Parker and Nils Wiklund remained unpublished until 1987 but all were well known in parapsychological circles. Sargent wrote a rebuttal to these criticisms (also not published until 1987) in which he did not deny what Blackmore had observed, but argued that her conclusions based on those observations were wrong and prejudiced. His co-workers also responded, saying that any deviation from protocol was the result of "random errors" rather than any concerted attempt at fraud. Carl Sargent stopped working in parapsychology after this and did not respond "in a timely fashion" when the Council of the Parapsychological Association asked for his data, and so his membership of that organization was allowed to lapse.

Writing for *Skeptical Inquirer* in 2018, Blackmore states that Sargent "deliberately violated his own protocols and in one trial had almost certainly cheated." Psychologists reading Daryl Bem's review in *Psychological Bulletin* would "not have a clue that serious doubt had been cast on more than a quarter of the studies involved" Sargent and Chuck Honortons. When Blackmore confronted Sargent, he told her "it wouldn't matter if some experiments were unreliable because, after all, we know that psi exists". Blackmore also recounts having a discussion with Bem at a consciousness conference where she challenged him on his support of Sargent and Honorton's research, he replied "it did not matter". Blackmore writes, "But it does matter. ... It matters because Bem's continued claims mislead a willing public into believing that there is reputable scientific evidence for ESP in the Ganzfeld when there is not".

Further reading

- "What's the story on "ganzfeld" experiments?"[548]. The Straight Dope, December 14, 2000.
- Andrew Colman. (1995). *Controversies in Psychology*. Longman Pub Group. ISBN 978-0582278035
- C. E. M. Hansel. (1989). *The Search for Psychic Power: ESP and Parapsychology Revisited*. Prometheus Books. ISBN 978-0879755331
- Terence Hines. (2003). *Pseudoscience and the Paranormal*. Prometheus Books. ISBN 978-1573929790
- Nicholas Humphrey. (1996). *Soul Searching: Human Nature and Supernatural Belief*. Vintage. ISBN 978-0099273417
- Ray Hyman (1995). "Evaluation of Program on Anomalous Mental Phenomena"[549]. *The Journal of Parapsychology*.
- Hyman Ray (2010). "Meta-analysis that conceals more than it reveals: Comment on Storm et al"[550] (PDF). *Psychological Bulletin*. **136**: 486–90. doi: 10.1037/a0019676[551]. Archived from the original[552] (PDF) on 2013-11-03.
- Paul Kurtz. (1985). *A Skeptic's Handbook of Parapsychology*. Prometheus Books. ISBN 978-0879753009
- Scott O. Lilienfeld (November–December 1999). "New Analyses Raise Doubts About Replicability of ESP Findings"[553]. *Skeptical Inquirer*.
- Scott O. Lilienfeld, Steven Jay Lynn, John Ruscio, Barry Beyerstein. (2009). *50 Great Myths of Popular Psychology*. Wiley-Blackwell. ISBN 978-1405131124
- David Marks. (2000). *The Psychology of the Psychic*. Prometheus Books. ISBN 978-1573927987

- Julie Milton, Richard Wiseman (2001). "Does psi exist? Reply to Storm and Ertel (2001)"[554] (PDF). *Psychological Bulletin.* **127**: 434–38. doi: 10.1037/0033-2909.127.3.434[555].
- Andrew Neher. (2011). *Paranormal and Transcendental Experience: A Psychological Examination.* Dover Publications. ISBN 978-0486261676
- Dean Radin (1997). *The Conscious Universe: The Scientific Truth of Psychic Phenomena.* HarperOne. ISBN 0-06-251502-0.
- Spencer Rathus. (2011). *Psychology: Concepts and Connections.* Cengage Learning. ISBN 978-1111344856
- Gordon Stein. (1996). *The Encyclopedia of the Paranormal.* Prometheus Books. ISBN 978-1573920216
- Victor Stenger. (1990). *Physics and Psychics: The Search for a World Beyond the Senses.* Prometheus Books. ISBN 978-0879755751
- Leonard Zusne and Warren Jones. (1989). *Anomalistic Psychology: A Study of Magical Thinking.* Psychology Press. ISBN 978-0805805086

External links

- Koestler Parapsychology Unit: Testing Psi[556]
- *The Skeptic's Dictionary*: "Ganzfeld"[557]

Remote viewing

Remote viewing

Remote viewing

Claims	The alleged paranormal ability to perceive a remote or hidden target without support of the senses.[558]
Year proposed	1970
Original proponents	Russell Targ and Harold Puthoff
Subsequent proponents	Ingo Swann, Joseph McMoneagle, Courtney Brown

Part of a series on the
Paranormal

- v
- t
- e[559]

Remote viewing (**RV**) is the practice of seeking impressions about a distant or unseen target, purportedly using extrasensory perception (ESP) or "sensing" with the mind.

Remote viewing experiments have historically been criticized for lack of proper controls and repeatability. There is no scientific evidence that remote viewing exists, and the topic of remote viewing is generally regarded as pseudoscience.

Typically a remote viewer is expected to give information about an object, event, person or location that is hidden from physical view and separated at some distance.

Physicists Russell Targ and Harold Puthoff, parapsychology researchers at Stanford Research Institute (SRI), are generally credited with coining the term "remote viewing" to distinguish it from the closely related concept of clairvoyance,[560] although according to Targ, the term was first suggested by Ingo Swann in December 1971 during an experiment at the American Society for Psychical Research in New York City.

Remote viewing was popularized in the 1990s upon the declassification of certain documents related to the Stargate Project, a $20 million research program that had started in 1975 and was sponsored by the U.S. government, in an attempt to determine any potential military application of psychic phenomena. The program was terminated in 1995 after it failed to produce any actionable intelligence information.

History

Early background

In early occult and spiritualist literature, remote viewing was known as telesthesia and travelling clairvoyance. Rosemary Guiley described it as "seeing remote or hidden objects clairvoyantly with the inner eye, or in alleged out-of-body travel."

The study of psychic phenomena by major scientists started in the mid-nineteenth century. Early researchers included Michael Faraday, Alfred Russel Wallace, Rufus Osgood Mason, and William Crookes. Their work predominantly involved carrying out focused experimental tests on specific individuals who were thought to be psychically gifted. Reports of apparently successful tests were met with much skepticism from the scientific community.

In the 1930s, J. B. Rhine expanded the study of paranormal performance into larger populations, by using standard experimental protocols with unselected human subjects. But, as with the earlier studies, Rhine was reluctant to publicize this work too early because of the fear of criticism from mainstream scientists.

This continuing skepticism, with its consequences for peer review and research funding, ensured that paranormal studies remained a fringe area of scientific exploration. However, by the 1960s, the prevailing counterculture attitudes muted some of the prior hostility. The emergence of New Age thinking-Wikipedia:Please clarify and the popularity of the Human Potential Movement provoked a mini-renaissance that renewed public interest in consciousness studies and psychic phenomena and helped to make financial support more available for research into such topics.

In the early 1970s, Harold Puthoff and Russell Targ joined the Electronics and Bioengineering Laboratory at Stanford Research Institute (SRI, now SRI International) where they initiated studies of the paranormal that were, at first, supported with private funding from the Parapsychology Foundation and the Institute of Noetic Sciences.

In the late 1970s, the physicists John Taylor and Eduardo Balanovski tested the psychic Matthew Manning in remote viewing and the results proved "completely unsuccessful".

One of the early experiments, lauded by proponents as having improved the methodology of remote viewing testing and as raising future experimental standards, was criticized as leaking information to the participants by inadvertently leaving clues.[561] Some later experiments had negative results when these clues were eliminated.[562]</ref>

The viewers' advice in the "Stargate project" was always so unclear and non-detailed that it has never been used in any intelligence operation.

Decline and termination

In the early 1990s, the Military Intelligence Board, chaired by DIA chief Soyster, appointed Army Colonel William Johnson to manage the remote viewing unit and evaluate its objective usefulness. Funding dissipated in late 1994 and the program went into decline. The project was transferred out of DIA to the CIA in 1995.

In 1995, the CIA hired the American Institutes for Research (AIR) to perform a retrospective evaluation of the results generated by the Stargate Project. Reviewers included Ray Hyman and Jessica Utts. Utts maintained that there had been a statistically significant positive effect, with some subjects scoring 5–15% above chance. Hyman argued that Utts' conclusion that ESP had been proven to exist, "is premature, to say the least." Hyman said the findings had yet to be replicated independently, and that more investigation would be necessary to "legitimately claim the existence of paranormal functioning". Based upon both of their studies, which recommended a higher level of critical research and tighter controls, the CIA terminated the $20 million project in 1995. *Time* magazine stated in 1995 that three full-time psychics were still working on a $500,000-a-year budget out of Fort Meade, Maryland, which would soon be shut down.

The AIR report concluded that no usable intelligence data was produced in the program. David Goslin, of the American Institute for Research said, "There's no documented evidence it had any value to the intelligence community".

UK government research

In 2001–2002 the UK government performed a study on 18 untrained subjects. The experimenters recorded the E field and H field around each viewer to see if the cerebral activity of successful viewings caused higher-than-usual fields to be emitted from the brain. However, the experimenters did not find any evidence that the viewers had accessed the targets in the data collection phase, the project was abandoned, and the data was never analyzed since no RV activity had happened. Some "narrow-band" E-fields were detected during the viewings, but they were attributed to external causes. The experiment was disclosed in 2007 after a UK Freedom of Information request.

PEAR's Remote Perception program

Following Utts' emphasis on replication and Hyman's challenge on interlaboratory consistency in the AIR report, the Princeton Engineering Anomalies Research Lab conducted several hundred trials to see if they could replicate the SAIC and SRI experiments. They created an analytical judgment methodology to replace the human judging process that was criticized in past experiments, and they released a report in 1996. They felt the results of the experiments were consistent with the SRI experiments. However, statistical flaws have been proposed by others in the parapsychological community and within the general scientific community. Hansen, Utts and Markwick concluded "The PEAR remote-viewing experiments depart from commonly accepted criteria for formal research in science. In fact, they are undoubtedly some of the poorest quality ESP experiments published in many years."

Scientific reception

A variety of scientific studies of remote viewing have been conducted. Early experiments produced positive results but they had invalidating flaws.[533] None of the more recent experiments have shown positive results when conducted under properly controlled conditions. This lack of successful experiments has led the mainstream scientific community to reject remote viewing, based upon the absence of an evidence base, the lack of a theory which would explain remote viewing, and the lack of experimental techniques which can provide reliably positive results.[563,564,565]

Science writers Gary Bennett, Martin Gardner, Michael Shermer and professor of neurology Terence Hines describe the topic of remote viewing as pseudoscience.

C. E. M. Hansel who evaluated the remote viewing experiments of parapsychologists such as Puthoff, Targ, John B. Bisha and Brenda. J. Dunne noted that there were a lack of controls and precautions were not taken to rule out the possibility of fraud. He concluded the experimental design was inadequately reported and "too loosely controlled to serve any useful function."

The psychologist Ray Hyman says that, even if the results from remote viewing experiments were reproduced under specified conditions, they would still not be a conclusive demonstration of the existence of psychic functioning. He blames this on the reliance on a negative outcome—the claims on ESP are based on the results of experiments not being explained by normal means. He says that the experiments lack a positive theory that guides as to what to control on them and what to ignore, and that "Parapsychologists have not come close to (having a positive theory) as yet".[566]</ref>

Hyman also says that the amount and quality of the experiments on RV are way too low to convince the scientific community to "abandon its fundamental ideas about causality, time, and other principles", due to its findings still not having been replicated successfully under careful scrutiny.[567]

Martin Gardner has written that the founding researcher Harold Puthoff was an active Scientologist prior to his work at Stanford University, and that this influenced his research at SRI. In 1970, the Church of Scientology published a notarized letter that had been written by Puthoff while he was conducting research on remote viewing at Stanford. The letter read, in part: "Although critics viewing the system Scientology from the outside may form the impression that Scientology is just another of many quasi-educational quasi-religious 'schemes,' it is in fact a highly sophistical and highly technological system more characteristic of modern corporate planning and applied technology". Among some of the ideas that Puthoff supported regarding remote viewing was the claim in the book *Occult Chemistry* that two followers of Madame Blavatsky, founder of theosophy, were able to remote-view the inner structure of atoms.

Michael Shermer investigated remote viewing experiments and discovered a problem with the target selection list. According to Shermer with the sketches only a handful of designs are usually used such as lines and curves which could depict any object and be interpreted as a "hit". Shermer has also written about confirmation and hindsight biases that have occurred in remote viewing experiments.[568]

Various skeptic organizations have conducted experiments for remote viewing and other alleged paranormal abilities, with no positive results under properly controlled conditions.

Sensory cues

The psychologists David Marks and Richard Kammann attempted to replicate Russell Targ and Harold Puthoff's remote viewing experiments that were carried out in the 1970s at the Stanford Research Institute. In a series of 35 studies, they were unable to replicate the results so investigated the procedure of the original experiments. Marks and Kammann discovered that the notes given to the judges in Targ and Puthoff's experiments contained clues as to which order they were carried out, such as referring to yesterday's two targets, or they had the date of the session written at the top of the page. They concluded that these clues were the reason for the experiment's high hit rates. According to Terence Hines:

<templatestyles src="Template:Quote/styles.css"/>

Examination of the few actual transcripts published by Targ and Puthoff show that just such clues were present. To find out if the unpublished transcripts contained cues, Marks and Kammann wrote to Targ and Puthoff requesting copies. It is almost unheard of for a scientist to refuse to provide his data for independent examination when asked, but Targ and Puthoff consistently refused to allow Marks and Kammann to see copies of the transcripts. Marks and Kammann were, however, able to obtain copies of the transcripts from the judge who used them. The transcripts were found to contain a wealth of cues.[569]

Thomas Gilovich has written:

<templatestyles src="Template:Quote/styles.css"/>

Most of the material in the transcripts consists of the honest attempts by the percipients to describe their impressions. However, the transcripts also contained considerable extraneous material that could aid a judge in matching them to the correct targets. In particular, there were numerous references to dates, times and sites previously visited that would enable the judge to place the transcripts in proper sequence... Astonishingly, the judges in the Targ-Puthoff experiments were given a list of target sites in the exact order in which they were used in the tests!

According to Marks, when the cues were eliminated the results fell to a chance level. Marks was able to achieve 100 per cent accuracy without visiting any of the sites himself but by using cues.[570]</ref> James Randi has written that controlled tests by several other researchers, eliminating several sources of cuing and extraneous evidence present in the original tests, produced negative results. Students were also able to solve Puthoff and Targ's locations from the clues that had inadvertently been included in the transcripts.

Marks and Kamman concluded: "Until remote viewing can be confirmed in conditions which prevent sensory cueing the conclusions of Targ and Puthoff remain an unsubstantiated hypothesis."[571] In 1980, Charles Tart claimed that a rejudging of the transcripts from one of Targ and Puthoff's experiments revealed an above-chance result. Targ and Puthoff again refused to provide copies of the transcripts and it was not until July 1985 that they were made available for study when it was discovered they still contained sensory cues. Marks and Christopher Scott (1986) wrote "considering the importance for the remote viewing hypothesis of adequate cue removal, Tart's failure to perform this basic task seems beyond comprehension. As previously concluded, remote viewing has not been demonstrated in the experiments conducted by Puthoff and Targ, only the repeated failure of the investigators to remove sensory cues."

The information from the Stargate Project remote viewing sessions was vague and included a lot of irrelevant and erroneous data, it was never useful in any intelligence operation, and it was suspected that the project managers in some cases changed the reports so they would fit background cues.[572]</ref>

Marks in his book *The Psychology of the Psychic* (2000) discussed the flaws in the Stargate Project in detail.[573] He wrote that there were six negative design features of the experiments. The possibility of cues or sensory leakage was not ruled out, no independent replication, some of the experiments were conducted in secret making peer-review impossible. Marks noted that the judge Edwin May was also the principal investigator for the project and this was problematic making huge conflict of interest with collusion, cuing and fraud being possible. Marks concluded the project was nothing more than a "subjective delusion" and after two decades of research it had failed to provide any scientific evidence for remote viewing.

Marks has also suggested that the participants of remote viewing experiments are influenced by subjective validation, a process through which correspondences are perceived between stimuli that are in fact associated purely randomly.

Professor Richard Wiseman, a psychologist at the University of Hertfordshire, and a fellow of the Committee for Skeptical Inquiry (CSI) has pointed out several problems with one of the early experiments at SAIC, including information leakage. However, he indicated the importance of its process-oriented approach and of its refining of remote viewing methodology, which meant that researchers replicating their work could avoid these problems. Wiseman later insisted there were multiple opportunities for participants on that experiment to be influenced by inadvertent cues and that these cues can influence the results when they appear.

Selected RV study participants

- Ingo Swann, a prominent research participant in remote viewing
- Pat Price, an early remote viewer
- Joseph McMoneagle, an early remote viewer See: Stargate Project
- Courtney Brown, political scientist and founder of the Farsight Institute
- David Marks, a critic of remote viewing, after finding sensory cues and editing in the original transcripts generated by Targ and Puthoff at Stanford Research Institute in the 1970s
- Uri Geller, the subject of a study by Targ and Puthoff at Stanford Research Institute

Further reading

- Alcock, James E.; Committee on Techniques for the Enhancement of Human Performance: Commission on Behavioral and Social Sciences Education: National Research Council (NRC) (1988). "Part VI. Parapsychological Techniques". *Enhancing Human Performance: Issues, Theories, and Techniques, Background Papers (Complete Set)*[574]. Washington, DC: National Academies Press.
- Brown, Courtney. (2005). *Remote Viewing: The Science and Theory of Nonphysical Perception*. Farsight Press. ISBN 0-9766762-1-4
- Gilovich, Thomas. (1993). *How We Know What isn't So: Fallibility of Human Reason in Everyday Life*. Free Press. ISBN 978-0-02-911706-4
- Gordon, Henry. (1988). *Extrasensory Deception: ESP, Psychics, Shirley MacLaine, Ghosts, UFOs*. Macmillan of Canada. ISBN 0-7715-9539-5
- Marks, David. (2000). *The Psychology of the Psychic* (2nd Edition). Prometheus Books. ISBN 1-57392-798-8
- McMoneagle, Joseph. (2002). *The Stargate Chronicles: Memoirs of a Psychic Spy*. Hampton Roads. ISBN 1-57174-225-5
- Randi, James. (1982). *Flim-Flam! Psychics, ESP, Unicorns, and Other Delusions*. Prometheus Books. ISBN 0-87975-198-3

External links

- Remote viewing[575] - Skeptic's Dictionary

Dream telepathy

Dream telepathy

Dream telepathy is the purported ability to communicate telepathically with another person while one is dreaming.[576] The first person in modern times to document telepathic dreaming was Sigmund Freud. In the 1940s it was the subject of the **Eisenbud-Pederson-Krag-Fodor-Ellis controversy**, named after the preeminent psychoanalysts of the time who were involved Jule Eisenbud, Geraldine Pederson-Krag, Nandor Fodor, and Albert Ellis.[577] There is no scientific evidence that dream telepathy is a real phenomenon. Parapsychological experiments into dream telepathy have not produced replicable results.[578]

History

The notion and speculation of communication via dreaming was first mooted in psychoanalysis by Sigmund Freud in 1921.[579] He produced a model to express his ideas about telepathic dreaming. His 1922 paper *Dreams and Telepathy* is reproduced in the book *Psychoanalysis and the Occult* (1953) and was intended to be a lecture to the Vienna Psycho-Analytical Society, although he never delivered it. Freud considered that a connection between telepathy and dreams could be neither proven nor disproven. He was distinctly suspicious of the whole idea, noting that he himself had never had a telepathic dream. (His two dreams that were potentially telepathic, where he dreamed of the deaths of a son and of a sister-in-law, which did not occur, he labeled as "purely subjective anticipations".) His ideas were not widely accepted at the time, but he continued to publicly express his interest and findings about telepathic dreaming. He also observed that he had not encountered any evidence of dream telepathy in his patients.[580] Freud claims neutrality about the phenomenon itself, states that the sleep milieu has special likely properties for it if it does exist, and discounts all of the cases presented to him on standard psychoanalytic grounds (e.g. neurosis, transference, etc.).[581]

Figure 42: *Montague Ullman was notable for conducting dream telepathy experiments. His results were never replicated.*[585]

In the 1940s Jule Eisenbud, Geraldine Pederson-Krag and Nandor Fodor described alleged cases of dream telepathy. Albert Ellis regarded their conclusions to have been based upon flimsy evidence, and that they could be better explained by bias, coincidence and unconscious cues than by dream telepathy. He also accused them of an emotional involvement in the notion, resulting in their observations and judgement being clouded.[582,583] Psychologist L. Börje Löfgren also criticised dream telepathy experiments of Eisenbud. He stated that coincidence was a more likely explanation and the "assumption of paranormal forces to explain them is unnecessary."[584]

Experiments

There have been many experiments done to test the validity of dream telepathy and its effectiveness, but with significant issues of blinding. Many test subjects find ways to communicate with others to make it look like telepathic communication. Attempts to cut off communication between the agent, sender, and receiver of information failed because subjects found ways to get around blindfolds no matter how intricate and covering they were.[586] In studies at the Maimonides Medical Center in Brooklyn, New York led by Stanley Krippner and Montague Ullman, patients were monitored and awakened after a period of REM then separated to study the claimed ability to communicate telepathically. They concluded the results from some of their experiments supported dream telepathy.

The picture target experiments that were conducted by Krippner and Ullman were criticized by C. E. M. Hansel. According to Hansel there were weaknesses in the design of the experiments in the way in which the agent became aware of their target picture. Only the agent should have known the target and no other person until the judging of targets had been completed; however, an experimenter was with the agent when the target envelope was opened. Hansel also wrote there had been poor controls in the experiment as the main experimenter could communicate with the subject.[587]

An attempt to replicate the experiments that used picture targets was carried out by Edward Belvedere and David Foulkes. The finding was that neither the subject nor the judges matched the targets with dreams above chance level.[588] Results from other experiments by Belvedere and Foulkes were also negative.

In 2003, Simon Sherwood and Chris Roe wrote a review that claimed support for dream telepathy at Maimonides.[589] However, James Alcock noted that their review was based on "extreme messiness" of data. Alcock concluded the dream telepathy experiments at Maimonides have failed to provide evidence for telepathy and "lack of replication is rampant."[590]

The psychologist and noted skeptic Richard Wiseman took part in a dream telepathy experiment. It was conducted by Caroline Watt at a sleep laboratory in an attempt to replicate the results of Krippner and Ullman. The experiment was a complete failure. According to Wiseman "after monitoring about twenty volunteers for several nights on end, the study didn't discover any evidence in support of the supernatural."[591]

Further reading

- Alcock, James (1981). *Parapsychology: Science or Magic? A Psychological Perspective*. Pergamon Press. ISBN 0-08-025772-0
- Devereux, George, ed. (1953). "The Eisenbud-Pederson-Krag-Fodor-Ellis controversy". *Psychoanalysis and the Occult*. Oxford, England: International Universities Press.
- Ellis, Albert (1947). "Telepathy and Psychoanalysis: A Critique of Recent Findings". *Psychiatric Quarterly*. **21**: 607–659. doi: 10.1007/bf01654321[592].
- Child, Irvin (November 1985). "Psychology and Anomalous Observations: The Question of ESP in Dreams". *American Psychologist*. **40** (11): 1219–1230. doi: 10.1037/0003-066X.40.11.1219[593].

Anomalistic psychology

Anomalistic psychology

In psychology, **anomalistic psychology** is the study of human behaviour and experience connected with what is often called the paranormal, with the assumption that there is nothing paranormal involved.

Early history

According to anomalistic psychology, paranormal phenomena have naturalistic explanations resulting from psychological and physical factors which have given the false impression of paranormal activity to some people.[594] There were many early publications that gave rational explanations for alleged paranormal experiences.

The physician John Ferriar wrote *An Essay Towards a Theory of Apparitions* in 1813 in which he argued that sightings of ghosts were the result of optical illusions. Later, the French physician Alexandre Jacques François Brière de Boismont published *On Hallucinations: Or, the Rational History of Apparitions, Dreams, Ecstasy, Magnetism, and Somnambulism* in 1845 in which he claimed sightings of ghosts were the result of hallucinations.[595] William Benjamin Carpenter, in his book *Mesmerism, Spiritualism, Etc: Historically and Scientifically Considered* (1877), wrote that Spiritualist practices could be explained by fraud, delusion, hypnotism and suggestion.[596] The British psychiatrist Henry Maudsley, in *Natural Causes and Supernatural Seemings* (1886), wrote that so-called supernatural experiences could be explained in terms of disorders of the mind and were simply "malobservations and misinterpretations of nature".[597]

In the 1890s, the German psychologist Max Dessoir and psychiatrist Albert Moll formed the "critical occultism" position. This viewpoint interpreted psychical phenomena naturalistically. All apparent cases were attributed to fraud,

Figure 43: *Henry Maudsley (1835–1918) an*
early researcher in anomalistic psychology.

suggestion, unconscious cues or psychological factors.[598] Moll wrote that practices such as Christian Science, Spiritualism and occultism were the result of fraud and hypnotic suggestion. Moll argued that suggestion explained the cures of Christian Science, as well as the apparently supernatural rapport between magnetisers and their somnambulists. He wrote that fraud and hypnotism could explain mediumistic phenomena.[599]

Lionel Weatherly (a psychiatrist) and John Nevil Maskelyne (a magician) wrote *The Supernatural?* (1891) which offered rational explanations for apparitions, paranormal and religious experiences and Spiritualism.[600] Karl Jaspers, in his book *General Psychopathology* (1913), stated that all paranormal phenomena are manifestations of psychiatric symptoms.[601]

The German *Zeitschrift für Kritischen Okkultismus* (Journal for Critical Occultism) operated from 1926-1928.[602] Psychologist Richard Baerwald was the editor, and the journal published articles by Dessoir, Moll and others. It contained "some of the most important skeptical investigations of claims of the paranormal".

Other early scientists who studied anomalistic psychology include Millais Culpin, Joseph Jastrow, Charles Arthur Mercier and Ivor Lloyd Tuckett.

Figure 44: *Chris French founder of the Anomalistic Psychology Research Unit.*

Modern research

The phrase "Anomalistic Psychology" was a term first suggested by the psychologists Leonard Zusne and Warren Jones in their book *Anomalistic Psychology: A Study of Magical Thinking* (1989) which systematically addresses phenomena of human consciousness and behaviors that may appear to violate the laws of nature when they actually do not.[603]

The Canadian psychologist Graham Reed published a major work on the subject *The Psychology of Anomalous Experience* (1972).[604]

Various psychological publications have explained in detail how reported paranormal phenomena such as mediumship, precognition, out-of-body experiences and psychics can be explained by psychological factors without recourse to the supernatural. Researchers involved with anomalistic psychology try to provide plausible non-paranormal accounts, supported by empirical evidence, of how psychological and physical factors might combine to give the impression of paranormal activity when there had been none. Apart from deception or self-deception such explanations might involve cognitive biases, anomalous psychological states, dissociative states, hallucinations, personality factors, developmental issues and the nature of memory.[605]

The psychologist David Marks wrote that paranormal phenomena can be explained by magical thinking, mental imagery, subjective validation, coincidence, hidden causes, and fraud.[606] Robert Baker wrote that many paranormal phenomena can be explained via psychological effects such as hallucinations, sleep paralysis and hidden memories, a phenomenon in which experiences that originally make little conscious impression are filed away in the brain to be suddenly remembered later in an altered form.[607]

Massimo Polidoro, a professor of Anomalistic Psychology at the University of Milano Bicocca, Italy, taught the course "Scientific Method, Pseudoscience and Anomalistic Psychology".[608] Another notable researcher is the British psychologist Chris French who set up the Anomalistic Psychology Research Unit (APRU) in the Department of Psychology at Goldsmiths, University of London.[609]

Hauntings

A psychological study (Klemperer, 1992) of ghosts wrote that visions of ghosts may arise from hypnagogic hallucinations ("waking dreams" which are experienced in the transitional states to and from sleep).[610] In an experiment (Lange and Houran, 1997) 22 subjects visited five areas of a performance theatre and were asked to take note of the environment. Half of the subjects were informed that the locations they were in were haunted, whilst the other half were told that the building was simply under renovation. The subjects' perceptions in both groups were recorded to an experiential questionnaire which contained 10 subscales related to psychological and physiological perceptions. The results showed more intense perceptual experiences on nine of the ten subscales from the group that was told the building was haunted, which has indicated that demand characteristics alone can stimulate paranormal experiences.[611]

A study (Lange and Houran, 1998) suggested that poltergeist experiences are delusions "resulting from the affective and cognitive dynamics of percipients' interpretation of ambiguous stimuli".[612]

Two experiments into alleged hauntings (Wiseman et al. 2003) discovered that the data supported the "notion that people consistently report unusual experiences in 'haunted' areas because of environmental factors, which may differ across locations." Some of these factors included "the variance of local magnetic fields, size of location and lighting level stimuli of which witnesses may not be consciously aware".[613]

Mediumship

Research and empirical evidence from psychology for over a hundred years has revealed that where there is not fraud, mediumship and Spiritualistic practices can be explained by psychological factors. Trance mediumship, which is claimed by the Spiritualists to be caused by discarnate spirits speaking through the medium, has been proven in some cases to be the emergence of alternate personalities from the medium's subconscious mind.[614]

The medium may obtain information about their clients, called sitters, by secretly eavesdropping on sitter's conversations or searching telephone directories, the internet and newspapers before the sittings.[615] Mediums are known for employing a technique called cold reading which involves obtaining information from the sitter's behavior, clothing, posture, and jewellery.[616,617]

In a series of fake seance experiments (Wiseman et al. 2003), an actor suggested to paranormal believers and disbelievers that a table was levitating when, in fact, it remained stationary. After the seance, approximately one third of the participants incorrectly reported that the table had moved. The results showed a greater percentage of believers reporting that the table had moved. In another experiment the believers had also reported that a handbell had moved when it had remained stationary and expressed their belief that the fake seances contained genuine paranormal phenomena. The experiments strongly supported the notion that in the seance room, believers are more suggestible than disbelievers to suggestions that are consistent with their belief in paranormal phenomena.[618]

An experiment (O'Keeffe and Wiseman, 2005) involving 5 mediums found no evidence to support the notion that the mediums under controlled conditions were able to demonstrate paranormal or mediumistic ability.[619]

Paranormal healing

A study in the British Medical Journal (Rose, 1954) investigated spiritual healing, therapeutic touch and faith healing. In a hundred cases that were investigated no single case revealed that the healer's intervention alone resulted in any improvement or cure of a measurable organic disability.[620]

A trial was carried out by a group of scientists (Beutler, 1988) to see whether three treatment groups, paranormal laying on of hands, paranormal healing at a distance and no paranormal healing to test if they might reduce blood pressure. The data did not reveal any paranormal effects as no significant differences between the three treatment groups were found. The results concluded that the fall in blood pressure in all three of the groups was caused by the psychosocial approach and the placebo effect of the trial itself.[621]

One form of paranormal healing known as psychic surgery has been discovered to be the result of sleight of hand tricks. Psychic surgeons pretend to reach into the patient's body but the skin is never punctured, there are no scars and the blood is released from packets hidden in the surgeon's hands.[622]

Psychokinesis

Cognitive biases have been found in some cases of psychokinesis. In an investigation of 380 studies a group of psychologists (Bösch *et al.* 2006) have written a meta-analysis on the subject. In their paper they wrote "statistical significance of the overall database provides no directive as to whether the phenomenon is genuine or not" and came to the conclusion that "publication bias appears to be the easiest and most encompassing explanation for the primary findings of the meta-analysis."[623]

According to Richard Wiseman there are a number of ways for faking psychokinetic metal bending (PKMB) these include switching straight objects for pre-bent duplicates, the concealed application of force, and secretly inducing metallic fractures. Research has also suggested that (PKMB) effects can be created by verbal suggestion. On this subject (Harris, 1985) wrote:

"   **"**

If you are doing a really convincing job, then you should be able to put a bent key on the table and comment, 'Look, it is still bending', and have your spectators really believe that it is. This may sound the height of boldness; however, the effect is astounding – and combined with suggestion, it does work.[624]

In an experimental study (Wiseman and Greening, 2005) two groups of participants were shown a videotape in which a fake psychic placed a bent key on a table. Participants in the first group heard the fake psychic suggest that the key was continuing to bend when it had remained stationary, whilst those in the second group did not. The results revealed that participants from the first group reported significantly more movement of the key than the second group. The findings were replicated in another study. The experiments had demonstrated that "testimony for PKMB after effects can be created by verbal suggestion, and therefore the testimony from individuals who have observed allegedly genuine demonstrations of such effects should not be seen as strong evidence in support of the paranormal".[625]

Remote viewing

Research has suggested that in cases the participants of remote viewing experiments are influenced by subjective validation, a process through which correspondences are perceived between stimuli that are in fact associated purely randomly. Sensory cues have also occurred in remote viewing experiments.[626]

Telepathy

Research has discovered that in some cases telepathy can be explained by a covariation bias. In an experiment (Schienle et al. 1996) 22 believers and 20 skeptics were asked to judge the covariation between transmitted symbols and the corresponding feedback given by a receiver. According to the results the believers overestimated the number of successful transmissions whilst the skeptics made accurate hit judgments.[627] The results from another telepathy experiment involving 48 undergraduate college students (Rudski, 2002) were explained by hindsight and confirmation biases.[628]

Relationship with parapsychology

Anomalistic psychology is sometimes described as a sub-field of parapsychology, however, anomalistic psychology rejects the paranormal claims of parapsychology. According to Chris French:

> The difference between anomalistic psychology and parapsychology is in terms of the aims of what each discipline is about. Parapsychologists typically are actually searching for evidence to prove the reality of paranormal forces, to prove they really do exist. So the starting assumption is that paranormal things do happen, whereas anomalistic psychologists tend to start from the position that paranormal forces probably don't exist and that therefore we should be looking for other kinds of explanations, in particular the psychological explanations for those experiences that people typically label as paranormal.[629]

Anomalistic psychology has been reported to be on the rise. It is now offered as an option on many psychology degree programmes and is also an option on the A2 psychology syllabus in the UK.[630]

Further reading

- Gustav Jahoda. (1974). *The Psychology of Superstition*. Jason Aronson, Inc. Publisher. ISBN 978-0876681855
- David Marks. (2000). *The Psychology of the Psychic*. Prometheus Books. ISBN 978-1573927987
- Andrew Neher. (2011). *Paranormal and Transcendental Experience: A Psychological Examination*. Dover Publications. ISBN 978-0486261676
- John Schumaker. (1990). *Wings of Illusion: The Origin, Nature and Future of Paranormal Belief*. Prometheus Books. ISBN 978-0879756246
- Etzel Cardeña, Steven Jay Lynn, Stanley Krippner. (2000). *Varieties of Anomalous Experience*. American Psychological Association. ISBN 978-1-55798-625-2

External links

	Look up *anomalistic* in Wiktionary, the free dictionary.

- What is Anomalistic Psychology?[631]
- Prof Chris French explains anomalistic psychology on Pulse Project Expert Explanations.[632]

Appendix

References

[1] //en.wikipedia.org/w/index.php?title=Template:Paranormal&action=edit

[2] • (Pigliucci, Boudry 2013) "Parapsychological research almost never appears in mainstream science journals." • (Odling-Smee 2007) "But parapsychologists are still limited to publishing in a small number of niche journals."

[3] //en.wikipedia.org/w/index.php?title=Template:Fringe_medicine_sidebar&action=edit

[4] Harvey J. Irwin, Caroline A. Watt. (2007). *An Introduction to Parapsychology*. McFarland. p. 6

[5] Charles M. Wynn, Arthur W. Wiggins. (2001). *Quantum Leaps in the Wrong Direction: Where Real Science Ends...and Pseudoscience Begins*. Joseph Henry Press. p. 152.

[6] Hines, Terence. (2003). *Pseudoscience and the Paranormal*. Prometheus Books. pp. 50-52.

[7] Podmore, Frank. (1897). *Studies in Psychical Research*. G. P. Putnam's Sons. pp. 48-49

[8] Podmore, Frank. (1902). *Modern Spiritualism: A History and a Criticism*. Methuen Publishing. pp. 234-235

[9] Podmore, Frank. (1897). *Studies in Psychical Research*. New York: Putnam. p. 47

[10] Stein, Gordon. (1996). *The Encyclopedia of the Paranormal*. Prometheus Books. p. 703. "Slade succeeded only on tests that allowed easy trickery, such of producing knots in cords that had their ends tied together and the knot sealed, putting wooden rings on a table leg, and removing coins from sealed boxes. He failed utterly on tests that did not permit deception. He was unable to reverse the spirals of snail shells. He could not link two wooden rings, one of oak, the other of alder. He could not knot an endless ring cut from a bladder, or put a piece of candle inside a closed glass bulb. He failed to change the optical handedness of tartaric dextro to levo. These tests would have been easy to pass if Slade's spirit controls had been able to take an object into the fourth dimension, then return it after making the required manipulations. Such successes would have created marvelous PPOs (permanent paranormal objects), difficult for skeptics to explain. Zöllner wrote an entire book in praise of Slade. Titled *Transcendental Physics* (1878), it was partly translated into English in 1880 by spiritualist Charles Carleton Massey. The book is a classic of childlike gullibility by a scientist incapable of devising adequate controls for testing paranormal powers."

[11] Mulholland, John. (1938). *Beware Familiar Spirits*. C. Scribner's Sons. pp. 111-112.

[12] Hyman, Ray. (1989). *The Elusive Quarry: A Scientific Appraisal of Psychical Research*. Prometheus Books. p. 209. "In the case of Zöllner's investigations of Slade, not only do we know that Slade was exposed before and after his sessions with Zöllner, but also there is ample reason to raise questions about the adequacy of the investigation. Carrington (1907), Podmore (1963), and Mrs. Sidgwick (1886-87) are among a number of critics who have uncovered flaws and loopholes in Zöllner's sittings with Slade."

[13] Thurschwell, Pamela. (2004). *Literature, Technology and Magical Thinking, 1880–1920*. Cambridge University Press. p. 16.

[14] McCorristine, Shane. (2010). *Spectres of the Self: Thinking about Ghosts and Ghost-Seeing in England, 1750-1920*. Cambridge University Press. p. 114.

[15] Douglas, Alfred. (1982). *Extra-Sensory Powers: A Century of Psychical Research*. Overlook Press. p. 76. "Phantasms of the Living was criticized by a number of scholars when it appeared, one ground for the attack being the lack of written testimony regarding the apparitions composed shortly after they had been seen. In many instances several years had elapsed between the occurrence and a report of it being made to the investigators from the SPR."

[16] Williams, William F. (2000). *Encyclopedia of Pseudoscience: From Alien Abductions to Zone Therapy*. Routledge. p. 49.

[17] C. E. M. Hansel. *The Search for a Demonstration of ESP*. In Paul Kurtz. (1985). *A Skeptic's Handbook of Parapsychology*. Prometheus Books. pp. 97-127.

[18] Edmunds, Simeon. (1966). *Spiritualism: A Critical Survey*. Aquarian Press. p. 115. "The early history of spirit photography was reviewed by Mrs Henry Sidgwick in the Proceedings of the

SPR in 1891. She showed clearly not only that Mumler, Hudson, Buguet and their ilk were fraudulent, but the way in which those who believed in them were deceived."

[19] Moreman, Christopher M. (2010). *Beyond the Threshold: Afterlife Beliefs and Experiences in World Religions.* Rowman & Littlefield Publishers, Inc. p. 163. "SPR investigators quickly found that many mediums were indeed, as skeptics had alleged, operating under cover of darkness in order to perpetrate scams. They used a number of tricks facilitated by darkness: sleight of hand was used to manipulate objects and touch people eager to make contact with deceased loved ones; flour or white lines would give the illusion of spectral white hands or faces; accomplices were even stashed under tables or in secret rooms to lent support in the plot... As the investigations of the SPR, and other skeptics, were made public, many fraudulent mediums saw their careers ruined and many unsuspecting clients were enraged at the deception perpetrated."

[20] Larsen, Egon. (1966). *The Deceivers: Lives of the Great Imposters.* Roy Publishers. pp. 130-132

[21] Berger, Arthur S. (1988). *Lives and Letters in American Parapsychology: A Biographical History,* 1850-1987. McFarland. pp. 75-107.

[22] Asprem, Egil. (2014). *The Problem of Disenchantment: Scientific Naturalism and Esoteric Discourse, 1900-1939.* Brill Academic Publishers. pp. 355-360.

[23] J. B. Rhine (1934). Extra-Sensory Perception. (4th ed.) Branden Publishing Company 1997.

[24] Jenny Hazelgrove. (2000). *Spiritualism and British Society Between the Wars.* Manchester University Press. p. 204.

[25] A. S. Russell, John Andrews Benn. (1938). *Discovery the Popular Journal of Knowledge.* Cambridge University Press. pp. 305-306

[26] Samuel Soal. *A Repetition of Dr. Rhine's work with Mrs. Eileen Garrett.* Proc. S.P.R. Vol. XLII. pp. 84-85. Also quoted in Antony Flew. (1955). *A New Approach To Psychical Research.* Watts & Co. pp. 90-92.

[27] Cited in C. E. M. Hansel *The Search for a Demonstration of ESP* in Paul Kurtz. (1985). *A Skeptic's Handbook of Parapsychology.* Prometheus Books. pp. 105-127. • Crumbaugh, J. C. (1938). *An experimental study of extra-sensory perception.* Masters thesis. Southern Methodist University. • Willoughby, R. R. (1938). *Further card-guessing experiments.* Journal of Psychology 18: 3-13.

[28] Alcock, James. (1981). *Parapsychology-Science Or Magic?: A Psychological Perspective.* Pergamon Press. 136.

[29] Joseph Jastrow. (1938). *ESP, House of Cards.* The American Scholar 8: 13-22.

[30] Harold Gulliksen. (1938). *Extra-Sensory Perception: What Is It?.* American Journal of Sociology. Vol. 43, No. 4. pp. 623-634. "Investigating Rhine's methods, we find that his mathematical methods are wrong and that the effect of this error would in some cases be negligible and in others very marked. We find that many of his experiments were set up in a manner which would tend to increase, instead of to diminish, the possibility of systematic clerical errors; and lastly, that the ESP cards can be read from the back."

[31] Charles M. Wynn, Arthur W. Wiggins. (2001). *Quantum Leaps in the Wrong Direction: Where Real Science Ends...and Pseudoscience Begins.* Joseph Henry Press. p. 156. "In 1940, Rhine coauthored a book, *Extrasensory Perception After Sixty Years* in which he suggested that something more than mere guess work was involved in his experiments. He was right! It is now known that the experiments conducted in his laboratory contained serious methodological flaws. Tests often took place with minimal or no screening between the subject and the person administering the test. Subjects could see the backs of cards that were later discovered to be so cheaply printed that a faint outline of the symbol could be seen. Furthermore, in face-to-face tests, subjects could see card faces reflected in the tester's eyeglasses or cornea. They were even able to (consciously or unconsciously) pick up clues from the tester's facial expression and voice inflection. In addition, an observant subject could identify the cards by certain irregularities like warped edges, spots on the backs, or design imperfections."

[32] Terence Hines. (2003). *Pseudoscience and the Paranormal.* Prometheus Books. p. 122. "The procedural errors in the Rhine experiments have been extremely damaging to his claims to have demonstrated the existence of ESP. Equally damaging has been the fact that the results have not replicated when the experiments have been conducted in other laboratories."

[33] Jonathan C. Smith. (2009). *Pseudoscience and Extraordinary Claims of the Paranormal: A Critical Thinker's Toolkit* https//books.google.com. Wiley-Blackwell. "Today, researchers discount the first decade of Rhine's work with Zener cards. Stimulus leakage or cheating could account for all his findings. Slight indentations on the backs of cards revealed the symbols embossed on card faces. Subjects could see and hear the experimenter, and note subtle but revealing facial expressions or changes in breathing."

[34] Milbourne Christopher. (1970). *ESP, Seers & Psychics.* Thomas Y. Crowell Co. pp. 24-28

[35] Robert L. Park. (2000). *Voodoo Science: The Road from Foolishness to Fraud.* Oxford University Press. pp. 40-43.

[36] Rhine, J.B. (1966). Foreword. In Pratt, J.G., Rhine, J.B., Smith, B.M., Stuart, C.E., & Greenwood, J.A. (eds.). *Extrasensory Perception After Sixty Years.* 2nd ed. Boston, US: Humphries.

[37] C. E. M. Hansel. (1980). *ESP and Parapsychology: A Critical Re-Evaluation.* Prometheus Books. pp. 125-140

[38] *Back from the Future: Parapsychology and the Bem Affair* http://www.csicop.org/specialarticles/show/back_from_the_future. *Skeptical Inquirer.* "Despite Rhine's confidence that he had established the reality of extrasensory perception, he had not done so. Methodological problems with his experiments eventually came to light, and as a result parapsychologists no longer run card-guessing studies and rarely even refer to Rhine's work."

[39] John Sladek. (1974). *The New Apocrypha: A Guide to Strange Sciences and Occult Beliefs.* Panther. pp. 172-174

[40] Peter Lamont. (2013). *Extraordinary Beliefs: A Historical Approach to a Psychological Problem.* Cambridge University Press. pp. 206-208.

[41] C. E. M. Hansel. (1989). *The Search for Psychic Power: ESP and Parapsychology Revisited.* Prometheus Books. p. 46.

[42] Bergen Evans. (1954). *The Spoor of Spooks: And Other Nonsense.* Knopf. p. 24

[43] C. E. M. Hansel. (1989). *The Search for Psychic Power: ESP and Parapsychology Revisited.* Prometheus Books. pp. 56-58.

[44] C. E. M. Hansel. (1989). *The Search for Psychic Power: ESP and Parapsychology Revisited.* Prometheus Books. p. 53. "First, the recording was not completely independent, since the flash of light in the experimenters' room could be varied in duration by the subject and thus provide a possible cue. Second, there were five different symbols in the target series, but the experimental record showed that two of these arose more frequently than the other three."

[45] An Evaluation of Remote Viewing: Research and Applications https://web.archive.org/web/20170113100257/http://www.lfr.org/lfr/csl/library/AirReport.pdf by Mumford, Rose and Goslin "*remote viewings have never provided an adequate basis for 'actionable' intelligence operations-that is, information sufficiently valuable or compelling so that action was taken as a result (...) a large amount of irrelevant, erroneous information is provided and little agreement is observed among viewers' reports. (...) remote viewers and project managers reported that remote viewing reports were changed to make them consistent with known background cues (...) Also, it raises some doubts about some well-publicized cases of dramatic hits, which, if taken at face value, could not easily be attributed to background cues. In at least some of these cases, there is reason to suspect, based on both subsequent investigations and the viewers' statement that reports had been "changed" by previous program managers, that substantially more background information was available than one might at first assume.*"

[46] (Odling-Smee 2007)
[47]

[18] Leonard Zusne, Warren H. Jones (1989). *Anomalistic Psychology: A Study of Magical Thinking.* Lawrence Erlbaum Associates.

[49] Julie Milton, Richard Wiseman. (2002). *A Response to Storm and Ertel (2002).* The Journal of Parapsychology. Volume 66: 183-186.

[50] Richard Wiseman, Matthew Smith, Diana Kornbrot. (1996). *Assessing possible sender-to-experimenter acoustic leakage in the PRL autoganzfeld.* Journal of Parapsychology. Volume 60: 97-128.

[51] Leonard Zusne, Warren H. Jones (1989). *Anomalistic Psychology: A Study of Magical Thinking.* Lawrence Erlbaum Associates. p. 167.

[52] Martin Bridgstock. (2009). *Beyond Belief: Skepticism, Science and the Paranormal*. Cambridge University Press. p. 106. "The explanation used by Marks and Kammann clearly involves the use of Occam's razor. Marks and Kammann argued that the 'cues' - clues to the order in which sites had been visited—provided sufficient information for the results, without any recourse to extrasensory perception. Indeed Marks himself was able to achieve 100 percent accuracy in allocating some transcripts to sites without visiting any of the sites himself, purely on the ground basis of the cues. From Occam's razor, it follows that if a straightforward natural explanation exists, there is no need for the spectacular paranormal explanation: Targ and Puthoff's claims are not justified".

[53] Terence Hines. (2003). *Pseudoscience and the Paranormal*. Prometheus Books. p. 136.

[54] Massimo Pigliucci. (2010). *Nonsense on Stilts: How to Tell Science from Bunk*. University of Chicago Press. pp. 77-80.

[55] Parker, Adrian. (1975). *States of Mind: ESP and Altered States of Consciousness*. Taplinger. p. 90.

[56] Hyman, Ray. (1986). *Maimonides dream-telepathy experiments*. Skeptical Inquirer 11: 91-92.

[57] Neher, Andrew. (2011). *Paranormal and Transcendental Experience: A Psychological Examination*. Dover Publications. p. 145.

[58] Hansel, C. E. M. *The Search for a Demonstration of ESP*. In Kurtz, Paul. (1985). *A Skeptic's Handbook of Parapsychology*. Prometheus Books. pp. 97-127.

[59] Ramakrishna Rao, K, Gowri Rammohan, V. (2002). *New Frontiers of Human Science: A Festschrift for K. Ramakrishna Rao*. McFarland. p. 135.

[60] Hansel, C. E. M. (1989). *The Search for Psychic Power: ESP and Parapsychology Revisited*. Prometheus Books. pp. 141-152.

[61] "In their article, Sherwood and Roe examine attempts to replicate the well-known Maimonides dream studies that began in the 1960s. They provide a good review of these studies of dream telepathy and clairvoyance, but if one thing emerges for me from their review, it is the extreme messiness of the data adduced. Lack of replication is rampant. While one would normally expect that continuing scientific scrutiny of a phenomenon should lead to stronger effect sizes as one learns more about the subject matter and refines the methodology, this is apparently not the case with this research."

[62] Lee Worth Bailey and Jenny L. Yates (1996). The near-death experience: a reader https//books. google.com Routledge, p. 26.

[63] Harvey J. Irwin (2004). *An Introduction to Parapsychology*. McFarland, p. 218.

[64] Ian Wilson. (1981). *Mind Out of Time: Reincarnation Investigated*. Gollancz.

[65] Robert Baker. (1996). *Hidden Memories: Voices and Visions from Within*. Prometheus Books.

[66] Robert Cogan. (1998). *Critical Thinking: Step by Step*. University Press of America. pp. 202-203. "Edwards catalogs common sense objections which have been made against reincarnation. 1) How does a soul exist between bodies? 2) Tertullian's objection: If there is reincarnation, why are not babies born with the mental abilities of adults? 3) Reincarnation claims an infinite series of prior incarnations. Evolution teaches that there was a time when humans did not yet exist. So reincarnation is inconsistent with modern science. 4) If there is reincarnation, then what is happening when the population increases? 5) If there is reincarnation, then why do so few, if any people, remember past lives?... To answer these objections believers in reincarnation must accept additional assumptions... Acceptance of these silly assumptions, Edwards says, amounts to a crucifixion of one's intellect." • Paul Edwards. (1996, reprinted in 2001). *Reincarnation: A Critical Examination*. Prometheus books.

[67] Simon Hoggart, Mike Hutchinson. (1995). *Bizarre Beliefs*. Richard Cohen Books. p. 145. "The trouble is that the history of research into psi is littered with failed experiments, ambiguous experiments, and experiments which are claimed as great successes but are quickly rejected by conventional scientists. There has also been some spectacular cheating."

[68] Robert Cogan. (1998). *Critical Thinking: Step by Step*. University Press of America. p. 227. "When an experiment can't be repeated and get the same result, this tends to show that the result was due to some error in experimental procedure, rather than some real causal process. ESP experiments simply have not turned up any repeatable paranormal phenomena."

[69] Charles M. Wynn, Arthur W. Wiggins. (2001). *Quantum Leaps in the Wrong Direction: Where Real Science Ends...and Pseudoscience Begins*. Joseph Henry Press. p. 165. "Extrasensory perception and psychokinesis fail to fulfill the requirements of the scientific method. They therefore must remain pseudoscientific concepts until methodological flaws in their study are eliminated, and repeatable data supporting their existence are obtained."

[70] Terence Hines. (2003). *Pseudoscience and the Paranormal*. Prometheus Books. p. 144. "It is important to realize that, in one hundred years of parapsychological investigations, there has never been a single adequate demonstration of the reality of any psi phenomenon."

[71] Victor Stenger. (1990). *Physics and Psychics: The Search for a World Beyond the Senses*. Prometheus Books. p. 166. "The bottom line is simple: science is based on consensus, and at present a scientific consensus that psychic phenomena exist is still not established."

[72] Eugene B. Zechmeister, James E. Johnson. (1992). *Critical Thinking: A Functional Approach*. Brooks/Cole Pub. Co. p. 115. "There exists no good scientific evidence for the existence of paranormal phenomena such as ESP. To be acceptable to the scientific community, evidence must be both valid and reliable."

[73] • Michael Shermer. (2003). *Psychic drift. Why most scientists do not believe in ESP and psi phenomena*. Scientific American 288: 2.

[74] Graham Reed. (1988). *The Psychology of Anomalous Experience: A Cognitive Approach*. Prometheus Books. Leonard Zusne, Warren H. Jones (1989). *Anomalistic Psychology: A Study of Magical Thinking*. Lawrence Erlbaum Associates.

[75] Donovan Rawcliffe. (1952). *The Psychology of the Occult*. Derricke Ridgway, London.

[76] C. E. M. Hansel. (1980). *ESP and Parapsychology: A Critical Reevaluation*. Prometheus Books.

[77] Ray Hyman. (1989). *The Elusive Quarry: A Scientific Appraisal of Psychical Research*. Prometheus Books.

[78] Andrew Neher. (2011). *Paranormal and Transcendental Experience: A Psychological Examination*. Dover Publications.

[79]

[80] "Parapsychology is the only realm of objective inquiry in which the phenomena are all negatively defined, defined in terms of ruling out normal explanations. Of course, ruling out all normal explanations is not an easy task. We may not be aware of all possible normal explanations, or we may be deceived by our subjects, or we may deceive ourselves. If all normal explanations actually could be ruled out, just what is it that is at play? What is psi? Unfortunately, it is just a label It has no substantive definition that goes beyond saying that all normal explanations have apparently been eliminated. Of course, parapsychologists generally presume that it has something to do with some ability of the mind to transcend the laws of nature as we know them, but all that is so vague as to be unhelpful in any scientific exploration."

[81] James Alcock, Jean Burns, Anthony Freeman. (2003). *Psi Wars: Getting to Grips with the Paranormal*. Imprint Academic. p. 25.

[82] Terence Hines. (2003). *Pseudoscience and the Paranormal*. Prometheus Books. p. 146.

[83] Antony Flew. (1989). *The problem of evidencing the improbable and the impossible*. In G. K. Zollschan, J. F. Schumaker & G. F. Walsh (Eds.), *Exploring the paranormal*. pp. 313–327. Dorset, England: Prism Press.

[84] Michael W. Friedlander. (1998). *At the Fringes of Science*. Westview Press. p. 122.

[85] Ray Hyman. (2008). "Anomalous Cognition? A Second Perspective" http://www.csicop.org/si/show/anomalous_cognition_a_second_perspective/. *Skeptical Inquirer*. Volume 32. Retrieved May 22, 2014.

[86] Mario Bunge. (1983). Treatise on Basic Philosophy: Volume 6: Epistemology & Methodology II: Understanding the World. Springer. p. 56.

[87] John Taylor. (1980). *Science and the Supernatural: An Investigation of Paranormal Phenomena Including Psychic Healing, Clairvoyance, Telepathy, and Precognition by a Distinguished Physicist and Mathematician*. Temple Smith.

[88] Susan Blackmore. (2001). *Why I Have Given Up* in Paul Kurtz. *Skeptical Odysseys: Personal Accounts by the World's Leading Paranormal Inquirers*. Prometheus Books. pp. 85-94.

[89] Mario Bunge. (1983). *Treatise on Basic Philosophy: Volume 6: Epistemology & Methodology II: Understanding the World*. Springer. pp. 225-226. • "Precognition violates the principle

of antecedence ("causality"), according to which the effect does not happen before the cause. Psychokinesis violates the principle of conservation of energy as well as the postulate that mind cannot act directly on matter. (If it did no experimenter could trust his own readings of his instruments.) Telepathy and precognition are incompatible with the epistemological principle according to which the gaining of factual knowledge requires sense perception at some point."

• "Parapsychology makes no use of any knowledge gained in other fields, such as physics and physiological psychology. Moreover, its hypotheses are inconsistent with some basic assumptions of factual science. In particular, the very idea of a disembodied mental entity is incompatible with physiological psychology; and the claim that signals can be transmitted across space without fading with distance is inconsistent with physics."

[90]Gilovich, Thomas (1993). *How We Know What Isn't So: The Fallibility of Human Reason in Everyday Life.* Simon & Schuster. pp. 160, 169, 174, 175.

[91]Milton A. Rothman. (1988). *A Physicist's Guide to Skepticism.* Prometheus Books. p. 193. "Transmission of information through space requires transfer of energy from one place to another. Telepathy requires transmission of an energy-carrying signal directly from one mind to another. All descriptions of ESP imply violations of conservation of energy in one way or another, as well as violations of all the principles of information theory and even of the principle of causality. Strict application of physical principles requires us to say that ESP is impossible."

[92]Charles M. Wynn, Arthur W. Wiggins. (2001). *Quantum Leaps in the Wrong Direction: Where Real Science Ends...and Pseudoscience Begins.* Joseph Henry Press. p. 165. "One of the reasons scientists have difficulty believing that psi effects are real is that there is no known mechanism by which they could occur. PK action-at-a-distance would presumably employ an action-at-a-distance force that is as yet unknown to science... Similarly, there is no known sense (stimulation and receptor) by which thoughts could travel from one person to another by which the mind could project itself elsewhere in the present, future, or past."

[93]John Taylor. (1980). *Science and the Supernatural: An Investigation of Paranormal Phenomena Including Psychic Healing, Clairvoyance, Telepathy, and Precognition by a Distinguished Physicist and Mathematician.* Temple Smith. pp. 27-30.

[94]Felix Planer. (1980). *Superstition.* Cassell. p. 242.

[95]Felix Planer. (1980). *Superstition.* Cassell. p. 254.

[96]

[97]Mario Bunge. (1983). *Treatise on Basic Philosophy: Volume 6: Epistemology & Methodology II: Understanding the World.* Springer. pp. 225-227.

[98]Mario Bunge. (1984). *What is Pseudoscience?.* The Skeptical Inquirer. Volume 9: 36-46.

[99]Arthur Newell Strahler. (1992). *Understanding Science: An Introduction to Concepts and Issues.* Prometheus Books. pp. 168-212.

[100]Terence Hines. (2003). *Pseudoscience and the Paranormal.* Prometheus Books. pp. 113-150.

[101]Raimo Tuomela *Science, Protoscience, and Pseudoscience* in Joseph C. Pitt, Marcello Pera (1987). *Rational Changes in Science: Essays on Scientific Reasoning.* Springer. pp. 83-102.

[102]James Alcock. (1981). *Parapsychology-Science Or Magic?: A Psychological Perspective.* Pergamon Press. p. 196.

[103]Thomas Gilovich. (1993). *How We Know What Isn't So: The Fallibility of Human Reason in Everyday Life.* Free Press. p. 160

[104]Terence Hines. (2003). *Pseudoscience and the Paranormal.* Prometheus Books. pp. 117-145.

[105]David Marks. (1986). *Investigating the Paranormal.* Nature. Volume 320: 119-124.

[106]French, Chris; Stone, Anna. (2014). *Anomalistic Psychology: Exploring Paranormal Belief and Experience.* Palgrave Macmillan. pp. 252-255.

[107]Dowden, Bradley. (1993). *Logical Reasoning.* Wadsworth Publishing Company. p. 392.

[108]Henry Gordon. (1988). *Extrasensory Deception: ESP, Psychics, Shirley MacLaine, Ghosts, UFOs.* Macmillan of Canada. p. 13. "The history of parapsychology, of psychic phenomena, has been studded with fraud and experimental error."

[109]Hyman, Ray. (1989). *The Elusive Quarry: A Scientific Appraisal of Psychical Research.* Prometheus Books. pp. 99-106.

[110]Stein, Gordon. (1996). *The Encyclopedia of the Paranormal.* Prometheus Books. p. 688.]

[111]Andrew Neher. (2011). *Paranormal and Transcendental Experience: A Psychological Examination* Dover Publications. p. 220.

[112] Betty Markwick. (1985). *The establishment of data manipulation in the Soal-Shackleton experiments*. In Paul Kurtz. *A Skeptic's Handbook of Parapsychology*. Prometheus Books. pp. 287-312.

[113] McBurney, Donald H; White, Theresa L. (2009). *Research Methods*. Wadsworth Publishing. p. 60.

[114] Neher, Andrew. (2011). *Paranormal and Transcendental Experience: A Psychological Examination*. Dover Publications. p. 144.

[115] Philip John Tyson, Dai Jones, Jonathan Elcock. (2011). *Psychology in Social Context: Issues and Debates*. Wiley-Blackwell. p. 199.

[116] Massimo Pigliucci. (2010). *Nonsense on Stilts: How to Tell Science from Bunk*. University Of Chicago Press. p. 82.

[117] Kendrick Frazier. (1991). *The Hundredth Monkey: And Other Paradigms of the Paranormal*. Prometheus Books. pp. 168-170.

[118] Lawrie Reznek. (2010). *Delusions and the Madness of the Masses*. Rowman & Littlefield Publishers. p. 54.

[119] Louisa Rhine. (1983). *Something Hidden*. McFarland & Company. p. 226.

[120] Mary Roach. (2010). *Spook: Science Tackles the Afterlife*. Canongate Books Ltd. pp. 122-130.

[121] Randi, J. (1983) The Project Alpha experiment: Part one: the first two years. *Skeptical Inquirer*, Summer issue, Pages 24-33 and Randi, J. (1983)The Project Alpha Experiment: Part two: Beyond the Laboratory," *Skeptical Inquirer* Fall issue, Pages 36-45

[122] Nicola Holt, Christine Simmonds-Moore, David Luke, Christopher French. (2012). *Anomalistic Psychology (Palgrave Insights in Psychology)*. Palgrave Macmillan.

[123] Interview with Chris French on Anomalistic psychology http://www.videojug.com/interview/anomalistic-psychology-2

[124] The rise of anomalistic psychology – and the fall of parapsychology? http://blogs.nature.com/soapboxscience/2011/12/19/the-rise-of-anomalistic-psychology-%E2%80%93-and-the-fall-of-parapsychology

[125] //doi.org/10.1017/s0140525x00054595

[126] http://www.medicine.virginia.edu/clinical/departments/psychiatry/sections/cspp/dops

[127] http://www.noetic.org/

[128] https://web.archive.org/web/20100310213612/http://www.parapsych.org/index.html

[129] http://www.rhine.org/

[130] http://www.spr.ac.uk/

[131] http://csicop.org/

[132] http://www.randi.org/site/

[133] https://web.archive.org/web/20080112045008/http://findarticles.com/p/search?qt=parapsychology

[134] https://curlie.org/Science/Social_Sciences/Psychology/Alternative/Parapsychology/

[135] //en.wikipedia.org/w/index.php?title=Template:Paranormal&action=edit

[136] Marks, David; Kammann, Richard. (2000). *The Psychology of the Psychic*. Prometheus Books. pp. 97-106.

[137] Hyman, Ray. *Evaluating Parapsychological Claims*. In Robert J. Sternberg, Henry L. Roediger, Diane F. Halpern. (2007). *Critical Thinking in Psychology*. Cambridge University Press. pp. 216-231.

[138] Telepathy http://www.collinsdictionary.com/dictionary/english/telepathy. CollinsDictionary.com. Collins English Dictionary - Complete & Unabridged 11th Edition. Retrieved December 06, 2012.

[139] Following the model of sym**pathy** and em**pathy**.

[140] Glossary of Parapsychological terms - Telepathy http://parapsych.org/glossary_s_z.html#t — Parapsychological Association. Retrieved December 19, 2006.

[141] Felix Planer. (1980). *Superstition*. Cassell. p. 218. "Many experiments have attempted to bring scientific methods to bear on the investigation of the subject. Their results based on literally millions of tests, have made it abundantly clear that there exists no such phenomenon as telepathy, and that the seemingly successful scores have relied either on illusion, or on deception."

[142] Spencer Rathus. (2011). *Psychology: Concepts and Connections*. Cengage Learning. p. 143. "There is no adequate scientific evidence that people can read other people's minds. Research has not identified one single indisputable telepath or clairvoyant."

[143] Oppenheim, Janet. (1985). *The Other World: Spiritualism and Psychical Research in England, 1850-1914*. Cambridge University Press. pp. 135-249.

[144] Luckhurst, Roger. (2002). *The Invention of Telepathy, 1870-1901*. Oxford University Press. pp. 9-51.

[145] Dingwall, Eric. (1985). *The Need for Responsibility in Parapsychology: My Sixty Years in Psychical Research*. In *A Skeptic's Handbook of Parapsychology*. Prometheus Books. pp. 161-174. "Let me give an example, such as thought-transference, which is as good as any. When the British SPR was founded, the public was led to believe that at least a scientific survey was to be made, and I have no doubt that even some of those closely associated with the early days thought so too. But Myers, among others, had no such intention and cherished no such illusion. He knew that the primary aim of the Society was not objective experimentation but the establishment of telepathy. (...) What was wanted was proof that mind could communicate with mind apart from the normal avenues, for if mental sharing was a fact when the persons concerned were incarnate it could plausibly be suggested that the same mechanism might operate when death had occurred. Thus the supernatural might be proved by science, and psychical research might become, in the words of Sir William Barrett, a handmaid to religion."

[146] Roger Luckhurst. (2002). *The Invention of Telepathy: 1870-1901*. Oxford University Press. p. 63.

[147] Richard Wiseman. (2011). *Paranormality: Why We See What Isn't There*. Macmillan. p. 140-142.

[148] Nicola Bown, Carolyn Burdett, Pamela Thurschwell. (2004). *The Victorian Supernatural*. Cambridge University Press. pp. 87-108.

[149] Ray Hyman. (1989). *The Elusive Quarry: A Scientific Appraisal of Psychical Research*. Prometheus Books. pp. 99-106

[150] Gordon Stein. (1996). *The Encyclopedia of the Paranormal*. Prometheus Books. p. 688

[151] Neher, Andrew. (2011). *Paranormal and Transcendental Experience: A Psychological Examination*. Dover Publications. p. 220.

[152] Payne, Kenneth Wilcox. (1928). *Is Telepathy all Bunk? Popular Science Monthly*. p. 119

[153] Couttie, Bob. (1988). *Forbidden Knowledge: The Paranormal Paradox*. Lutterworth Press. p. 129. "In the early 1900s Gilbert Murray, who died in 1957, carried out some experiments in ESP in which he was in one room and the sender in a hallway, often with an open door between them. These experiments were successful. Most of the time the target was spoken aloud. When it was not, there were negative results. This is suggestive of a hyperacuity of hearing, especially since on at least one occasion Murray complained about noise coming from a milk-cart in the street next to the one in which the experiments were being carried out."

[154] Mauskopf, Seymour H; McVaugh, Michael Rogers. (1980). *The Elusive Science: Origins of Experimental Psychical Research*. Johns Hopkins University Press. p. 331.

[155] Zusne, Leonard; Jones, Warren H. (1989). *Anomalistic Psychology: A Study of Magical Thinking*. Lawrence Erlbaum Associates, Inc. p. 155.

[156] Anderson, Rodger. (2006). *Psychics, Sensitives and Somnambules: A Biographical Dictionary with Bibliographies*. McFarland. p. 126.

[157] Christopher, Milbourne. (1971). *ESP, Seers & Psychics*. Crowell. p. 19.

[158] Berger, Arthur S. (1988). *Lives and Letters in American Parapsychology: A Biographical History, 1850-1897*. McFarland. p. 66.

[159] Luckhurst, Roger. (2002). *The Invention of Telepathy: 1870-1901*. Oxford University Press. p. 269.

[160] Hannan, Caryn. (2008 edition). *Connecticut Biographical Dictionary*. State History Publications. p. 526. "On his return to Harvard in 1916, one of his first enterprises was an investigation of telepathy in the psychology laboratory, which gave negative results."

[161] Asprem, Egil. (2014). *The Problem of Disenchantment: Scientific Naturalism and Esoteric Discourse, 1900-1939*. Brill Academic Publishers. pp. 362-364.

[162] John Booth. (1986). *Psychic Paradoxes*. Prometheus Books. p. 8

[163] Gault, Robert H. (August, 1924). *Telepathy Put to the Test. Popular Science*. pp. 114-115

[164] Mauskopf, Seymour H; McVaugh, Michael Rogers. (1980). *The Elusive Science: Origins of Experimental Psychical Research*. Johns Hopkins University Press. pp. 36-38.

[165] Edmunds, Simeon. (1965). *Miracles of the Mind: An Introduction to Parapsychology*. C. C. Thomas. pp. 26-28

[166] Martin Gardner, *Fads & Fallacies in the Name of Science* (Courier Dover Publications, 1957) Chapter 25: *ESP and PK*, available online https://books.google.com/books?id= TwP3SGAUsnkC&; accessed July 25, 2010.

[167] John Sladek. (1974). The New Apocrypha: A Guide to Strange Sciences and Occult Beliefs. Panther. pp. 172-174

[168] Bergen Evans. (1954). *The Spoor of Spooks: And Other Nonsense*. Knopf. p. 24

[169] C. E. M. Hansel. (1989). *The Search for Psychic Power: ESP and Parapsychology Revisited*. Prometheus Books. pp. 56-58.

[170] Simon Nasht. (2006). *The Last Explorer: Hubert Wilkins, Hero of the Great Age of Polar Exploration*. Arcade Publishing. pp. 267-268

[171] Hubert Wilkins, Harold Sherman. (2004). *Thoughts through Space: A Remarkable Adventure in the Realm of Mind*. Hampton Roads Publishing.

[172] John Booth. (1986). *Psychic Paradoxes*. Prometheus Books. p. 69

[173] Steiner, Lee R. (1942). *Review of Thoughts Through Space*. American Journal of Orthopsychiatry 12 (4): 745.

[174] Lamont, Peter. (2013). *Extraordinary Beliefs: A Historical Approach to a Psychological Problem*. Cambridge University Press. p. 220.

[175] Lawrie Reznek. (2010). *Delusions and the Madness of the Masses*. Rowman & Littlefield Publishers . pp. 54-55

[176] C. E. M. Hansel. (1980). *ESP and Parapsychology: A Critical Reevaluation*. Prometheus Books. p. 165

[177] Betty Markwick. (1985). *The establishment of data manipulation in the Soal-Shackleton experiments*. In Paul Kurtz. *A Skeptic's Handbook of Parapsychology*. Prometheus Books. pp. 287-312

[178] Glossary of Parapsychological terms - ESP http://parapsych.org/glossary_e_k.html#e , Parapsychological Association. Retrieved December 19, 2006.

[179] Rennie, John (1845), "Test for Telepathy", *Scientific American*, V3#1 (1847-09-25)

[180] Plazo, Joseph R., (2002) "Psychic Seduction." pp.112-114

[181] St. Claire, David., (1989) "Instant ESP." pp.40-50

[182] Jonathan C. Smith. (2009). *Pseudoscience and Extraordinary Claims of the Paranormal: A Critical Thinker's Toolkit* https//books.google.co.uk. Wiley-Blackwell. "Today, researchers discount the first decade of Rhine's work with Zener cards. Stimulus leakage or cheating could account for all his findings. Slight indentations on the backs of cards revealed the symbols embossed on card faces. Subjects could see and hear the experimenter, and note subtle but revealing facial expressions or changes in breathing."

[183] Milbourne Christopher. (1970). *ESP, Seers & Psychics*. Thomas Y. Crowell Company. p. 28

[184] James Alcock. (2011). *Back from the Future: Parapsychology and the Bem Affair* http://www.csicop.org/specialarticles/show/back_from_the_future. *Skeptical Inquirer*. "Despite Rhine's confidence that he had established the reality of extrasensory perception, he had not done so. Methodological problems with his experiments eventually came to light, and as a result parapsychologists no longer run card-guessing studies and rarely even refer to Rhine's work."

[185] Parker, Adrian. (1975). *States of Mind: ESP and Altered States of Consciousness*. Taplinger. p. 90.

[186] Hyman, Ray. (1986). *Maimonides dream-telepathy experiments*. Skeptical Inquirer 11: 91-92.

[187] Neher, Andrew. (2011). *Paranormal and Transcendental Experience: A Psychological Examination*. Dover Publications. p. 145.

[188] Hansel, C. E. M. *The Search for a Demonstration of ESP*. In Kurtz, Paul. (1985). *A Skeptic's Handbook of Parapsychology*. Prometheus Books. pp. 97-127.

[189] Hansel, C. E. M. (1989). *The Search for Psychic Power: ESP and Parapsychology Revisited*. Prometheus Books. pp. 141-152.

[190] *The Conscious Universe: The Scientific Truth of Psychic Phenomena* by Dean I. Radin Harper Edge,

[191] Julie Milton, Richard Wiseman. (2002). *A Response to Storm and Ertel (2002)*. The Journal of Parapsychology. Volume 66: 183-186.

[192] Ray Hyman. *Evaluating Parapsychological Claims* in Robert J. Sternberg, Henry L. Roediger, Diane F. Halpern. (2007). *Critical Thinking in Psychology*. Cambridge University Press. pp. 216-231.

[193] Richard Wiseman, Matthew Smith, Diana Kornbrot. (1996). *Assessing possible sender-to-experimenter acoustic leakage in the PRL autoganzfeld*. Journal of Parapsychology. Volume 60: 97-128.

[194] Robert Todd Carroll. (2014). "Ganzfeld http://www.skepdic.com/ganzfeld.html" in The Skeptic's Dictionary.

[195] Hyman, R. (2010). *Meta-analysis that conceals more than it reveals: Comment on Storm et al* http://drsmorey.org/bibtex/upload/Hyman:2010.pdf . (2010). Psychological Bulletin, 136. pp. 486-490.

[196] Hupp, Stephen; Jewell, Jeremy. (2015). *Great Myths of Child Development*. Wiley. pp. 10-16.

[197] Wiseman, Richard. (2011). *Paranormality: Why We See What Isn't There*. Macmillan. p. 54.

[198] "The Riddle of Twin Telepathy" http://www.livescience.com/45405-twin-telepathy.html. Retrieved 2014-06-06.

[199] Simon Hoggart, Mike Hutchinson. (1995). *Bizarre Beliefs*. Richard Cohen Books. p. 145. "The trouble is that the history of research into psi is littered with failed experiments, ambiguous experiments, and experiments which are claimed as great successes but are quickly rejected by conventional scientists. There has also been some spectacular cheating."

[200] Robert Cogan. (1998). *Critical Thinking: Step by Step*. University Press of America. p. 227. "When an experiment can't be repeated and get the same result, this tends to show that the result was due to some error in experimental procedure, rather than some real causal process. ESP experiments simply have not turned up any repeatable paranormal phenomena."

[201] Terence Hines. (2003). *Pseudoscience and the Paranormal*. Prometheus Books. p. 144. "It is important to realize that, in one hundred years of parapsychological investigations, there has never been a single adequate demonstration of the reality of any psi phenomenon."

[202] Thomas Gilovich. (1993). *How We Know What Isn't So: The Fallibility of Human Reason in Everyday Life*. Free Press. p. 160

[203] Daisie Radner, Michael Radner. (1982). *Science and Unreason*. Wadsworth. pp. 38-66.

[204] Michael W. Friedlander. (1998). *At the Fringes of Science*. Westview Press. p. 119. "Parapsychology has failed to gain general scientific acceptance even for its improved methods and claimed successes, and it is still treated with a lopsided ambivalence among the scientific community. Most scientists write it off as pseudoscience unworthy of their time."

[205] Massimo Pigliucci, Maarten Boudry. (2013). *Philosophy of Pseudoscience: Reconsidering the Demarcation Problem*. University Of Chicago Press p. 158. "Many observers refer to the field as a "pseudoscience". When mainstream scientists say that the field of parapsychology is not scientific, they mean that no satisfying naturalistic cause-and-effect explanation for these supposed effects has yet been proposed and that the field's experiments cannot be consistently replicated."

[206] Charles M. Wynn, Arthur W. Wiggins. (2001). *Quantum Leaps in the Wrong Direction: Where Real Science Ends...and Pseudoscience Begins*. Joseph Henry Press. p. 165. "One of the reasons scientists have difficulty believing that psi effects are real is that there is no known mechanism by which they could occur. PK action-at-a-distance would presumably employ an action-at-a-distance force that is as yet unknown to science... Similarly, there is no known sense (stimulation and receptor) by which thoughts could travel from one person to another by which the mind could project itself elsewhere in the present, future, or past."

[207] Mario Bunge. (1983). *Treatise on Basic Philosophy: Volume 6: Epistemology & Methodology II: Understanding the World*. Springer. pp. 225-226. • "Precognition violates the principle of antecedence ("causality"), according to which the effect does not happen before the cause. Psychokinesis violates the principle of conservation of energy as well as the postulate that mind cannot act directly on matter. (If it did no experimenter could trust his own readings of his instruments.) Telepathy and precognition are incompatible with the epistemological principle according to which the gaining of factual knowledge requires sense perception at some point."
• "Parapsychology makes no use of any knowledge gained in other fields, such as physics and

physiological psychology. Moreover, its hypotheses are inconsistent with some basic assumptions of factual science. In particular, the very idea of a disembodied mental entity is incompatible with physiological psychology; and the claim that signals can be transmitted across space without fading with distance is inconsistent with physics."

[208] John Taylor. (1980). *Science and the Supernatural: An Investigation of Paranormal Phenomena Including Psychic Healing, Clairvoyance, Telepathy, and Precognition by a Distinguished Physicist and Mathematician*. Temple Smith. p. 84.

[209] Sutherland, Stuart. (1994). *Irrationality: The Enemy Within*. p. 314. Penguin Books.

[210] Graham Reed. (1988). *The Psychology of Anomalous Experience*. Prometheus Books. pp. 38-42.

[211] Skepdic.com on ESP http://www.skepdic.com/esp.html. Retrieved February 22, 2007.

[212] Leonard Zusne, Warren H. Jones. (1989). *Anomalistic Psychology: A Study of Magical Thinking*. Psychology Press.

[213] Ian Rowland. (1998). *The Full Facts Book of Cold Reading*. Ian Rowland Limited: 4th Revised edition.

[214] Derren Brown. (2007). *Tricks of the Mind*. Channel 4: New edition.

[215] Richard Noll. (2007). *The Encyclopedia of Schizophrenia and Other Psychotic Disorders*. Facts on File. p. 359.

[216] Graham Pickup. (2006). *Cognitive Neuropsychiatry*. Volume 11, Number 2, Number 2/March 2006. pp. 117-192

[217] Andrew Gumley, Matthias Schwannauer. (2006). *Staying Well After Psychosis: A Cognitive Interpersonal Approach to Recovery and Relapse Prevention*. Wiley. p. 187. "Schizotypy refers to a normal personality construct characterised by an enduring tendency to experience attenuated forms of hallucinatory (e.g. hearing one's own thoughts) and delusional experiences (e.g. beliefs in telepathy)."

[218] Mary Townsend. (2013). *Essentials of Psychiatric Mental Health Nursing: Concepts of Care in Evidence-Based Practice*. F. A. Davis Company. p. 613. "Individuals with schizotypal personality disorder are aloof and isolated and behave in a bland and apathetic manner. Magical thinking, ideas of reference, illusions, and depersonalization are part of their everybody world. Examples include superstitiousness, belief in clairvoyance, telepathy, or "six sense;" and beliefs that "others can feel my feelings.""

[219] https://archive.org/stream/folliesfraudsofs00manniala#page/130/mode/2up

[220] https//books.google.co.uk

[221] http://www.dana.org/Cerebrum/Default.aspx?id=39113

[222] http://www.skepdic.com/telepath.html

[223] http://skepdic.com/soalgoldney.html

[224] http://www.psicoanalisi.it/psicoanalisi/psicosomatica/articoli/psomaing1117.htm

[225] //en.wikipedia.org/w/index.php?title=Template:Paranormal&action=edit

[226] Inglis (1985), Chapter on "Precognition"

[227] Aristotle. (350 BC). On Prophesying by Dreams. Trans. J.I. Beare http://classics.mit.edu/Aristotle/prophesying.html, MIT. (Retrieved 5 September 2018).

[228] Dunne (1927).

[229] Flew, Antony; "The Sources of Serialism, *in Shivesh Thakur (Ed)*. Philosophy and Psychical Research, *George Allen & Unwin Ltd. 1976, pp. 81-96.*

[230] Sean O'Donnell, *The Paranormal Explained*. Lulu 2007.

[231] Brian Inglis; *The Paranormal: An Encyclopedia of Psychic Phenomena*. Paladin (Grafton), 1986, p.92.

[232] Dunne (1927), 3rd Edition, Faber, 1934, *Appendix III: The new experiment.*

[233] C. D. Broad; "The Philosophical Implications of Foreknowledge", *Proceedings of the Aristotelian Society, Supplementary Volumes*, Vol. 16, Knowledge and Foreknowledge (1937), pp. 177-209

[234] Harold Gulliksen. (1938). *Extra-Sensory Perception: What Is It?*. American Journal of Sociology. Vol. 43, No. 4. pp. 623-634. "Investigating Rhine's methods, we find that his mathematical methods are wrong and that the effect of this error would in some cases be negligible and in others very marked. We find that many of his experiments were set up in a manner which would

tend to increase, instead of to diminish, the possibility of systematic clerical errors; and lastly, that the ESP cards can be read from the back."

[235] Wynn & Wiggins (2001), p. 156: "It is now known that the experiments conducted in his laboratory contained serious methodological flaws. Tests often took place with minimal or no screening between the subject and the person administering the test. Subjects could see the backs of cards that were later discovered to be so cheaply printed that a faint outline of the symbol could be seen. Furthermore, in face-to-face tests, subjects could see card faces reflected in the tester's eyeglasses or cornea. They were even able to (consciously or unconsciously) pick up clues from the tester's facial expression and voice inflection. In addition, an observant subject could identify the cards by certain irregularities like warped edges, spots on the backs, or design imperfections."

[236] Hines (2003), pp. 78–81. "The procedural errors in the Rhine experiments have been extremely damaging to his claims to have demonstrated the existence of ESP. Equally damaging has been the fact that the results have not replicated when the experiments have been conducted in other laboratories."

[237] Betty Markwick. (1985). *The establishment of data manipulation in the Soal-Shackleton experiments*. In Paul Kurtz. *A Skeptic's Handbook of Parapsychology*. Prometheus Books. pp. 287-312.

[238] C. E. M. Hansel. (1980). *ESP and Parapsychology: A Critical Re-Evaluation*. Prometheus Books. pp. 222-232. Hansel found that in the experiments of Schmidt there was no presence of an observer or second-experimenter in any of the experiments, no counterchecking of the records and no separate machines used for high and low score attempts.

[239] Brian Inglis; *The Paranormal: An Encyclopedia of Psychic Phenomena*. Paladin (Grafton), 1986, p.90.

[240] Priestley (1964).

[241] Francis Spufford, " I Have Been Here Before http://www.bbc.co.uk/programmes/b04h7lr0", *Sunday Feature*, BBC Radio 3, 14 Sep 2014.

[242] Ryback, David, PhD. "Dreams That Came True". New York: Bantam Doubleday Dell Publishing Group, 1988.

[243] James Alcock, *Back from the Future: Parapsychology and the Bem Affair* http://www.csicop. org/specialarticles/show/back_from_the_future, March/April 2011 Skeptical Inquirer, January 6, 2011.

[244] Wynn & Wiggins (2001), p. 165. "One of the reasons scientists have difficulty believing that psi effects are real is that there is no known mechanism by which they could occur. PK action-at-a-distance would presumably employ an action-at-a-distance force that is as yet unknown to science... Similarly, there is no known sense (stimulation and receptor) by which thoughts could travel from one person to another by which the mind could project itself elsewhere in the present, future, or past."

[245] Alcock, James. (1981). *Parapsychology-Science Or Magic?: A Psychological Perspective* Pergamon Press. pp. 3-6.

[246] Zusne, Leonard; Jones, Warren H. (1989). *Anomalistic Psychology: A Study of Magical Thinking*. Lawrence Erlbaum Associates, Inc. p. 151.

[247] Ciccarelli, Saundra E; Meyer, Glenn E. *Psychology*. (2007). Prentice Hall Higher Education. p. 118. "Precognition is the supposed ability to know something in advance of its occurrence or to predict a future event."

[248] Bunge, Mario. (1983). *Treatise on Basic Philosophy: Volume 6: Epistemology & Methodology II: Understanding the World*. Springer. pp. 225-226.

[249] Taylor, John. (1980). *Science and the Supernatural: An Investigation of Paranormal Phenomena Including Psychic Healing, Clairvoyance, Telepathy, and Precognition by a Distinguished Physicist and Mathematician*. Temple Smith. p. 83.

[250] Merali, Zeeya. " Back From the Future http://discovermagazine.com/2010/apr/01-back-from-the-future". *Discover*, April 2010. (recovered 5 September 2018).

[251] Hines (2003).

[252] via Hines (2003).

[253] via

[254] Wiseman, Richard. (2011). *Paranormality: Why We See What Isn't There*. Macmillan. pp. 163-167.

[255] Sutherland, Stuart. (1994). *Irrationality: The Enemy Within*. pp. 312-313. Penguin Books.

[256] Peake, Anthony; *The Labyrinth of Time*, Arcturus, 2012, Chapter 10: "Dreams and precognition".

[257] Anon,; "Obituary: Mr. J. W. Dunne, Philosopher and Airman", *The Times*, August 27, 1949, Page 7.

[258] Stewart, V.; "J. W. Dunne and literary culture in the 1930s and 1940s", *Literature and History*, Volume 17, Number 2, Autumn 2008, pp. 62-81, Manchester University Press.

[259] Vladimir Nabokov (ed. Gennady Barabtarlo); *Insomniac Dreams: Experiments with Time*, Princeton University Press, 2018.

[260] https://www.theguardian.com/science/2012/mar/15/precognition-studies-curse-failed-replications

[261] //en.wikipedia.org/w/index.php?title=Template:Paranormal&action=edit

[262] Britannica Online Encyclopedia http://www.britannica.com/ebc/article-9364105, Retrieved 2007-10-07. The ESP entry includes clairvoyance

[263] Carroll, Robert Todd. (2003). "Clairvoyance" http://www.skepdic.com/clairvoy.html. Retrieved 2014-04-30.

[264] • Bunge, Mario. (1983). *Treatise on Basic Philosophy: Volume 6: Epistemology & Methodology II: Understanding the World*. Springer. p. 226. "Despite being several thousand years old, and having attracted a large number of researchers over the past hundred years, we owe no single firm finding to parapsychology: no hard data on telepathy, clairvoyance, precognition, or psychokinesis." • Stenger, Victor. (1990). *Physics and Psychics: The Search for a World Beyond the Senses*. Prometheus Books. p. 166. "The bottom line is simple: science is based on consensus, and at present a scientific consensus that psychic phenomena exist is still not established." • Zechmeister, Eugene; Johnson, James. (1992). *Critical Thinking: A Functional Approach*. Brooks/Cole Pub. Co. p. 115. "There exists no good scientific evidence for the existence of paranormal phenomena such as ESP. To be acceptable to the scientific community, evidence must be both valid and reliable." • Hines, Terence. (2003). *Pseudoscience and the Paranormal*. Prometheus Books. p. 144. "It is important to realize that, in one hundred years of parapsychological investigations, there has never been a single adequate demonstration of the reality of any psi phenomenon."

[265] Melton, John. (2001). *The Encyclopedia of Occultism & Parapsychology*. p. 297. Gale Group, Detroit.

[266] S. A. Jain 1992, p. 16.

[267] Taves, Ann. (1999). *Fits, Trances, and Visions: Experiencing Religion and Explaining Experience from Wesley to James*. Princeton University Press. p. 126.

[268] Hyman, Ray. (1985). *A Critical Historical Overview of Parapsychology*. In Kurtz, Paul. *A Skeptic's Handbook of Parapsychology*. Prometheus Books. pp. 3-96.

[269] Roeckelein, Jon. (2006). *Elsevier's Dictionary of Psychological Theories*. Elsevier Science. p. 450.

[270] Hansel, C. E. M. *The Search for a Demonstration of ESP*. In Paul Kurtz. (1985). *A Skeptic's Handbook of Parapsychology*. Prometheus Books. pp. 97-127.

[271] McCabe, Joseph. (1920). *Is Spiritualism Based On Fraud? The Evidence Given By Sir A. C. Doyle and Others Drastically Examined*. Chapter *The Subtle Art of Clairvoyance*. London: Watts & Co. pp. 93-108

[272] Tuckett, Ivor Lloyd. (1911). *The Evidence for the Supernatural: A Critical Study Made with "Uncommon Sense"*. Chapter *Telepathy and Clairvoyance*. K. Paul, Trench, Trübner. pp. 107-142

[273] Baker, Robert A. (1996). *Hidden Memories: Voices and Visions From Within*. Prometheus Books. p. 234.

[274] Christopher, Milbourne. (1996). *The Illustrated History of Magic*. Greenwood Publishing Group. p. 264.

[275] Jastrow, Joseph. (1938). *ESP, House of Cards*. The American Scholar. Vol. 8, No. 1. pp. 13-22. "Rhine's results fail to be confirmed. At Colgate University (40, 000 tests, 7 subjects), at Chicago (extensive series on 315 students), at Southern Methodist College (75, 000 tests), at

Glasgow, Scotland (6, 650 tests), at London University (105, 000 tests), not a single individual was found who under rigidly conducted experiments could score above chance. At Stanford University it has been convincingly shown that the conditions favorable to the intrusion of subtle errors produce above-chance records which come down to chance when sources of error are eliminated."

[276] Hansel, C. E. M. *The Search for a Demonstration of ESP*. In Paul Kurtz. (1985). *A Skeptic's Handbook of Parapsychology*. Prometheus Books. pp. 105-127. • Crumbaugh, J. C. (1938). *An experimental study of extra-sensory perception*. Masters thesis. Southern Methodist University. • Willoughby, R. R. (1938). *Further card-guessing experiments. Journal of Psychology* 18: 3-13.

[277] Gulliksen, Harold. (1938). *Extra-Sensory Perception: What Is It?. American Journal of Sociology*. Vol. 43, No. 4. pp. 623-634. "Investigating Rhine's methods, we find that his mathematical methods are wrong and that the effect of this error would in some cases be negligible and in others very marked. We find that many of his experiments were set up in a manner which would tend to increase, instead of to diminish, the possibility of systematic clerical errors; and lastly, that the ESP cards can be read from the back."

[278] Wynn, Charles; Wiggins, Arthur. (2001). *Quantum Leaps in the Wrong Direction: Where Real Science Ends...and Pseudoscience Begins*. Joseph Henry Press. p. 156. "In 1940, Rhine coauthored a book, *Extrasensory Perception After Sixty Years* in which he suggested that something more than mere guess work was involved in his experiments. He was right! It is now known that the experiments conducted in his laboratory contained serious methodological flaws. Tests often took place with minimal or no screening between the subject and the person administering the test. Subjects could see the backs of cards that were later discovered to be so cheaply printed that a faint outline of the symbol could be seen. Furthermore, in face-to-face tests, subjects could see card faces reflected in the tester's eyeglasses or cornea. They were even able to (consciously or unconsciously) pick up clues from the tester's facial expression and voice inflection. In addition, an observant subject could identify the cards by certain irregularities like warped edges, spots on the backs, or design imperfections."

[279] Hines, Terence. (2003). *Pseudoscience and the Paranormal*. Prometheus Books. p. 122. "The procedural errors in the Rhine experiments have been extremely damaging to his claims to have demonstrated the existence of ESP. Equally damaging has been the fact that the results have not replicated when the experiments have been conducted in other laboratories."

[280] Hazelgrove, Jenny. (2000). *Spiritualism and British Society Between the Wars*. Manchester University Press. p. 204.

[281] Russell, A. S; Benn, John Andrews. (1938). *Discovery the Popular Journal of Knowledge*. Cambridge University Press. pp. 305-306

[282] Soal, Samuel. *A Repetition of Dr. Rhine's work with Mrs. Eileen Garrett*. Proc. S.P.R. Vol. XLII. pp. 84-85. Also quoted in Antony Flew. (1955). *A New Approach To Psychical Research*. Watts & Co. pp. 90-92.

[283] Blom, Jan. (2009). *A Dictionary of Hallucinations*. Springer. p. 451.

[284] Bridgstock, Martin. (2009). *Beyond Belief: Skepticism, Science and the Paranormal*. Cambridge University Press. p. 106. "The explanation used by Marks and Kammann clearly involves the use of Occam's razor. Marks and Kammann argued that the 'cues' – clues to the order in which sites had been visited—provided sufficient information for the results, without any recourse to extrasensory perception. Indeed Marks himself was able to achieve 100 percent accuracy in allocating some transcripts to sites without visiting any of the sites himself, purely on the ground basis of the cues. From Occam's razor, it follows that if a straightforward natural explanation exists, there is no need for the spectacular paranormal explanation: Targ and Puthoff's claims are not justified".

[285] Terence Hines. (2003). *Pseudoscience and the Paranormal*. Prometheus Books. p. 136.

[286] Rawcliffe, Donovan. (1988). *Occult and Supernatural Phenomena*. Dover Publications. pp. 367-463.

[287] Reed, Graham. (1988). *The Psychology of Anomalous Experience: A Cognitive Approach*. Prometheus Books.

[288] Zusne, Leonard; Jones, Warren. (1989). *Anomalistic Psychology: A Study of Magical Thinking*. Lawrence Erlbaum Associates. pp. 152-168.

[289] Friedlander, Michael W. (1998). *At the Fringes of Science*. Westview Press. p. 119. "Parapsychology has failed to gain general scientific acceptance even for its improved methods and claimed successes, and it is still treated with a lopsided ambivalence among the scientific community. Most scientists write it off as pseudoscience unworthy of their time."

[290] Pigliucci, Massimo; Boudry, Maarten. (2013). *Philosophy of Pseudoscience: Reconsidering the Demarcation Problem*. University Of Chicago Press p. 158. "Many observers refer to the field as a "pseudoscience". When mainstream scientists say that the field of parapsychology is not scientific, they mean that no satisfying naturalistic cause-and-effect explanation for these supposed effects has yet been proposed and that the field's experiments cannot be consistently replicated."

[291] Gilovich, Thomas. (1993). *How We Know What Isn't So: The Fallibility of Human Reason in Everyday Life*. Free Press. p. 160.

[292] French, Chis; Wilson, Krissy. (2007). *Cognitive Factors Underlying Paranormal Beliefs and Experiences*. In Sala, Sergio. *Tall Tales About the Mind and Brain: Separating Fact From Fiction*. Oxford: Oxford University Press. pp. 3-22.

[293] Myers, David. (2006). *Psychology*. Worth Publishers; 8th edition.

[294] https://archive.org/details/Reality_JMT

[295] https://books.google.co.in/books?id=uRIaAAAAMAAJ

[296] https://archive.org/stream/onothersideoffoo00dutcrich#page/n3/mode/2up

[297] https://books.google.com/books?id=DvkhAwAAQBAJ&pg=PA140

[298] https://archive.org/stream/isspiritualismba00mccarich#page/93/mode/2up

[299] http://www.csicop.org/sb/show/springer_psychic_a_study_in_clairvoyance/

[300] https://www.sciencedaily.com/releases/2014/01/140114092142.htm

[301] http://skepdic.com/clairvoy.html

[302] //en.wikipedia.org/w/index.php?title=Template:Paranormal&action=edit

[303] Bunge, Mario (1983). *Treatise on Basic Philosophy: Volume 6: Epistemology & Methodology II: Understanding the World*. Springer. p. 226. "Despite being several thousand years old, and having attracted a large number of researchers over the past hundred years, we owe no single firm finding to parapsychology: no hard data on telepathy, clairvoyance, precognition, or psychokinesis."

[304] Robert Scharff. (1968). *The Las Vegas Experts' Gambling Guide*. Grosset & Dunlap. p. 26.

[305] Carruthers, Peter. (2004). *The Nature of the Mind: An Introduction*. Routledge. 135-136.

[306] Study conducted by the Gallup Organization between October 8, 2005 and December 12, 2005 on behalf of the Baylor Institute for Studies of Religion, Baylor University, of Waco, Texas, in the United States.

[307] Fodor, Nandor. (1934). *These Mysterious People*. Rider. Chapter 21.

[308] Description page at a stock photo agency representing the Mary Evans Picture Library, where the date is also given as 1909. She visited the researcher in 1908 and 1909; hence, the exact year is uncertain and reported as 1908 elsewhere.

[309] Elmer Green's description of Swami Rama's alleged psychokinetic demonstration (with illustrations).

[310] https://curlie.org/Society/Paranormal/Psychic/Psychokinesis/

[311] Egger, Victor (1896). "Le moi des mourants", *Revue Philosophique*, XLI : 26–38.

[312] Green, C., *Out-of-the-body Experiences*, London: Hamish Hamilton, 1968.

[313]

[314] Greyson, Bruce (2003) "Near-Death Experiences in a Psychiatric Outpatient Clinic Population". Psychiatric Services, December, Vol. 54 No. 12. The American Psychiatric Association

[315] Kennard, Mary J. "A Visit from an Angel." The American Journal of Nursing 98.3 (1998): 48–51

[316] Ring, K. (1980). Life at death: A scientific investigation of the near-death experience. New York: Coward, McCann, & Geoghegan., p. 40

[317] Kenneth Ring, quoted in Ketamine—Near Death and Near Birth Experiences Dr Karl Jansen http://lila.info/document_view.phtml?document_id=91

[318] theatlantic.com https://www.theatlantic.com/magazine/archive/2015/04/the-science-of-near-death-experiences/386231/

[319]Ring, Kenneth. *Heading toward Omega. In search of the Meaning of Near-Death Experience*, 1984, p. 45. "Subsequent research on suicide-related NDEs by Stephen Franklin and myself [Ring] and by Bruce Greyson has also confirmed my earlier tentative findings the NDEs following suicide attempts, however induced, conform to the classic prototype."

[320]Lindley, JH; Bryan, S & Conley, B. (1981). 'Near-death experiences in a Pacific Northwest population: The Evergreen study – Anabiosis 1. p. 109.

[321]Morse M, Castillo P, Venecia D, Milstein J, Tyler DC. (1986) "Childhood near-death experiences". *American Journal of Diseases of Children*, Nov;140(11):1110–4.

[322]Ring, K. "Life at death. A scientific investigation of the near-death experience." 1980, New York: Coward McCann and Geoghenan.

[323]Jimo Borjigina *et al.* (2013). "Surge of Neurophysiological Coherence and Connectivity in the Dying Brain" http://www.pnas.org/content/early/2013/08/08/1308285110.full.pdf+html. Proceedings of the National Academy of Sciences. Vol. 110, Issue 35. pp. 14432–14437.

[324]"Near-death experiences are 'electrical surge in dying brain'" https://www.bbc.co.uk/news/science-environment-23672150. BBC News.

[325]"Could a final surge in brain activity after death explain near-death experiences?" http://www.nature.com/scitable/blog/brain-metrics/could_a_final_surge_in. Nature.

[326]"Near-death experiences exposed: Surge of brain activity after the heart stops may trigger paranormal visions" http://www.dailymail.co.uk/sciencetech/article-2390236/Near-death-experiences-explained-Surge-brain-activity-trigger-paranormal-visions.html. Daily Mail.

[327]//en.wikipedia.org/w/index.php?title=Near-death_experience&action=edit

[328]UK Clinical Trials Gateway. Primary Trial ID Number 17129 https://web.archive.org/web/20160509201054/https://www.ukctg.nihr.ac.uk/trials/trial-details/trial-details?trialId=31651, entitled "AWARE II (AWAreness during REsuscitation) A Multi-Centre Observational Study of the Relationship between the Quality of Brain Resuscitation and Consciousness, Neurological, Functional and Cognitive Outcomes following Cardiac Arrest" Last updated May 3, 2016. Page archived May 9, 2016

[329]French, Chris. (2009). *Near-Death Experiences and the Brain https://www.novapublishers. com/catalog/product_info.php?products_id=10186*. In Craig Murray. *Psychological Scientific Perspectives on Out-of-Body and Near-Death Experiences*. Nova Science Publishers. pp. 187–203.

[330]Noyes, R. and Slymen, D. (1978–1979) *The subjective response to life-threatening danger. Omega* 9: 313–321.

[331]Mayank and Mukesh, 2004; Jansen, 1995; Thomas, 2004; Fenwick and Fenwick 2008

[332]Leaving Body And Life Behind: lnco.epfl.ch http//lnco.epfl.ch

[333]Whinnery, J. E. (1997). *Psychophysiologic correlates of unconsciousness and near-death experiences*. J. Near Death Stud 15: 231–258.

[334]Engmann, Birk. (2008). *Near-death Experiences: A review on the thesis of pathoclisis, neurotransmitter abnormalities, and psychological aspects*. MMW-Fortschr.Med.Nr.51-52/2008(150.Jg.) pp.42–43.

[335]Vogt C, Vogt O. (1922). *Erkrankungen der Großhirnrinde im Lichte der Topistik, Pathoklise und Pathoarchitektonik*. Journal für Psychologie und Neurologie; Bd. 28. Joh.- Ambr.- Barth-Verlag. Leipzig. (German).

[336]http://www.iands.org/

[337]https://www.susanblackmore.co.uk/chapters/near-death-experiences/

[338]https://www.scientificamerican.com/article/peace-of-mind-near-death/

[339]http://www.skepdic.com/nde.html

[340]//doi.org/10.1192/bjp.153.5.607

[341]//www.ncbi.nlm.nih.gov/pubmed/3076496

[342]https://www.scientificamerican.com/article/why-near-death-experience-isnt-proof-heaven/

[343]//doi.org/10.1038/scientificamerican0413-86

[344]//www.ncbi.nlm.nih.gov/pubmed/23539795

[345]http://www.csicop.org/si/show/darkness_tunnels_and_light

[346]//en.wikipedia.org/w/index.php?title=Template:Paranormal&action=edit

[347]Norman C. McClelland 2010, pp. 24–29, 171.

[348]Mark Juergensmeyer & Wade Clark Roof 2011, pp. 271–272.

[349] Stephen J. Laumakis 2008, pp. 90–99.

[350] Norman C. McClelland 2010, pp. 102–103.

[351] see Charles Taliaferro, Paul Draper, Philip L. Quinn, *A Companion to Philosophy of Religion*. John Wiley and Sons, 2010, page 640, Google Books https://books.google.com/books?id=SSCx-67Tk6cC&pg=PA640&dq=reincarnation+and+rebirth&cd=8#v=onepage&q=reincarnation%20and%20rebirth&f=false

[352] Gananath Obeyesekere, *Imagining Karma: Ethical Transformation in Amerindian, Buddhist, and Greek Rebirth*. University of California Press, 2002, page 15.

[353] Hitti, Philip K (2007) [1924]. *Origins of the Druze People and Religion, with Extracts from their Sacred Writings (New Edition)*. Columbia University Oriental Studies. **28**. London: Saqi. pp. 13–14.

[354] Heindel, Max (1985) [1939, 1908] *The Rosicrucian Christianity Lectures (Collected Works)*: The Riddle of Life and Death http://www.rosicrucian.com/rcl/rcleng01.htm#lecture1. Oceanside, California. 4th edition.

[355] An important recent work discussing the mutual influence of ancient Greek and Indian philosophy regarding these matters is *The Shape of Ancient Thought* by Thomas McEvilley

[356] metempsychosis http://www.etymonline.com/index.php?term=metempsychosis, Etymology Dictionary, Douglas Harper (2015)

[357] Carl Huffman (2014), Pythagoras, 4.1 The Fate of the Soul—Metempsychosis http://plato.stanford.edu/entries/pythagoras/ Stanford Encyclopedia of Philosophy, Stanford University

[358] Keown 2013, pp. 35–40.

[359] John Bowker 2014, pp. 84–85.

[360] Gavin Flood (2010), Brill's Encyclopedia of Hinduism (Editor: Knut Jacobsen), Volume II, Brill, , pages 881–884

[361] Klaus Klostermaier, Mokṣa and Critical Theory, Philosophy East and West, Vol. 35, No. 1 (Jan., 1985), pages 61–71

[362] Norman E. Thomas (April 1988), Liberation for Life: A Hindu Liberation Philosophy, Missiology, Volume 16, Number 2, pp 149–160;
Gerhard Oberhammer (1994), La Délivrance dès cette vie: Jivanmukti, Collège de France, Publications de l'Institut de Civilisation Indienne. Série in-8°, Fasc. 61, Édition-Diffusion de Boccard (Paris), , pages 1–9

[363] Obeyesekere 2005, p. 1-2, 108, 126–128.

[364] Mark Juergensmeyer & Wade Clark Roof 2011, pp. 272–273.

[365] Diodorus Siculus thought the Druids might have been influenced by the teachings of Pythagoras. Diodorus Siculus v.28.6; Hippolytus *Philosophumena* i.25.

[366] one modern scholar has speculated that Buddhist missionaries had been sent to Britain by the Indian king Ashoka. Donald A.Mackenzie, *Buddhism in pre-Christian Britain* (1928:21).

[367] M. Dillon and N. Chadwick, *The Celtic Realms*, Weidenfeld & Nicolson, London,

[368] Ara, Mitra (2008). *Eschatology in the Indo-Iranian traditions: The Genesis and Transformation of a Doctrine* https://books.google.com/books?id=NQ12k9delf4C. Peter Lang Publishing Inc., New York, USA. pp. 99–100.

[369] Flood, Gavin. Olivelle, Patrick. 2003. *The Blackwell Companion to Hinduism*. Malden: Blackwell. pg. 273-4. "The second half of the first millennium BCE was the period that created many of the ideological and institutional elements that characterize later Indian religions. The renouncer tradition played a central role during this formative period of Indian religious history....Some of the fundamental values and beliefs that we generally associate with Indian religions in general and Hinduism in particular were in part the creation of the renouncer tradition. These include the two pillars of Indian theologies: samsara – the belief that life in this world is one of suffering and subject to repeated deaths and births (rebirth); moksa/nirvana – the goal of human existence....."

[370] Gavin D. Flood, *An Introduction to Hinduism*, Cambridge University Press (1996), UK p. 86 – "A third alternative is that the origin of transmigration theory lies outside of vedic or sramana traditions in the tribal religions of the Ganges valley, or even in Dravidian traditions of south India."

[371] Stephen J. Laumakis 2008, p. 90.

[372] A.M. Boyer (1901), Etude sur l'origine de la doctrine du samsara, Journal Asiatique, Volume 9, Issue 18, pages 451–453, 459–468

[373] Padmanabh Jaini 1980, pp. 217–236.

[374] Padmanabh Jaini 1980, pp. 226-228.

[375] Padmanabh Jaini 1980, pp. 227-228.

[376] ; **Quote:** "Buddhist doctrine holds that until they realize nirvana, beings are bound to undergo rebirth and redeath due to their having acted out of ignorance and desire, thereby producing the seeds of karma".

[377] , **Quote:** "Nirvana is the *raison d'être* of Buddhism, and its ultimate justification."

[378] Paul Williams, Anthony Tribe, *Buddhist thought: a complete introduction to the Indian tradition.* Routledge, 2000, page 84.

[379] , **Quote:** "For a vast majority of Buddhists in Theravadin countries, however, the order of monks is seen by lay Buddhists as a means of gaining the most merit in the hope of accumulating good karma for a better rebirth."

[380] Jessica Frazier & Gavin Flood 2011, pp. 84–86.

[381] Yuvraj Krishan (1988), Is Karma Evolutionary?, Journal of Indian Council of Philosophical Research, Volume 6, pages 24–26

[382] Paul Williams, Anthony Tribe & Alexander Wynne 2012, pp. 30–42.

[383] [a]
[b] , **Quote:** "(...) anatta is the doctrine of non-self, and is an extreme empiricist doctrine that holds that the notion of an unchanging permanent self is a fiction and has no reality. According to Buddhist doctrine, the individual person consists of five skandhas or heaps – the body, feelings, perceptions, impulses and consciousness. The belief in a self or soul, over these five skandhas, is illusory and the cause of suffering."
[c] , **Quote:** "(...) Buddha's teaching that beings have no soul, no abiding essence. This 'no-soul doctrine' (anatta-vada) he expounded in his second sermon."

[384] [a] Anatta http://www.britannica.com/topic/anatta, Encyclopedia Britannica (2013), Quote: "Anatta in Buddhism, the doctrine that there is in humans no permanent, underlying soul. The concept of anatta, or anatman, is a departure from the Hindu belief in atman ('the self').";
[b] Steven Collins (1994), Religion and Practical Reason (Editors: Frank Reynolds, David Tracy), State Univ of New York Press, , page 64; "Central to Buddhist soteriology is the doctrine of not-self (Pali: anattā, Sanskrit: anātman, the opposed doctrine of ātman is central to Brahmanical thought). Put very briefly, this is the [Buddhist] doctrine that human beings have no soul, no self, no unchanging essence.";
[c] Edward Roer (Translator), to *Brihad Aranyaka Upanishad*, pages 2–4;
[d] Katie Javanaud (2013), Is The Buddhist 'No-Self' Doctrine Compatible With Pursuing Nirvana? https://philosophynow.org/issues/97/Is_The_Buddhist_No-Self_Doctrine_Compatible_With_Pursuing_Nirvana, Philosophy Now;
[e] David Loy (1982), Enlightenment in Buddhism and Advaita Vedanta: Are Nirvana and Moksha the Same?, International Philosophical Quarterly, Volume 23, Issue 1, pages 65–74;
[f] KN Jayatilleke (2010), Early Buddhist Theory of Knowledge, , pages 246–249, from note 385 onwards;

[385] John C. Plott et al (2000), Global History of Philosophy: The Axial Age, Volume 1, Motilal Banarsidass, , page 63, Quote: "The Buddhist schools reject any Ātman concept. As we have already observed, this is the basic and ineradicable distinction between Hinduism and Buddhism".

[386] Kalupahana 1992, pp. 38-39.

[387] Schibli, S., Hermann, Pherekydes of Syros, p. 104, Oxford Univ. Press 2001

[388] "The dates of his life cannot be fixed exactly, but assuming the approximate correctness of the statement of Aristoxenus (ap. Porph. *V.P.* 9) that he left Samos to escape the tyranny of Polycrates at the age of forty, we may put his birth round about 570 BCE, or a few years earlier. The length of his life was variously estimated in antiquity, but it is agreed that he lived to a fairly ripe old age, and most probably he died at about seventy-five or eighty." William Keith Chambers Guthrie, (1978), *A history of Greek philosophy, Volume 1: The earlier Presocratics and the Pythagoreans*, page 173. Cambridge University Press

[389] Linforth, Ivan M. (1941) *The Arts of Orpheus* Arno Press, New York,

[390] Long, Herbert S. (1948) *A Study of the doctrine of metempsychosis in Greece, from Pythagoras to Plato* (Long's 1942 Ph.D. dissertation) Princeton, New Jersey,

[391] Long, Herbert S. (16 February 1948) "Plato's Doctrine of Metempsychosis and Its Source" *The Classical Weekly* 41(10): pp. 149—155

[392] Menander, *The Inspired Woman*

[393] Lucian, *Gallus*, 18 et seq.

[394] Poesch, Jessie (1962) "Ennius and Basinio of Parma" *Journal of the Warburg and Courtauld Institutes* 25(1/2): pp. 116—118, page 117, FN15

[395] Lucretius, (i. 124)

[396] Horace, *Epistles*, II. i. 52

[397] Virgil, *The Aeneid*, vv. 724 et seq.

[398] The book *Reincarnation in Christianity*, by the theosophist Geddes MacGregor (1978) asserted that Origen believed in reincarnation. MacGregor is convinced that Origen believed in and taught about reincarnation but that his texts written about the subject have been destroyed. He admits that there is no extant proof for that position. The allegation was also repeated by Shirley MacLaine in her book *Out On a Limb*. Origen does discuss the concept of transmigration (*metensomatosis*) from Greek philosophy, but it is repeatedly stated that this concept is not a part of the Christian teaching or scripture in his Comment on the Gospel of Matthew (which survives only in a 6th-century Latin translatio): "In this place [when Jesus said Elijah was come and referred to John the Baptist] it does not appear to me that by Elijah the soul is spoken of, lest I fall into the doctrine of transmigration, which is foreign to the Church of God, and not handed down by the apostles, nor anywhere set forth in the scriptures" (13:1:46–53, see Commentary on Matthew, Book XIII

[399] Much of this is documented in R.E. Slater's book *Paradise Reconsidered.*

[400] Richard Foltz, *Religions of the Silk Road*, New York: Palgrave Macmillan, 2010

[401] Julius Caesar, "De Bello Gallico", VI

[402] *Essential Judaism: A Complete Guide to Beliefs, Customs & Rituals*, By George Robinson, Simon and Schuster 2008, page 193

[403] "Mind in the Balance: Meditation in Science, Buddhism, and Christianity", p. 104, by B. Alan Wallace

[404] "Between Worlds: Dybbuks, Exorcists, and Early Modern Judaism", p. 190, by J. H. Chajes

[405] *Jewish Tales of Reincarnation'*, By Yonasson Gershom, Yonasson Gershom, Jason Aronson, Incorporated, 31 Jan 2000

[406] Yonasson Gershom (1999), *Jewish Tales of Reincarnation*. Northvale, NJ: Jason Aronson.

[407] Steven Runciman, *The Medieval Manichee: A Study of the Christian Dualist Heresy*, 1982, , Cambridge University Press, *The Bogomils*, Google Books https://books.google.com/books?id=d1LGB7u5iD0C&printsec=frontcover&dq=mediaeval+manichee&cd=1

[408] For example Dondaine, Antoine. O.P. *Un traite neo-manicheen du XIIIe siecle: Le Liber de duobus principiis, suivi d'un fragment de rituel Cathare* (Rome: Institutum Historicum Fratrum Praedicatorum, 1939)

[409] "the souls must always be the same, for if none be destroyed they will not diminish in number." Republic X, 611. The Republic of Plato By Plato, Benjamin Jowett Edition: 3 Published by Clarendon press, 1888.

[410] In a letter to his friend George Whatley written May 23, 1785: Jennifer T. Kennedy, Death Effects: Revisiting the conceit of Franklin's *Memoir, Early American Literature*, 2001. JSTOR https://www.jstor.org/pss/25057231

[411] Marsilio Ficino, *Platonic Theology*, 17.3–4

[412] "Again, Rosalind in "As You Like It" (Act III., Scene 2), says: *I was never so be-rhimed that I can remember since Pythagoras's time, when I was an Irish rat"* — alluding to the doctrine of the transmigration of souls." William H. Grattan Flood, quoted at Libraryireland.com http://www.libraryireland.com/IrishMusic/XVII-2.php

[413] Boulting, 1914. pp. 163–64

[414] Schopenhauer, A: "Parerga und Paralipomena" (Eduard Grisebach edition), On Religion, Section 177

[415] Nietzsche and the Doctrine of Metempsychosis, in J. Urpeth & J. Lippitt, *Nietzsche and the Divine*, Manchester: Clinamen, 2000

[416] David Hammerman, Lisa Lenard, *The Complete Idiot's Guide to Reincarnation*, Penguin, p.34. For relevant works by James, see; William James, *Human Immortality: Two Supposed Objections to the Doctrine (the Ingersoll Lecture, 1897)*, The Will to Believe, Human Immortality (1956) Dover Publications, , *The Varieties of Religious Experience: A Study in Human Nature* (1902), , *Essays in Radical Empiricism* (1912) Dover Publications 2003,

[417] Richmal Crompton, *More William*, George Newnes, London, 1924, XIII. William and the Ancient Souls http://www.gutenberg.org/files/17125/17125-h/17125-h.htm; "The memory usually came in a flash. For instance, you might remember in a flash when you were looking at a box of matches that you had been Guy Fawkes."

[418] Théodore Flournoy, Des Indes à la planète Mars http://www.psychanalyse-paris.com/-Des-Indes-a-la-planete-Mars-.html, Étude sur un cas de somnambulisme avec glossolalie, Éditions Alcan et Eggimann, Paris et Genève, 1900

[419] Mark Juergensmeyer & Wade Clark Roof 2011, p. 272.

[420] Jeaneane D. Fowler 1997, p. 10.

[421] Christopher Chapple (1986), Karma and creativity, State University of New York Press, , pages 60-64

[422] Jeaneane D. Fowler 1997, p. 11.

[423] Jacobsen, Knut A. "Three Functions Of Hell In The Hindu Traditions." Numen 56.2–3 (2009): 385–400. ATLA Religion Database with ATLASerials. Web. 16 Sept. 2012.

[424] Jeaneane D. Fowler 1997, pp. 111-112.

[425] Harold Coward 2008, p. 129.

[426] Harold Coward 2008, pp. 129, also see pages 130–155.

[427] Chapple 2010, p. 98.

[428] Chapple 2010, p. 107.

[429] Chapple 2010, p. 582.

[430] Trainor 2004, p. 58, **Quote:** "Buddhism shares with Hinduism the doctrine of Samsara, whereby all beings pass through an unceasing cycle of birth, death and rebirth until they find a means of liberation from the cycle. However, Buddhism differs from Hinduism in rejecting the assertion that every human being possesses a changeless soul which constitutes his or her ultimate identity, and which transmigrates from one incarnation to the next..

[431] (M.1.256) "Post-Classical Developments in the Concepts of Karma and Rebirth in Theravada Buddhism." by Bruce Matthews. in *Karma and Rebirth: Post-Classical Developments* State Univ of New York Press: 1986 pg 121

[432] Collins, Steven. *Selfless persons: imagery and thought in Theravāda Buddhism* Cambridge University Press, 1990. pg 215, Google Books https//books.google.com

[433] (D.3.105) "Post-Classical Developments in the Concepts of Karma and Rebirth in Theravada Buddhism. by Bruce Matthews. in Karma and Rebirth: *Post-Classical Developments* State Univ of New York Press: 1986 pg 125

[434] His Holiness the Dalai Lama, *How to Practice: The Way to a Meaningful Life* (New York: Atria Books, 2002), p. 46

[435] Bruce Matthews in Ronald Wesley Neufeldt, editor, *Karma and Rebirth: Post Classical Developments*. SUNY Press, 1986, page 125. Google.com https://books.google.com/books?id=iaRWtgXjpIQC&pg=PA126&dq=Bija+Niyama&lr=#PPA125,M1

[436] Peter Harvey, *The Selfless Mind*. Curzon Press 1995, page 247.

[437] The Connected Discourses of the Buddha. A Translation of the Samyutta Nikaya, Bhikkhu Bodhi, Translator. Wisdom Publications. Sutta 44.9

[438] Trainor 2004, pp. 210–211.

[439] Trainor 2004, pp. 62–63.

[440] *Transform Your Life*: A Blissful Journey, page 52), Tharpa Publications (2001, US ed. 2007)

[441] Padmanabh Jaini 1980, pp. 226–228.

[442] Kuhn, Hermann (2001) pp. 226–230

[443] Krishan, Yuvraj (1997): p. 43.

[444] Kuhn, Hermann (2001) pp.70–71

[445] Kuhn, Hermann (2001) pp.64–66

[446] Kuhn, Hermann (2001) p.15

[447] Rankin, Aidan (2006) p.67

[448] Jaini, Padmanabh (1998) p.108

[449] The Jain hierarchy of life classifies living beings on the basis of the senses: five-sensed beings like humans and animals are at the top, and single sensed beings like microbes and plants are at the bottom.

[450] Jaini, Padmanabh (1998) pp.108–09

[451] Jaini, Padmanabh (2000) p.130

[452] Krishan, Yuvraj (1997) p.44

[453] Kuhn, Hermann (2001) p.28

[454] Kuhn, Hermann (2001) p.69

[455] Kuhn, Hermann (2001) pp.65–66, 70–71

[456] //en.wikipedia.org/w/index.php?title=Template:Kabbalah&action=edit

[457] Kabbalah for Dummies

[458] *Sha'ar Ha'Gilgulim, The Gate of Reincarnations*, Chaim Vital

[459] "The Big Book of Reincarnation", by Roy Stemman, p. 14

[460] Cross, F. L., and Elizabeth A. Livingstone. *The Oxford Dictionary of the Christian Church* (Second Edition). New York: Oxford University Press, 1984. p. 1009.

[461] Norman C. McClelland 2010, pp. 122–123.

[462] Norman C. McClelland 2010, pp. 122-123.

[463] //en.wikipedia.org/w/index.php?title=Template:Shia_Islam&action=edit

[464] Wilson, Peter Lamborn, *Scandal: Essays in Islamic Heresy*, Brooklyn, NY: Autonomedia. (1988). hardcover 0-936756-12-2 paperback

[465] Alawis http://countrystudies.us/syria/32.htm, Countrystudies.us, U.S. Library of Congress.

[466] see his *To Die Before Death: The Sufi Way of Life*

[467] Gnostic liberation front http://www.gnosticliberationfront.com/sufi_message_of_hazrat_ inayat%20khan.htm The Sufi Message of Hazrat Inayat Khan

[468] //en.wikipedia.org/w/index.php?title=Template:Druze&action=edit

[469] Seabrook, W. B., *Adventures in Arabia*, Harrap and Sons 1928, (chapters on Druze religion)

[470] Dwairy, Marwan (2006) "The Psychosocial Function Of Reincarnation Among Druze In Israel" *Culture, Medicine and Psychiatry*, page 29 – 53

[471] Jutta Woods. "The Theosophical Heritage in Modern Astrology." *The Mountain Astrologer*. Aug/Sept 2013

[472] See e.g. *Reincarnation and Karma* by Steiner

[473] Steiner, *Karmic Relationships*, volumes 1–6

[474] Baba, Meher (1967), *Discourses* http://www.discoursesbymeherbaba.org, Volume III, Sufism Reoriented, 1967, , p. 96.

[475] Encyclopedia of Wicca and Witchcraft, Raven Grimassi

[476] Cadoret, Remi. Book Review: European Cases of the Reincarnation Type http://ajp. psychiatryonline.org/article.aspx?articleid=177497 *The American Journal of Psychiatry*, April 2005.

[477] Rockley, Richard. (2002). "Book Review: Children who Remember Previous Lives" http: //www.skepticreport.com/sr/?p=482. SkepticReport. Retrieved 2014-10-11.

[478] Edwards, Paul. (1996, reprinted in 2001). *Reincarnation: A Critical Examination*. Prometheus Books.

[479] Thomason, Sarah G.. "Xenoglossy" http://www-personal.umich.edu/~thomason/papers/ xenogl.pdf. In Gordon Stein. (1996). *The Encyclopedia of the Paranormal*. Prometheus Books.

[480] Wilson, Ian. (1981). *Mind Out of Time: Reincarnation Investigated*. Gollancz.

[481] Baker, Robert A. (1996). *Hidden Memories: Voices and Visions from Within*. Prometheus Books.

[482] Cogan, Robert. (1998). *Critical Thinking: Step by Step*. University Press of America. pp. 202–203. "Edwards catalogs common sense objections which have been made against reincarnation. 1) How does a soul exist between bodies? 2) Tertullian's objection: If there is reincarnation, why are not babies born with the mental abilities of adults? 3) Reincarnation claims an infinite series of prior incarnations. Evolution teaches that there was a time when humans did not yet exist. So reincarnation is inconsistent with modern science. 4) If there is reincarnation, then what is happening when the population increases? 5) If there is reincarnation, then why do

so few, if any people, remember past lives?... To answer these objections believers in reincarnation must accept additional assumptions... Acceptance of these silly assumptions, Edwards says, amounts to a crucifixion of one's intellect." • Edwards, Paul. (1996, reprinted in 2001). *Reincarnation: A Critical Examination*. Prometheus Books.

[483] Tony Walter and Helen Waterhouse, " A Very Private Belief: Reincarnation in Contemporary England http://socrel.oxfordjournals.org/content/60/2/187.full.pdf". *Sociology of Religion*, Vol. 60, 1999

[484] "The Boundaries of Knowledge in Buddhism, Christianity, and Science", by Paul David Numrich, p. 13, Vandenhoeck & Ruprecht,

[485] Jane Henry (2005). Parapsychology: research on exceptional experiences https//books.google.com Routledge, p. 224.

[486] https://books.google.com/books?id=Te9wBAAAQBAJ

[487] https://books.google.com/books?id=COuy5CDAqt4C

[488] https://books.google.com/books?id=LkE_8uch5P0C

[489] https://books.google.com/books?id=RmGKHu20hA0C

[490] https://books.google.com/books?id=4WZIj3M71y0C

[491] https://books.google.com/books?id=_QXX0Uq29aoC

[492] https://books.google.com/books?id=WwJzAwAAQBAJ

[493] https://books.google.com/books?id=_29ZDAcUEwYC

[494] https://books.google.com/books?id=S_Leq4U5ihkC

[495] http://www.revistas.usp.br/filosofiaantiga/article/view/56475

[496] https://books.google.com/books?id=_PrloTKuAjwC

[497] https://books.google.com/books?id=NOLfCgAAQBAJ

[498] http://www.discoursesbymeherbaba.org

[499] http://www.rosicrucian.com/rcc/rcceng04.htm

[500] http://wn.rsarchive.org/Lectures/KarmReII/Karm01_index.html

[501] http://www.grailforum.com/whybornbook.html

[502] https://web.archive.org/web/20080821030150/http://www.bartleby.com/65/tr/transmig.html

[503] http://www.newadvent.org/cathen/10234d.htm

[504] http://www.chabad.org/search/keyword.asp?scope=6198&kid=6569

[505] http://www.krasnostup.com/wp-content/uploads/2017/11/en_Philosophy_of_Incarnation.pdf

[506] Bennett 1939.

[507] Gurney, E., Myers, F.W.H. and Podmore, F. (1886). *Phantasms of the Living*, Vols. I and II. London: Trubner and Co.

[508] Sidgwick, Eleanor; Johnson, Alice; and others (1894). Report on the Census of Hallucinations, London: *Proceedings of the Society for Psychical Research*, Vol. X.

[509] Myers, F.W.H. (1903). *Human Personality and its Survival of Bodily Death*. London: Longmans Green. Reissued: Charlottesville, VA: Hampton Roads, 2002

[510] Tyrell & Price 1943.

[511] Tyrell & Price 1943, pp. 53—60.

[512] Tyrell & Price 1943, pp. 101—103.

[513] Green & McCreery 1975.

[514] Green & McCreery 1975, pp. 200—203.

[515] Green & McCreery 1975, p. 123.

[516] Green & McCreery 1975, pp. 150—155.

[517] Green & McCreery 1975, pp. 95—101.

[518] Gibson, J.J. (1950). *The Perception of the Visual World*. Boston: Houghton Mifflin.

[519] Bennett 1939, pp. 173—177.

[520] See, for example, Claridge, G. and Beech, T. (1995). 'Fully and quasi-dimensional constructions of schizotypy.' In Raine, A., Lencz, T., and Mednick, S.A., Schizotypal Personality. Cambridge: Cambridge University Press.

[521] Drever, (1952). *A Dictionary of Psychology*. London: Penguin.

[522] Gibson, J.J. (1979). *The Ecological Approach to Visual Perception.*. Boston: Houghton Mifflin.

[523] Horowitz 1964, pp. 513—523.

[524] Horowitz 1964, p. 513.

[525] Cf. Green, C.E. (1968). *Lucid Dreams*. London: Hamish Hamilton, pp. 70-78.

[526] Cf. Green, C.E. (1968). *Out-of-the-Body Experiences*. London: Hamish Hamilton, pp. 71-80.

[527] McCreery, C. (2006). "Perception and Hallucination: the Case for Continuity." *Philosophical Paper No. 2006-1*. Oxford: Oxford Forum. Online PDF http://www.celiagreen.com/charlesmccreery/perception.pdf

[528] //doi.org/10.1097/00005053-196406000-00002

[529] Frazier, Kendrick. (1991). *The Hundredth Monkey: And Other Paradigms of the Paranormal*. Prometheus Books. pp. 143–48.

[530] Hyman, Ray. (1996). *The Evidence for Psychic Functioning: Claims vs. Reality* http://www.csicop.org/si/show/evidence_for_psychic_functioning_claims_vs._reality/. *The Skeptical Inquirer*. pp. 24–26. Retrieved November 4, 2013.

[531] Smith, Jonathan. (2009). *Pseudoscience and Extraordinary Claims of the Paranormal: A Critical Thinker's Toolkit* https://books.google.com. Wiley-Blackwell. Retrieved November 1, 2013.

[532] Rathus, Spencer. (2011). *Psychology: Concepts and Connections*. Cengage Learning. p. 143.

[533] Marks, David; Kammann, Richard. (2000). *The Psychology of the Psychic*. Prometheus Books. pp. 97–106.

[534] Philip John Tyson, Dai Jones, Jonathan Elcock. (2011). *Psychology in Social Context: Issues and Debates*. Wiley-Blackwell. pp. 199–200.

[535] Milton, J., & Wiseman, R. (2002). *A response to Storm and Ertel (2002)*. The Journal of Parapsychology, 66. pp. 183–86.

[536] Ray Hyman. *Evaluating Parapsychological Claims* in Robert J. Sternberg, Henry L. Roediger, Diane F. Halpern. (2007). *Critical Thinking in Psychology*. Cambridge University Press. pp. 216–31.

[537] Hyman, R., and Honorton, C. (1986). *A joint communiqué: the psi ganzfeld controversy*. Journal of Parapsychology, 50. pp. 351–64.

[538] Neher, Andrew (2011). *Paranormal and Transcendental Experience: A Psychological Examination*. Dover Publications. p. 307.

[539] Honorton, C., Berger, R.E., Varvoglis, M.P., Quant, M., Derr, P., Schechter, E.I., & Ferrari, D.C. (1990). *Psi Communication in the Ganzfeld*. Journal of Parapsychology, 54. pp. 99–139.

[540] Wiseman, R., Smith, M. and Kornbrot, D. (1996). *Exploring possible sender-to-experimenter acoustic leakage in the PRL autoganzfeld experiments*. Journal of Parapsychology, 60. pp. 97–128.

[541] Humphrey, Nicholas. (1996). *Soul Searching: Human Nature and Supernatural Belief*. Vintage. p. 136. "Richard Wiseman, a friend and former colleague of Honorton, has subsequently reanalysed the raw data trial by trial and shown that all the positive results can be attributed to those trials in which one or other of these sources of 'sensory leakage' was at least a possibility. In fact, in the relatively few trials (100 in all) where such leakage of information would not have been possible the receivers did no better than chance (26 per cent correct)."

[542] Storm, L.. & Ertel, S. (2001). *Does psi exist? Comments on Milton and Wiseman's (1999) meta-analysis of ganzfeld research*. Psychological. Bulletin, 127. pp. 424–33.

[543] Milton, J. and Wiseman, R. (2001). *Does psi exist? Reply to Storm and Ertel (2001)* http://homepage.psy.utexas.edu/homepage/class/Psy391P/Does%20Psi%20Exist%20II%EF%80%A5.pdf. Psychological Bulletin, 127. pp. 434–38.

[544] James Alcock, Jean Burns and Anthony Freeman. (2003). *Psi Wars: Getting to Grips with the Paranormal*. p. 59. Imprint Academic.

[545] Hansel, C. E. M. *The Search for a Demonstration of ESP* in Kurtz, Paul. (1985). *A Skeptic's Handbook of Parapsychology*. Prometheus Books. pp. 97–127

[546] Hines, Terence. (2003). *Pseudoscience and the Paranormal*. Prometheus Books. pp. 131–38.

[547] Lilienfeld, Scott O; Lynn, Steven Jay; Ruscio, John; Beyerstein, Barry L. (2009). *Myth #3 Extrasensory Perception (ESP) Is a Well Established Scientific Phenomenon*. *In 50 Great Myths of Popular Psychology: Shattering Widespread Misconceptions About Human Behavior*. *Wiley-Blackwell*.

[548] http://www.straightdope.com/mailbag/mganzfeld.html

[549] http://www.mceagle.com/remote-viewing/refs/science/air/hyman.html

[550] https://web.archive.org/web/20131103081111/http://drsmorey.org/bibtex/upload/Hyman%3A2010.pdf

[551] //doi.org/10.1037/a0019676

[552] http://drsmorey.org/bibtex/upload/Hyman:2010.pdf

[553] http://www.csicop.org/si/show/new_analyses_raise_doubts_about_replicability_of_esp_findings/

[554] http://homepage.psy.utexas.edu/homepage/class/Psy391P/Does%20Psi%20Exist%20II%EF%80%A5.pdf

[555] //doi.org/10.1037/0033-2909.127.3.434

[556] http://www.koestler-parapsychology.psy.ed.ac.uk/Psi.html

[557] http://www.skepdic.com/ganzfeld.html

[558] Blom, Jan. (2009). *A Dictionary of Hallucinations*. Springer. p. 451.

[559] //en.wikipedia.org/w/index.php?title=Template:Paranormal&action=edit

[560] Kendrick Frazier. *Science Confronts the Paranormal https://books.google.com/books?id=i2Nm8OyXpyQC&pg=PA94*. Prometheus Books, Publishers; . p. 94–.

[561]

* Obtained from listing of research papers on Wiseman's website http://www.richardwiseman.com/research/papers.html

[562] From *An Encyclopedia of Claims, Frauds, and Hoaxes of the Occult and Supernatural* by James Randi: "The data of Puthoff and Targ were reexamined by the other researchers, and it was found that their students were able to solve the locations without use of any psychic powers, using only the clues that had inadvertently been included in the Puthoff and Targ transcripts."<ref name="randi_encyclopedia">

[563]

[564]

[565]

[566] Ray Hyman wrote in an article in *Skeptical Inquirer*: "Because even if Utts and her colleagues are correct and we were to find that we could reproduce the findings under specified conditions, this would still be a far cry from concluding that psychic functioning has been demonstrated. This is because the current claim is based entirely upon a negative outcome—the sole basis for arguing for ESP is that extra-chance results can be obtained that apparently cannot be explained by normal means. But an infinite variety of normal possibilities exist and it is not clear than one can control for all of them in a single experiment. You need a positive theory to guide you as to what needs to be controlled, and what can be ignored. Parapsychologists have not come close to this as yet."<ref name="hyman claims v reality">

[567] Hyman also says in the *Skeptical Inquirer* article: "What seems clear is that the scientific community is not going to abandon its fundamental ideas about causality, time, and other principles on the basis of a handful of experiments whose findings have yet to be shown to be replicable and lawful."Blom, Jan. (2009). *A Dictionary of Hallucinations*. Springer. p. 451.

[568] Shermer, Michael. (2001). *The Borderlands of Science: Where Sense Meets Nonsense*. Oxford University Press. pp. 8-10.

[569] Hines, Terence. (2003). *Pseudoscience and the Paranormal*. Prometheus Books. p. 135.

[570] Martin Bridgstock wrote in *Beyond Belief: Skepticism, Science and the Paranormal*: "The explanation used by Marks and Kammann clearly involves the use of Occam's razor. Marks and Kammann argued that the 'cues' - clues to the order in which sites had been visited—provided sufficient information for the results, without any recourse to extrasensory perception. Indeed Marks himself was able to achieve 100 percent accuracy in allocating some transcripts to sites without visiting any of the sites himself, purely on the ground basis of the cues. From Occam's razor, it follows that if a straightforward natural explanation exists, there is no need for the spectacular paranormal explanation: Targ and Puthoff's claims are not justified".<ref>

[571] Hansel, C. E. M. (1980). *ESP and Parapsychology: A Critical Reevaluation*. Prometheus Books. p. 293

[572]

[573] Marks, David. (2000). *The Psychology of the Psychic* (2nd Edition). Prometheus Books. pp. 71-96.

[574] http://books.nap.edu/openbook.php?record_id=778&page=601

[575] http://skepdic.com/remotevw.html

[576] Krippner, Stanley; Franasso, Cheryl. (2011). *Dreams, Telepathy, and Various States of Consciousness*. NeuroQuantology 9 (1): 4.

[577] Devereux, George, ed. (1953). "The Eisenbud-Pederson-Krag-Fodor-Ellis Controversy". In *Psychoanalysis and the Occult*. Oxford, England: International Universities Press.

[578] Hansel, C. E. M. (1989). *The Search for Psychic Power: ESP and Parapsychology Revisited*. Prometheus Books. pp. 141-152.

[579] Eshel, Ofra (December 2006). "Where are you, my beloved?: On absence, loss, and the enigma of telepathic dreams". *The International Journal of Psychoanalysis* 87 (6): 1603–1627.

[580] Frieden, Ken (1990). *Freud's dream of interpretation*. SUNY series in modern Jewish literature and culture. SUNY Press. pp. 102-103.

[581] Freud, S. Collected Papers, V. IV pp 408-435 International Psychoanalytic Library No. 7, Ed 1, Basic Books 1959 *"Have I given you the impression that I am secretly inclined to support the reality of telepathy in the occult sense? If so, I should very much regret that it is so difficult to avoid giving such an impression. In reality, however, I was anxious to be strictly impartial. I have every reason to be so, for I have no opinion; I know nothing about it."* p. 435. Here Freud explicitly refers to the conflation of telepathy as such with clairvoyance and other occult elements

[582] Ellis, Albert. (1947). *Telepathy and Psychoanalysis: A Critique of Recent Findings*. Psychiatric Quarterly 21: 607-659.

[583] Ellis, Albert. (1949). *Re-analysis of an alleged telepathic dream*. Psychiatric Quarterly: 23: 116-126.

[584] Löfgren, L. B. (1968). *Recent Publications on Parapsychology. Journal of the American Psychoanalytic Association* 16: 146-178.

[585]

[586] McBroom, Patricia. (1967). *Dreams, Art and Mental Telepathy*. Science News 92: 424.

[587] Hansel, C. E. M. *The Search for a Demonstration of ESP*. In Paul Kurtz. (1985). *A Skeptic's Handbook of Parapsychology*. Prometheus Books. pp. 97-127.

[588] Belvedere, E., Foulkes, D. (1971). *Telepathy and Dreams: A Failure to Replicate*. Perceptual and Motor Skills 33: 783–789.

[589] Sherwood, S. J; Roe, C. A. (2003). *A Review of Dream ESP Studies Conducted Since the Maimonides Dream ESP Programme*. Journal of Consciousness Studies, 10: 85-109.

[590] Alcock, James. (2003). *Give the Null Hypothesis a Chance: Reasons to Remain Doubtful about the Existence of Psi*. Journal of Consciousness Studies 10: 29-50. "In their article, Sherwood and Roe examine attempts to replicate the well-known Maimonides dream studies that began in the 1960s. They provide a good review of these studies of dream telepathy and clairvoyance, but if one thing emerges for me from their review, it is the extreme messiness of the data adduced. Lack of replication is rampant. While one would normally expect that continuing scientific scrutiny of a phenomenon should lead to stronger effect sizes as one learns more about the subject matter and refines the methodology, this is apparently not the case with this research."

[591] Wiseman, Richard. (2014). *Night School: Wake Up to the Power of Sleep*. Macmillan. pp. 200-201.

[592] //doi.org/10.1007/bf01654321

[593] //doi.org/10.1037/0003-066X.40.11.1219

[594] Nicola Holt, Christine Simmonds-Moore, David Luke, Christopher French. (2012). *Anomalistic Psychology (Palgrave Insights in Psychology)*. Palgrave Macmillan.

[595] Shane McCorristine. (2010). *Spectres of the Self: Thinking About Ghosts and Ghost-Seeing in England, 1750–1920*. Cambridge University Press. pp. 44–56.

[596] William Benjamin Carpenter. (1877). *Mesmerism, Spiritualism, Etc: Historically and Scientifically Considered*. Cambridge University Press.

[597] Ivan Leudar, Philip Thomas. (2000). *Voices of Reason, Voices of Insanity: Studies of Verbal Hallucinations*. Routledge. pp. 106–107.

[598] Wolffram, Heather. (2009). *The Stepchildren of Science: Psychical Research and Parapsychology in Germany, C. 1870-1939*. Rodopi. pp. 83-130.

[599] Wolffram, Heather. (2012). *Trick', 'Manipulation' and 'Farce': Albert Moll's Critique of Occultism* https://www.ncbi.nlm.nih.gov/pmc/articles/PMC3381525/. Medical History 56(2): 277–295.

[600] Lionel Weatherly, John Nevil Maskelyne. (2011). *The Supernatural? (Cambridge Library Collection – Spiritualism and Esoteric Knowledge)*. Cambridge University Press.

[601] Karl Jaspers. (1913). *General Psychopathology*. Baltimore. MD: Johns Hopkins.

[602] Kurtz, Paul. (1985). *A Skeptic's Handbook of Parapsychology*. Prometheus Books. p. 487.

[603] Leonard Zusne, Warren H. Jones. (1989). *Anomalistic Psychology: A Study of Magical Thinking*. Psychology Press.

[604] Graham Reed. (1972). *The Psychology of Anomalous Experience: A Cognitive Approach*. Hutchinson University Library.

[605] What is Anomalistic Psychology? http://www.gold.ac.uk/apru/what/

[606] Marks, David. (1988). *The psychology of paranormal beliefs*. Experientia, 44, 332–337.

[607] Robert Baker. (1996). *Hidden Memories: Voices and Visions from Within*. Prometheus Books.

[608] Biography of Massimo Polidoro http://www.massimopolidoro.com/english-version/bio-notes

[609] Anomalistic psychology: What is it and why bother? by Chris French http://www.psychologytoday.com/blog/weird-science/200909/anomalistic-psychology-what-is-it-and-why-bother

[610] Klemperer, Frances. (1992). *Ghosts, Visions, And Voices: Sometimes Simply Perceptual Mistakes* http://pubmedcentralcanada.ca/pmcc/articles/PMC1884722/pdf/bmj00105-0010.pdf. *BMJ: British Medical Journal, Vol. 305, No. 6868 (Dec. 19–26), pp. 1518–1519.*

[611] Lange, R., and J. Houran. (1997). *Context-induced paranormal experiences: Support for Houran and Lange's model of haunting phenomena*. Perceptual and Motor Skills, 84, 1455–1458.

[612] Lange, R., Houran, J. (1998). *Delusions of the paranormal: A haunting question of perception*. Journal of Nervous and Mental Disease, 186 (10), 637–645.

[613] Wiseman, R., C. Watt, P. Stevens, et al. (2003). *An investigation into alleged "hauntings"* http://www.richardwiseman.com/resources/BJP-hauntings.pdf. British Journal of Psychology, 94: 195–211.

[614] Millais Culpin. (1920). *Spiritualism and the New Psychology, an Explanation of Spiritualist Phenomena and Beliefs in Terms of Modern Knowledge*. Kennelly Press.

[615] Ian Rowland. (1998). *The Full Facts Book of Cold Reading*. London, England: Ian Roland.

[616] Brad Clark (2002). *Spiritualism*. pp. 220–226 in Michael Shermer. *The Skeptic Encyclopedia of Pseudoscience*. ABC-CLIO.

[617] Jonathan Smith. (2009). *Pseudoscience and Extraordinary Claims of the Paranormal: A Critical Thinker's Toolkit*. Wiley-Blackwell. pp. 141–241.

[618] Wiseman, R., Greening, E., and Smith, M. (2003). *Belief in the paranormal and suggestion in the seance room* https://uhra.herts.ac.uk/dspace/bitstream/2299/2278/1/103252.pdf. British Journal of Psychology, 94 (3): 285–297.

[619] O'Keeffe, C. & Wiseman, R. (2005). *Testing alleged mediumship: Methods and results* http://www.richardwiseman.com/resources/MediumBJP.pdf. British Journal of Psychology, Vol. 96, 165–179.

[620] Louis Rose. (1954). *Some Aspects Of Paranormal Healing*. British Medical Journal, Vol. 2, No. 4900, pp. 1329–1332.

[621] Beutler, J., Attevelt, J., Schouten, S., Faber, J., Mees, E., & Geijskes, G. (1988). *Paranormal healing and hypertension*. British Medical Journal, 296, 1491–1494.

[622] Randy Moore. (1992). *Debunking the Paranormal: We Should Teach Critical Thinking as a Necessity for Living, Not Just as a Tool for Science*. The American Biology Teacher, Vol. 54, No. 1, pp. 4–9.

[623] Bösch, H., Steinkamp, F., Boller, E. (2006). *Examining Psychokinesis: The Interaction of Human Intention with Random Number Generators. A Meta-Analysis Examining Psychokinesis: The Interaction of Human Intention with. Random Number Generators. A Meta-Analysis* http://www.ebo.de/publikationen/pk_ma.pdf. Psychological Bulletin, 132 (4): 497–523.

[624] Ben Harris. (1985). *Gellerism Revealed: The Psychology and Methodology Behind the Geller Effect*. Calgary: Micky Hades International.

[625] Wiseman, R. & Greening, E. (2005). *It's still bending': verbal suggestion and alleged psychokinetic ability* http://www.richardwiseman.com/resources/BJP-key.pdf. British Journal of Psychology, 96, 115–127.

[626] Marks, David. (1981). *Sensory cues invalidate remote viewing experiments*. Nature 292: 177.

[627] Schienle, A., Vaitl, D., and Stark, R. (1996). *Covariation bias and paranormal belief*. Psychological Reports, 78, 291–305.

[628] Rudski, J. M. (2002). *Hindsight and confirmation biases in an exercise in telepathy*. Psychological Reports, 91, 899–906.

[629] Interview with Chris French on Anomalistic psychology http://www.videojug.com/interview/anomalistic-psychology-2

[630] The rise of anomalistic psychology – and the fall of parapsychology? http://blogs.nature.com/soapboxscience/2011/12/19/the-rise-of-anomalistic-psychology-%E2%80%93-and-the-fall-of-parapsychology

[631] https://web.archive.org/web/20090523100130/http://www.goldsmiths.ac.uk/apru/what.php

[632] http://www.pulse-project.org/node/388

Article Sources and Contributors

The sources listed for each article provide more detailed licensing information including the copyright status, the copyright owner, and the license conditions.

Parapsychology *Source:* https://en.wikipedia.org/w/index.php?oldid=860053364 *License:* Creative Commons Attribution-Share Alike 3.0 *Contributors:*   425mike, A little angry, Allforrous, Amirgown, AnonFromDiscord, Bender235, Blorg, Brian Josephson, Brough87, BullRangifer, CFCF, Cannolis, Cantanchorus, CecilWard, ClueBot NG, CommonsDelinker, Ctxppc, Dan cole, David in DC, Dcirovic, Deacon Vorbis, Drnol, Donner60, Drobertpowell, Edaham, Ethanbas, Finlay McWalter, Flamingtorch372, Flyte35, Graham87, Grayfell, Hairhorn, Happydrafting, Hillbillyholiday, Home Lander, Iph, IronGargoyle, Ixocactus, Jeraphine Gryphon, Jess, Joefromrandb, Johnuniq, Johnvr4, Jontel, Joseph Rowe, JuliaHunter, JustAMuggle, Jxm, JzG, KBH96, Kaobear, Karyn Devlin, Keith D, Knaveknight, Krelnik, Laird Shaw, LuckyLouie, Mann jess, Materialscientist, Maunus, McGeddon, McSly, Me, Myself, and I are Here, Meticulo, Miistermagico, Morenono, MrBill3, NadirAli, Narssarssuaq, Natuur12, Nederlandse Leeuw, Nightscream, Nobiasherenope, North Shoreman, Novoneiro, OlejzMaku, OnBeyondZebrax, Orduin, Oshwah, Ost316, Paine Ellsworth, PaleoNeonate, ParanormalHope, Permstrump, Presearch, Prolumbo, Qzd, RichardMaurice, Rico402, Rjwilmsi, Ronz, Roxy the dog, RuDrAv's, SK infos, SMcCandlish, Schwede66, Siddhi.powers, Simonm223, Sjö, Sro23, Staszek Lem, Tallscreen, Tgeorgescu, The Evil IP address, TheRedPenOfDoom, Thegreatgrabber, Tom.Reding, Trappist the monk, TreeTrailer, Tunsa, Vsmith, WOSlinker, Ymblanter, You're No Longer You, Zedshort, 177 anonymous edits 1

Telepathy *Source:* https://en.wikipedia.org/w/index.php?oldid=859145159 *License:* Creative Commons Attribution-Share Alike 3.0 *Contributors:* 29twenty-nine29, 3primetime3, 5Q5, Al.w.hog, Alex Dunnett, Alxeedo, Amccann421, Anaxial, AndrewOne, AndyTheGrump, Ankhsn, Antandrus, Aquillion, Arjayay, Ayanna10p, Ayanna9p, BD2412, BU Rob13, Bender235, Bitsandbites23, BullRangifer, CAPTAIN RAJU, Ciphers, ClueBot NG, DatGuy, Dave Andrew, David.moreno72, Demon of Demons, Dodgewc25, Dominus Vobisdu, Donner60, Eameece, Ekips39, Epicwikierror, Erieberry, Felix558, Fixuture, FoCuSandLeArN, Frosty, Georgekeeling, Gilliam, Glane23, Goblin Face, Gobonobo, Goseahawks101, Hindi aalekh, Hob Gadling, Home Lander, IllaZilla, Ixocactus, J 1982, Jackfork, Jdcomix, Jerodlycett, Jim1138, Jmcgnh, Joe Heato, John farthing, Johnuniq, JuliaHunter, Julie wagner, JzG, KatieJ0nes123, I adyshelby, Lipsiquid, Liz olvera, LuckyLouie, Materialscientist, McSly, Mean as custard, Mojoworker, MrBill3, Mysterdee, Nederlandse Leeuw, NeilN, Nick Moyes, Nick5990, Omnipaedista, OnBeyondZebrax, Oshwah, Ospalh, Packer1028, Pinethicket, Pleiotrop3, Pradip Balapnde, Rap Chart Mike, Rinum.nassah, Rjwilmsi, Rp2006, Science Student99, Seagull123, Serols, Shin881217, Simplexity22, Solarra, Stefana.palade, Stephenb, Steve the Skeptic, Suhasbhokare, TYelliot, Theexposure1, ToBeFree, Tom.Reding, Tony^600, Toreightyone, Trafford09, Transphasic, TreeTrailer, Trovatore, Vanamonde93, Vasu333999, Widefox, Wikisheff, Yunshui, Zxcvbnm, 153 anonymous edits 37

Precognition *Source:* https://en.wikipedia.org/w/index.php?oldid=859113677 *License:* Creative Commons Attribution-Share Alike 3.0 *Contributors:* Aeternus, Allecher, Arthur Rubin, Asarlaí, Ashish98420, Beaumont877, Bender235, Bob Burkhardt, Borock, Cattas, Clearlight1, ClueBot NG, D'SuperHero, DH85868993, DMacks, Davidkinnen, DirectBeak, Dcirovic, Dennis7114, Diannaa, Discospinster, Drewmutt, Edoe, EronMain, Fraggle81, Geekdiva, GenQuest, GeneralizationsAreBad, Gilliam, Goblin Face, GreenUniverse, Gronk Oz, Guyonthesubway, Haon 2.0, Hisuphello4, I dream of horses, Jeraphine Gryphon, Jerodlycett, Jess, Jim1138, Johnevella, Keltrus, Kortoso, KylieTastic, Lipsquid, Lova Falk, LuckyLouie, Mann jess, Manul, MartinPoulter, MauSalamander, Maurice Carbonaro, McGeddon, Mgiganteus1, Mjesfahani, MrBill3, My name is not dave, Nihiltres, NuclearWarfare, Omnipaedista, Oshwah, PavonisStar, Pkalas, Power~enwiki, RA0808, Ramurf, Rjwilmsi, Robert the Magician, Sbmeirow, Seb77~enwiki, Second Quantization, Seleukos256, Shhhnotsoloud, Six words, Skylark777, Slightsmile, Smalljim, Steelpillow, TAnthony, Tedgoertzel, Tgeorgescu, The Anome, Timothy Gu, TopAce, TreeTrailer, Unreal7, Vsmith, WOSlinker, Yngln, 125 anonymous edits 50

Clairvoyance *Source:* https://en.wikipedia.org/w/index.php?oldid=855432123 *License:* Creative Commons Attribution-Share Alike 3.0 *Contributors:* 1exec1, Acather96, Ad Orientem, Agent007bond, AndyTheGrump, Annalisa Ventola, Anthon St Maarten, Atlantia, BU Rob13, Basilicofresco, Bender235, Bishonen, BullRangifer, CLCStudent, Carnby, Cathry, Cforrester101, Chris the speller, ChrisGualtieri, Citation bot 1, Cjwilky, Clairvoyant-fourm, Clarityfiend, ClockworkRebel, ClueBot NG, DASHBotAV, Daisy6116, Dan6hell66, Debouch, Dewritech, DexDor, Discospinster, Dispenser, DocWatson42, Donner60, DrRC, Dream of Nyx, Emily Matweow, Emotionlessthug, Fluffernutter, Froglich, Gco, Gerald daniels, GoatGod, Goblin Face, Gogo Dodo, Going Under I, GreenMeansGo, Hallows AG, Hans Adler, Happykg, Hyacinth, Hydrargyrum, Ian.thomson, Ihardlythinkso, JMyrleFuller, Jarble, Jdsg1, Jellyfish10, Jerodlycett, Jess, Jim1138, Jmcgnh, Johnbs, JonRichfield, JuliaHunter, K6ka, KH-1, Keen2write, Kerusnos, Kesmoore, Keyuria, Knightnr, Knowitahl, Lentower, Leszek Jańczuk, Lojbanist, Lotje, LuK3, LuckyLouie, MONGO, Mabalu, Magioladitis, Mann jess, Martinevans123, Me, Myself, and I are Here, Mean as custard, Michaeldsquare, Mild Bill Hiccup, Monique Saunders, MrBill3, Nanophosis, Nederlandse Leeuw, Nihil novi, Njames0, Ohnoitsjamie, Orangemarlin, Paine Ellsworth, Pharaoh of the Wizards, Pk dba, Powerover, RañkiSykes, Reesorville, Rjmail, Rjwilmsi, SERGEJ2011, SF007, Sbmeirow, Schwede66, Sesginnews, SkepticalRaptor, Slazenger, Steve1849, Suwa, TAnthony, TMNTfoeva, TakuyaMurata, Tgeorgescu, ThirdDolphin, This lousy T-shirt, Tillman, Trappist the monk, Verbal, Vihelik, आ, 145 anonymous edits 56

Psychokinesis *Source:* https://en.wikipedia.org/w/index.php?oldid=854870818 *License:* Creative Commons Attribution-Share Alike 3.0 *Contributors:* 7&6=thirteen, A little angry, Amaury, Amortias, Anaxial, AndyTheGrump, Ankhsn, Anonymous111Ann, Arash1971, Avernarius, Bender235, Bomb319, Bovineboy2008, BullRangifer, CAPTAIN RAJU, Cgarza3, Chris goulet, ClueBot NG, CuriousEric, DRodgers11, Dcirovic, Denisarona, Dlohcierekim, Dragescu, Dylan620 II, EditorSin, Ematica, Flyer22 Reborn, Gilliam, Headbomb, Isambard Kingdom, Ixocactus, J 1982, Jerodlycett, Jess, Jmcgnh, Joe Heato, Johnuniq, Jonathan vodini, Jonesey95, JuliaHunter, JzG, KH-1, LoudLizard, LuckyLouie, MLODROB, Mann jess, Mark Arsten, MatthewHoobin, McSly, Mcewan, MelbourneStar, Montanabw, NadirAli, Napolee007, Neil916, NeilN, Nelatti, Omnipaedista, Pigs1111, Plumitife, Quebec99, RA0808, RG72, Rich Farmbrough, Rjwilmsi, Robert the Magician, Roxy the dog, SERGEJ2011, ScrapIronIV, SemiHypercube, Shellwood, Sigma.4292, Signedzzzz, Skepticatheist, SkyWarrior, Slightsmile, Stargazingstanza, Synchro27, TAnthony, TheRedPenOfDoom, Theanswerman109, Thnidu, Tom.Reding, Treysand, Twilight100, Wavelength, Wikiway, WikiPen313, Wtmitchell, Xavier Combelle, Zerogravity89, Zxcvbnm, ಡಿಡಿ, 200 anonymous edits 63

Near-death experience *Source:* https://en.wikipedia.org/w/index.php?oldid=860502454 *License:* Creative Commons Attribution-Share Alike 3.0 *Contributors:* Aadelsberger, Alexbrn, Amallick87, Apokrif, Aquillion, Atvelonis, Augurar, Bellerophon5685, Benjamin Lanowski, Bohbot366, C Apple D, Claire.Poggi, Cyrej, DagosNavy, David J Johnson, Eagleash, Edward321, Edwin trinh14, Fixuture, Florian Blaschke, Flyer22 Reborn, Gongshow, GünniX, Ironrage, Jeremy68, JimVC3, John of Reading, Johnuniq, Josezetabal, Joshua Jonathan, Jytdog, Keith D, Lancebretthall, Lekatt2204, Lontjr, Magioladitis, Merry medievalist, Morphdog, MrBill3, MrX, My objective, N. Harmonik, Nat965, Onel5969, PaleoNeonate, Perky28, Pissadogood, Rabbitflyer, Rebecca Bird, Rjwilmsi, Roxy the dog, Rp2006, Seeker718, Serols, ShakespeareFan00, Shellwood, Skeptic from Britain, Smasongarrison, Smkolins, Soli58, Somedifferentstuff, Steelpillow, Sy036267, The Editor's Apprentice, The EpicGamerYT, Toni 001, Wega14, WikiGuide, Xbony2, ಡಿಡಿ, 78 anonymous edits 77

Reincarnation *Source:* https://en.wikipedia.org/w/index.php?oldid=860186896 *License:* Creative Commons Attribution-Share Alike 3.0 *Contributors:* Afterwriting, Alexb102072, Amallick87, Amccann421, Arjayay, Avaya1, Barek, Bender235, Bjorn87, Chdogskiss, Carrieann82, Ceosad, Clean Copy, ClueBot NG, Crystallizedcarbon, Cyberbot II, Cynulliad, D4iNa4, DadaNeem, Dallen Abel, DanielTYT, Dcirovic, Dewritech, Dr.K., Duncanhill, EPadmirateur, Editor2020, El C, Emir of Wikipedia, Excirial, Fastez, Fixuture, Galway50, Gilliam, Gluons12, God's World23, GL, Dun-lumeemee, GwydionM, Harizotoh9, Hijiri88, Home Lander, IkonicDeath, Ira Leviton, JarrahTree, Jdcomix, Jeraphine Gryphon, Jessicapierce, Jewish1234, Jim1138, Jmcgnh, John of Reading, Johnbs, Jonesey95, Josve05a, Junny980f, K kisses, KAP03, Kaobear, L293D, Linder89, Liridon, LordShozin, Lotje, LuckyLouie, MBlaze Lightning, MS0017, Magioladitis, MagistraMundi, Manishkrisna108, Materialscientist, Mcc1789, Me, Myself, and I are Here, Mean as custard, Miodrag1963, Modernist, Mohammed Akmal, Monica Ali, Montanabw, Motivação, Ms Sarah Welch, NadirAli, Nelatti, NewEnglandYankee, Nick Moyes, Oliver697, Oluwa2Chainz, Onel5969, Oshwah, PaleoNeonate, PatGallacher, Pfhorrest, Plank, PohranicniStraze, Pratyk321, Premeditated Chaos, Psychlohexane, Q Chris, Qzd, Realphi, Risto hot sir, Robot psychiatrist, Rp2006, Rubbish computer, Ruchi04, SJ Defender, Samsbanned, Sandstone, ScrapIronIV, Shantavira, Sheila Ki Jawani, Soler97, Solomon7968, Spartaz, Subashbhokare, TAnthony, Tachs, The Almightey Drill, Theinstantmatrix, Theroadislong, Tom.Reding, Trollworkout, Trutheyeness, Uanfala, Verbum Veritas, W.AndrzejZiarno, Wario-Man, Wbm, Wikishovel, Will to meaning, Yngvadottir, ZariaNest, Zechariah16, Znuzz, 140 anonymous edits 93

Apparitional experience *Source:* https://en.wikipedia.org/w/index.php?oldid=843905999 *License:* Creative Commons Attribution-Share Alike 3.0 *Contributors:* 1exec1, Anachronist, Anonymous Dissident, BD2412, Banno, Bookgrrl, Bovineboy2008, Bped1985, Casliber, Chockyegg, Cmon Avaro, ClueBot NG, Cowman109, DO11.10, Dbachmann, Deacon of Pndapetzim, Dexterous, Dona-Hue, DreamGuy, Editor2020, Elonka, FWadel, Gerkerath, GreenUniverse, HealthyGirl, JaGa, Jim1138, Jmackaeronspace, Johnfos, JustAGal, KathrynLybarger, Kilidiplomus, Maelnuneb, Magioladitis, Mark Ironie, Martinphi, Mattisse, Mertozoro, Michael Hardy, Morning277, Morton Shumway, Nealparr, Noah Salzman, Noted Seven, Oct13, PaleoNeonate, Permstrump, Peter Damian (original account), RA0808, Randy Bot, Redheylin, Reedy, Requestion, Rjwilmsi, Sardanaphalus, Sol1, Srleffler, Staszek Lem, Synergy, Tofutwitch11, Twinsday, UrsusArctosL71, V-Man737, Velella, Verbal, Westfalr3, Wikideaman, Yobmod, 33 anonymous edits 129

Ganzfeld experiment *Source:* https://en.wikipedia.org/w/index.php?oldid=846928931 *License:* Creative Commons Attribution-Share Alike 3.0 *Contributors:* 22hj19206jk, Amillar, Andycjp, Andyhowlett, Arch dude, Asdjha, BD2412, Bfinn, Bgwhite, Blysse, BullRangifer, Carmichael, Citation bot 1, ClueBot NG, Coach.eric, CommonsDelinker, Dan the speller, David Woodward, Dcirovic, Dolfrog, Donmike10, Donner60, Eric Corbett, Ersby, Gazsa, Gilliam, Goblin Face, GreenMeansGo, Harizotoh9, Hob Gadling, Insomnia dream, Issuesixty soulsgreat, JamesMLane, John85, Johnfos, Julesd, JzG, Kortoso, L Kensington, Leon C, LuckyLouie, Machinarium, MagistraMundi, Mann jess, Maunus, Maurice Carbonaro, McGeddon, Mjarsulic, MrBill3, Natuur12, Nurg, Nwillard, OxygenBlue, Philosi4, Racerx11, RadioElectric, Riotrocket8676, Rjwilmsi, Ronhjones, Ronz, Ruby Murray, SanGavinoEN, Sbmeirow, Schwede66, Sgerbic, Shirt58, Skeptic5757, Skysmith, Srich32977, Tesseract2, TheRedPenOfDoom, Tim1357, Trancestate, TreeTrailer, Twipley, Vanished user oerjio4kdm3, Xanzzibar, ಡಿಡಿ, 118 anonymous edits 135

Image Sources, Licenses and Contributors

The sources listed for each image provide more detailed licensing information including the copyright status, the copyright owner, and the license conditions.

Figure 1 *Source:* https://en.wikipedia.org/w/index.php?title=File:Paraghost.gif *License:* Public Domain *Contributors:* BotMultichill, Firsfron, Gbarta, Jochen Burghardt, Lone Wolfs, Man vyi, Staszek Lem, Wikidudeman, 1 anonymous edits 2
Image *Source:* https://en.wikipedia.org/w/index.php?title=File:Outline-body-aura.svg *License:* Creative Commons Zero *Contributors:* Artoria2e5, Cathy Richards, 1 anonymous edits 2
Figure 2 *Source:* https://en.wikipedia.org/w/index.php?title=File:Henry_Slade_with_Zöllner.png *License:* Public Domain *Contributors:* Aschroet, JuliaHunter, Lone Wolfs, Rebecca Bird 4
Figure 3 *Source:* https://en.wikipedia.org/w/index.php?title=File:Zener_cards_(color).svg *License:* GNU Free Documentation License *Contributors:* Mikhail Ryazanov (talk) 01:30, 1 April 2014 (UTC) 6
Figure 4 *Source:* https://en.wikipedia.org/w/index.php?title=File:Hubert_Pearce_with_J._B._Rhine.png *License:* Public Domain *Contributors:* Aschroet, JuliaHunter, Lone Wolfs, Rebecca Bird 7
Figure 5 *Source:* https://en.wikipedia.org/w/index.php?title=File:Mr._Zirkle_and_Miss_Ownbey_ESP_experiment.png *License:* Public Domain *Contributors:* Aschroet, JuliaHunter, Lone Wolfs, Rebecca Bird 8
Figure 6 *Source:* https://en.wikipedia.org/w/index.php?title=File:Bernard-carr.jpg *License:* Creative Commons Attribution-Sharealike 3.0 *Contributors:* Auntof6, BotMultichillT, Docu, Ilovebernardcarr, Jochen Burghardt, Lone Wolfs 12
Figure 7 *Source:* https://en.wikipedia.org/w/index.php?title=File:Ganzfeld.jpg *License:* Public Domain *Contributors:* Original uploader was Nealparr at en.wikipedia 15
Figure 8 *Source:* https://en.wikipedia.org/w/index.php?title=File:Russell_Targ_physicist.jpg *License:* Public Domain *Contributors:* Ankry, Brian Josephson, Krd, Lone Wolfs, NahidSultan, Rebecca Bird, Shakko, Simisa, Túrelio 16
Figure 9 *Source:* https://en.wikipedia.org/w/index.php?title=File:Hieronymus_Bosch_013.jpg *License:* Public Domain *Contributors:* Boo-Boo Baroo, BotMultichill, Carlodell, EDUCA33E, File Upload Bot (Eloquence), KillOrDie, L'inesprimibile nulla, Marsupium, Mattes, Palazzogrimani, Salix, Semofa, Shakko, Vincent Steenberg, Wst, 1 anonymous edits 20
Figure 10 *Source:* https://en.wikipedia.org/w/index.php?title=File:James_Alcock.jpg *License:* Creative Commons Attribution-Sharealike 3.0 *Contributors:* User:Sgerbic 22
Figure 11 *Source:* https://en.wikipedia.org/w/index.php?title=File:Hyman_LeeRoss_DarylBem_VictorBenassi.jpg *Contributors:* Jdx, Lone Wolfs, Natuur12, RobertoTenore, 1 anonymous edits 24
Figure 12 *Source:* https://en.wikipedia.org/w/index.php?title=File:MarioBungesmall.jpg *License:* Creative Commons Attribution-Sharealike 3.0 *Contributors:* User:Guandalug 27
Figure 13 *Source:* https://en.wikipedia.org/w/index.php?title=File:James_Randi_crop.jpg *License:* Creative Commons Attribution 2.0 *Contributors:* ensceptico 30
Figure 14 *Source:* https://en.wikipedia.org/w/index.php?title=File:Ganzfeld.jpg *License:* Public Domain *Contributors:* Original uploader was Nealparr at en.wikipedia 38
Figure 15 *Source:* https://en.wikipedia.org/w/index.php?title=File:Gilbert_Murray.jpg *License:* Public Domain *Contributors:* Aloneinthewild, Jonathan Groß, Kersti Nebelsiek, Lone Wolfs, Marcus Cyron, Rebecca Bird 39
Figure 16 *Source:* https://en.wikipedia.org/w/index.php?title=File:Frederick_Marion_mentalist.png *License:* Public Domain *Contributors:* Aschroet, HealthyGirl, Lone Wolfs, Rebecca Bird 41
Figure 17 *Source:* https://en.wikipedia.org/w/index.php?title=File:Zener_cards_(color).svg *License:* GNU Free Documentation License *Contributors:* Mikhail Ryazanov (talk) 01:30, 1 April 2014 (UTC) 44
Image *Source:* https://en.wikipedia.org/w/index.php?title=File:Wikisource-logo.svg *License:* Creative Commons Attribution-Sharealike 3.0 *Contributors:* ChrisiPK, Guillom, INeverCry, Jarekt, JuTa, Leyo, Lokal Profil, MichaelMaggs, NielsF, Rei-artur, Rocket000, Romaine, Steinsplitter 55
Figure 18 *Source:* https://en.wikipedia.org/w/index.php?title=File:Character_reader_and_Clairvoyant.jpg *Contributors:* Tyne & Wear Archives & Museums 58
Image *Source:* https://en.wikipedia.org/w/index.php?title=File:Wiktionary-logo-en-v2.svg *Contributors:* User:Dan Polansky, User:Smurrayinchester 62
Figure 19 *Source:* https://en.wikipedia.org/w/index.php?title=File:Poltergeist-Therese_Selles.jpg *Contributors:* unknown staff artist 64
Figure 20 *Source:* https://en.wikipedia.org/w/index.php?title=File:Kellar_levitation_poster.jpg *License:* Public Domain *Contributors:* Strobridge Lithographing Co. 69
Figure 21 *Source:* https://en.wikipedia.org/w/index.php?title=File:Médium_et_Aksakof002.jpg *License:* Public Domain *Contributors:* Fran6fran6 71
Figure 22 *Source:* https://en.wikipedia.org/w/index.php?title=File:Edouard-Isidore-Buguet-PK-spirit-photographer.jpg *Contributors:* Édouard Isidore Buguet 72
Figure 23 *Source:* https://en.wikipedia.org/w/index.php?title=File:Stanisława_Tomczyk_and_William_Marriott.png *License:* Public Domain *Contributors:* Fodor Fan, Lone Wolfs, OgreBot 2, Rebecca Bird, WFinch, Yngvadottir 73
Figure 24 *Source:* https://en.wikipedia.org/w/index.php?title=File:Uri_Geller_in_Russia.jpg *License:* Creative Commons Attribution-Sharealike 3.0 *Contributors:* Dmitry Rozhkov 75
Figure 25 *Source:* https://en.wikipedia.org/w/index.php?title=File:Hieronymus_Bosch_013.jpg *License:* Public Domain *Contributors:* Boo-Boo Baroo, BotMultichill, Carlodell, EDUCA33E, File Upload Bot (Eloquence), KillOrDie, L'inesprimibile nulla, Marsupium, Mattes, Palazzogrimani, Salix, Semofa, Shakko, Vincent Steenberg, Wst, 1 anonymous edits 78
Figure 26 *Source:* https://en.wikipedia.org/w/index.php?title=File:Pim_van_Lommel-1.jpg *License:* Creative Commons Attribution-Sharealike 3.0 *Contributors:* Pim_van_Lommel.JPG: Siegfried Hornecker derivative work: Hic et nunc (talk) 83
Figure 27 *Source:* https://en.wikipedia.org/w/index.php?title=File:Temporal_lobe_animation.gif *Contributors:* Polygon data were generated by Database Center for Life Science(DBCLS). 88
Image *Source:* https://en.wikipedia.org/w/index.php?title=File:Commons-logo.svg *License:* logo *Contributors:* Anomie, Callanecc, CambridgeBayWeather, Jo-Jo Eumerus, RHaworth 92
Figure 28 *Source:* https://en.wikipedia.org/w/index.php?title=File:Gati_or_existences.jpg *License:* Public Domain *Contributors:* Shree Diwakar Prakashan (Owner Mr. Sanjay Surana) (Website:http://www.jainbooks.in) 94
Figure 29 *Source:* https://en.wikipedia.org *License:* Attribution *Contributors:* Giovanni Dall'Orto. 102
Figure 30 *Source:* https://en.wikipedia.org/w/index.php?title=File:Ed0027.jpg *License:* Public Domain *Contributors:* Bukk, Haukurth, Holt, Redheylin, Sigo 102
Figure 31 *Source:* https://en.wikipedia.org/w/index.php?title=File:Wm_james.jpg *License:* Public Domain *Contributors:* Casliber, Dcflyer, DrKay, Ineuw, Infrogmation, Krupski Oleg, Lone Wolfs, Materialscientist, Prattflora, Rebecca Bird, Sergejpinka, Tholme, Wouterhagens 104
Figure 32 *Source:* https://en.wikipedia.org/w/index.php?title=File:Reincarnation2.jpg *License:* Creative Commons Attribution-Sharealike 2.5 *Contributors:* User:Himalayan_Academy_Publications#Copyright_permissions 105
Figure 33 *Source:* https://en.wikipedia.org/w/index.php?title=File:Buddhist_Wheel_of_Life.jpg *Contributors:* User:Laurent Bélanger 107
Figure 34 *Source:* https://en.wikipedia.org/w/index.php?title=File:Shamon_jigoku_zōshi.jpg *License:* Public Domain *Contributors:* Banise, Binabik, Daderot, Werieth 108
Figure 35 *Source:* https://en.wikipedia.org/w/index.php?title=File:Seven_Jain_Hells.jpg *License:* Public Domain *Contributors:* Anishshah19 109
Image *Source:* https://en.wikipedia.org/w/index.php?title=File:Tree_of_life_bahir_Hebrew.svg *License:* Public Domain *Contributors:* User:AnonMoos 112
Figure 36 *Source:* https://en.wikipedia.org/w/index.php?title=File:The_Childrens_Museum_of_Indianapolis_-_Egungun_masquerade_dance_garment.jpg *Contributors:* Judithcomm, LoriLee, Lotje, Missvain, Sgconlaw 114
Image *Source:* https://en.wikipedia.org/w/index.php?title=File:Basmala.svg *License:* Public Domain *Contributors:* AnonMoos, Baba66, BotMultichill, Cathy Richards, Ceyhun.044, Cirt, Escondites, Graphium, Jdx, Kalki, Mohamadrezadnz, RadiX, Wst, خالد, 19 anonymous edits 117
Image *Source:* https://en.wikipedia.org/w/index.php?title=File:Ghadir_logo.png *Contributors:* User:Mhhossein 117
Image *Source:* https://en.wikipedia.org/w/index.php?title=File:Druze_star.svg *License:* Public Domain *Contributors:* Erin Silversmith 118
Image *Source:* https://en.wikipedia.org/w/index.php?title=File:P_religion_world.svg *License:* GNU Free Documentation License *Contributors:* Achim55, Anime Addict AA, AnonMoos, Cathy Richards, Chris-martin, Gerrit Erasmus, Herbythyme, Jean-Frédéric, Jonund, Little Savage, MGA73bot2, Marcus Cyron, 3 anonymous edits 118

License

Index